THE
Sense
OF
Grammar

THE
Sense
OF
Grammar

LANGUAGE AS SEMEIOTIC

Michael Shapiro

Indiana University Press
Bloomington

This book was brought to publication with the assistance of a grant
from the Andrew W. Mellon Foundation.

Manufactured in the United States of America

Library of Congress Cataloging in Publication Data

Shapiro, Michael, 1939-
    The sense of grammar.

    Bibliography: p.
    Includes index.
    1. Semiotics. 2. Peirce, Charles Santiago Sanders,
1839-1914—Linguistics. 3. Grammar, Comparative and
general. I. Title.
P99.S46   1983   401'.41   82-49244
ISBN 0-253-35173-1
1 2 3 4 5 87 86 85 84 83

to my mother

I am satisfied that in the present state of the subject, there is but one General science of the nature of Signs. If we were to separate it into two,—then, according to my idea that a "science," as scientific men use the word, implies a social group of devotees, we should be in imminent danger of erecting two groups of one member each! Whereas, if you and I stick together, we are, at least, two of us. I remember in my college days that the Statutes of Harvard defined a "group" as *three* persons or more convening together. We shall have to try to seduce one of the linguists to our more fundamental study.

—From a partial draft of a letter dated 28 December 1908, from Charles Sanders Peirce to Victoria Lady Welby (*Collected Papers* 8.378)

CONTENTS

PREFACE

This book is an attempt to found a Peircean linguistics. By this I mean a reorientation of linguistic theory, and the ultimate goals of linguistic analysis, along lines suggested by Peirce's semeiotic in the context of his entire philosophy. As with all efforts of the kind, mine is necessarily partial, and the reader will not find treated all the subjects ordinarily encompassed by the very broad discipline of linguistics.

The book's focus is also defined to a considerable extent by the desire to present a synoptic view of my research over the past fifteen years (Part 2 is constituted largely by revised versions of previously published material). One subject directly affected thereby is syntax, though some syntactic data are included by way of illustrating general theoretical points. There is no doubt today (as Peirce himself foresaw) that the syntax of natural languages is particularly suited to semeiotic analysis, and the methodological compass implicit in a Peircean theory of grammar certainly invites applications by specialists in this popular field.

I have made a conscious decision to avoid polemics and concentrate instead on presenting a homogeneous point of view, to which not all other approaches are equally pertinent. Practically, this means that the definitiveness of a semeiotic analysis is intended to transpire from the discussion of concrete material without comparison and contrast to the currently more favored analytical mode. In lieu of a detailed critique of my own (but cf. my earlier book *Asymmetry* [1976]), I refer the reader to the admirably forceful and comprehensive opening chapter of Talmy Givon's *On Understanding Grammar* (1979), which can now stand as representing the views of all linguists who recognize the fundamental failures of transformational-generative grammar.

Linguistic analysis carried out in an explicitly semeiotic frame cannot boast a voluminous literature, a situation perhaps belied by the growing interest in semiotics. Even less developed is the study of language structure in the light of Peirce's theory of signs. For their part, Peirce studies have traditionally been preoccupied with textual exegesis—with good reason. We are still very much at the stage today of trying to clarify not only what Peirce meant to say, but what he in fact did say.

The difficulties of giving a comprehensive summary of Peirce's semeiotic that would square with all the divergent authorial versions, as well as with numerous modern interpretations, are well-known to students of Peirce. Chapter 1, which can stand on its own as an account of semeiotic, has been drawn with an eye toward reconciling, to the extent possible, some of the main differences between the theory of signs as Peirce held it before and after 1906. In attempting this task, I have relied on my own understanding of Peirce, aided in significant measure by the work of two interpreters, David Savan and T.L. Short, whose construal of semeiotic I have found preeminently valuable (even though they do not agree in all respects). Neither scholar is responsible, of course, for any shortcomings of my summary.

Because Peirce chose continually to reformulate his thoughts, in numerous drafts spanning several decades, we possess on most points a whole series of versions which amounts to an auto-commentary. Considering this to be a particularly valuable source for the understanding of semeiotic, I have included more than the customary number of direct quotations, as a deliberate procedure calculated to bring out as many of the variegated ramifications of Peirce's thought as possible.

It has not been my aim to illustrate all details of Peirce's system with linguistic examples, or to clothe traditional terminology in semeiotic dress. This circumstance is particularly important in the case of Chapters 3 and 4, which are meant to be read primarily as illustrations of the way a reoriented linguistics comes to grips with real data. I have striven to imbue linguistic analysis with the *attitude* toward language that Peirce's philosophical enterprise leads the analyst to adopt. To some extent, semeiotic and the structural analysis of language form a natural partnership which attenuates some of the terminological antagonism that tends to grow when disciplines are cross-pollinated.

Although Peirce himself spelled the name of his general theory of signs in a number of ways, he seems to have preferred *semeiotic,* and this is the spelling I have used consistently when referring to Peirce's doctrine (except in direct quotations). The more familiar contemporary spelling *semiotic* is restricted to non-Peircean references; the same distinction applies to *semeiosis* and *semiosis.*

References of the form 1.187 are to the *Collected Papers of Charles Sanders Peirce* by volume and paragraph number (2nd printing, 8 volumes in 4, vols. 1-6 edited by Charles Hartshorne and Paul Weiss, vols. 7-8 edited by Arthur Burks, Cambridge, Mass.: Harvard University Press, 1965-66). References of the form NE 4:241 are to *The New Elements of Mathematics by Charles S. Peirce* (4 volumes in 5, edited by Carolyn Eisele, The Hague: Mouton; Atlantic Highlands, N.J.: Humanities Press, 1976), by volume and page number. References of the form H 34 are to the pages of *Semiotic and Significs: The Correspondence between Charles S. Peirce and Victoria Lady Welby* (edited by Charles S. Hardwick, Bloomington: Indiana University Press, 1977). References of the form MS 915:1 and L25 are to the microfilm edition of the *Charles S. Peirce Papers* (Cambridge, Mass.: Harvard University Library Photographic Service, 1966) by manuscript and letter number and page. These numbered materials are described in Richard S. Robin's *Annotated Catalogue of the Papers of Charles S. Peirce* (Amherst: University of Massachusetts Press, 1967).

I would like to express my special thanks to my friend and former colleague Raimo Anttila, with whom I have had many profitable discussions on the subjects of this book. His *Introduction to Historical and Comparative Linguistics* (1972) was the first text of its kind to give emphasis to the Peircean perspective on grammar, and his subsequent research (in the light of Gestalt psychology) has continued to be a valuable stimulus.

It gives me genuine pleasure to acknowledge my considerable debt to David Savan, whose analysis of Peircean semeiotic has been determinative in helping me shape my own. His unflagging support of my work in general was invaluable in bringing this project to completion.

I have also benefited from the incisive comments of T. L. Short on parts of the 'Theoretical Prolegomena.' Members of the Peirce Edition Project, particularly Max H. Fisch and Christian J. W. Kloesel, were generous in their assistance to me during my brief research visit to Indianapolis as well as on other occasions. Institutional support was provided by UCLA in the form of Research Grants, and the completion of the manuscript was aided by an Individual Study and Research Fellowship from the National Endowment for the Humanities.

New York, N.Y.   M. S.

THE
Sense
OF
Grammar

Introduction

Plato's *Cratylus,* the matchless dialogue on the relationship between words and things, is the first work in which one finds a detailed discussion of the question which preoccupied philosophers of language in Ancient Greece like no other, namely that of 'the correctness of names' (*orthotes onomaton*). The eponymous hero of Plato's work, Cratylus, takes the position, espoused before him by Heraclitus, that language attaches form to content 'by nature' (*physei*), whereas his opponent, Hermogenes, follows Democritus in maintaining that things get their (Greek) names 'by convention' (*thesei*). Socrates, who inclines towards the position of Cratylus, is called upon by Hermogenes to demonstrate in his accustomed manner just how words are suited naturally to represent the things they name. For his part as moderator, Socrates, after adducing a series of examples calculated to vindicate Cratylus, comes in the latter section of the dialogue to conclude that the apparent superiority of representation by likeness over the use of arbitrary signs must be attenuated by the complementary presence of 'custom' (*ethos*) or conventionality. Cratylus accepts the view of Socrates, and the question which so engaged the protagonists remains unresolved.

Later Greek philosophy continues to be preoccupied with this controversy, the Epicureans and Stoics aligning themselves with the *physei* side and the Sceptics with the *thesei* side. In the Hellenistic period the topic reappears in a somewhat altered guise as a dispute over whether language is governed by 'analogy' (the Alexandrian grammarians) or by 'anomaly' (the Stoics of Pergamum). (Roughly, as far as linguistics is concerned, these terms were used to mean something like 'regularity' and 'irregularity.')

Although the controversy ceased to have the theoretical acuity it enjoyed among Greek philosophers and grammarians in the subsequent history of linguistics, one or another form of it is implicit in thinking about the foundations of language throughout the medieval and modern period. A kind of benchmark as far as the nineteenth century is concerned is an article by the pioneering American linguist William Dwight Whitney in the *Transactions of the American Philological Association* (1879) entitled '*Physei* or *Thesei*—Natural or Conventional,' in which the ancient argument is raised anew. Whitney comes down on the side of those, like Plato's Hermogenes, who view language as a system of arbitrary signs based on custom, habit, and convention. In fact, Whitney propagated this view in a number of books of the 1860s and 1870s which had a profound influence on the course of linguistic theorizing in Europe. Most prominent among those who accepted the doctrine of the arbitrariness of the linguistic sign was the Swiss, Ferdinand de Saussure.

Saussure, who along with the Poles Jan Baudouin de Courtenay and Mikołaj Kruszewski (teacher and student) is considered to be a founder of structural linguistics, made the notion of arbitrariness into a dogma of his conception of linguistic structure, which was set forth in the posthumous *Cours de linguistique générale* (1st edition, 1916) compiled by Saussure's students from lecture notes. Citing Whitney at a number of points, Saussure declared the bond linking signifier (*signifiant*) and signified (*signifié*) in the linguistic sign to be arbitrary. After the publication of the *Cours,* this Saussurian principle became a staple of thinking about the nature of language and was endorsed by such important linguists as Charles Bally, Antoine Meillet, Joseph Vendryes, and Leonard Bloomfield.

However, even at its publication Saussure's principle did not meet with unanimous acceptance. The prominent Danish linguist Otto Jespersen in his review of the *Cours* was quick to express the opinion that the role of arbitrariness in language had been grossly exaggerated. The most influential and oft-cited rejoinder of the inter-war period was Emile Benveniste's article (1939) 'La nature du signe linguistique,' which showed that what was arbitrary from the viewpoint of the outsider was necessary from that of the native speaker. Relations between components of the linguistic sign which appear to be mere accidents to the person with no knowledge of the language involved are seen as quite natural by the person to whom no other means of expression are available. Roman Jakobson, who himself contributed significantly to amending the Saussurian doctrine, repeats the anecdote of the Swiss-German peasant woman who was supposed to have queried her French-speaking countrymen as to why cheese was called *fromage*, remarking: 'Käse ist doch viel natürlicher!' ('*Käse* is so much more natural!'). He reminds us also (echoing Franz Boas) that languages differ not in what they *can* express but in what they *must* express.

Despite the vigor and insistence which accompanied Saussure's espousal of the doctrine of arbitrariness, there are passages in the *Cours* that represent a qualified retreat from the monolithic position usually ascribed to Saussure's teachings. A distinction between absolute and relative arbitrariness is introduced (part 2, chapter 6, section 3), which attenuates the fundamental principle by allowing degrees of arbitrariness and a concomitant gradedness in the unmotivated nature of the linguistic sign. Not all signs are completely unmotivated; indeed, where words have constituent structure along the syntagmatic axis and an attendant identification of such constituents as members of paradigms, Saussure speaks of the 'limiting of arbitrariness.' In what seems like a striking about-face, the best possible way of approaching the study of language as a system is identified with this revisionist methodological tenet. Relative motivation is a necessary consequence of the human mind's natural propensity to introduce order into the mass of irrational facts, argues Saussure, and language structure must therefore oscillate in actuality between two impossible extremes, complete arbitrariness and total motivatedness. On this view, a typology could be articulated whereby languages would be classified according to where they were judged to lie along the continuum between 'a minimum of organization and a minimum of arbitrariness.' Using strictly morphological criteria, Saussure ranges Sanskrit, for instance, as an ultra-grammatical type near one end and Chinese as an ultra-lexical type at the other end. They conform in structure to the two drifts he identifies in language, the tendency to prefer the grammatical instrument (contructional rule), on the one hand, and the opposing preference for the lexical tool, or unmotivated sign, on the other.

Even with the introduction of relative arbitrariness ('degrees of arbitrariness') into the scheme, Saussure remains unequivocally biased towards an absolutism which is basically incompatible with naturalist tendencies, and steadfastly regards absolute arbitrariness to be indeed 'the proper condition of the linguistic sign.'

In the 1930s efforts were made to overcome this bias, notable among which (besides the Benveniste article mentioned earlier) was J. R. Firth's book *Speech* (1930), where the term *phonaestheme* is coined and applied for the first time to describe the 'partial' or 'submorphemic' element *sl-* with affective meaning in words like *slack, slouch, slush, sludge, slime, slosh,* etc. Several studies by Dwight Bolinger dating from the late 1940s and early 1950s take up and develop Firth's idea, giving added impetus to Benjamin Lee Whorf's contention that 'the *patternment* aspect of language always overrides and controls the *lexation* or name-giving aspect.' However, these efforts concentrate on evidence that is at the periphery of language, on what is very much of a piece with the phenomenon known as onomatopoeia (sound imitation), of which Saussure himself was not unmindful (together with a long list of predecessors stretching back into antiquity).

A series of studies by Roman Jakobson from the 1950s and 1960s put the doctrine of the arbitrariness of the linguistic sign in a fundamentally new perspective. Where previous investigators had left unchanged the recognition of the sign's basic arbitrariness, Jakobson succeeded in uncovering facts of language structure (primarily, Russian) that demonstrated the extensive patterns of similarity and difference in the phonic shape of grammatical morphemes corresponding to relations of similarity and difference in their meanings. In a path-breaking article, 'Quest for the Essence of Language' (1965), he cited several examples of such correspondences; for instance, the relationship between singular and plural forms in all languages of the world: where the plural is formed by adding a morpheme, the singular is never distinguished from the plural by an additional morpheme. Moreover, the plural tends generally to be longer than the singular, reproducing the numeral increment by an increase in the length of the form. As pointed out by Jakobson, syntax resorts to a mimetic (imitative) representation of the order of events, with regard to time or to rank, when it records the progression of Caesar's acts by *Veni, vedi, vici*, or reflects the unequal status of the subjects in a coordinated sequence like 'the President and the Secretary of State attended the meeting.' The mirroring of content relations in relations of linguistic expression can be seen *en gros* in the relationship between lexical and grammatical morphemes in all languages. A pervasive pattern dictates that the semantically more restricted class of grammatical affixes be expressed by the smaller class of sounds—vowels; and the semantically less restricted class of lexical roots be expressed by the correspondingly larger class of sounds—consonants. English is a good example of this phenomenon: only two consonants, *s* and *t* and their combination *-st*, occur among the productive inflectional morphemes. Russian, with an inventory of twenty-four obstruents (true consonants), limits their use in the system of inflectional suffixes to just four. Moreover, corresponding to the opposition 'plural' vs. 'singular,' Russian nouns display a relatively greater vs. lesser number of segments (sounds) in case desinences (endings) implementing these two numbers. Regardless of the specific shape of the desinences, each plural desinence contains one more segment than the corresponding singular.

Jakobson's discussion of such correspondences in 'Quest for the Essence of Language' represents a major achievement in the search for principles of organization in the structure of language. His recognition that a system of sound units may diagram relations in the corresponding system of meaning units establishes in a most concrete way that *the content system of language is indeed a structure,* not just a purely additive code like an alphabet or Morse code. The use of the word 'diagram' here is not fortuitous, for one of the important methodological advances Jakobson made in this programmatic essay was to couch his strictly linguistic analysis in terms of the *semeiotic,* or theory of signs, of the American philosopher-scientist Charles Sanders Peirce, who gives 'diagram' a precise definition: a species of sign in which the relations of the parts of a thing are represented by analogous relations in parts of the sign itself. The main aspect of this definition of diagrams is the representation of relations by relations. For linguistics, this means the reflection of the relations at the content level (the level of meaning) in relations at the expression level (the level of sounds).

Peirce investigated semeiotic over a span of nearly fifty years (from around 1867 till his death in 1914), taking the name from Locke's *Essay Concerning Human Understanding,* where the Greek *semeiotike* is adopted by Locke to mean 'the doctrine of signs, the most usual whereof being words.' Peirce, with whose work the study of signs may be said to have received the most thorough philosophical grounding and the richest source of insights for application to diverse fields uninvestigated by Peirce himself, carefully defined semeiotic as 'the doctrine of the essential nature and fundamental varieties of possible semiosis.' He was equally careful to define precisely what he meant by the word *semeiosis,* calling it 'an action, or influence, which is, or involves a coöperation of *three* subjects, such as a sign, its object, and its interpretant, this tri-relative influence not being in any way resolvable into actions between pairs.' The great bulk of what Peirce actually wrote on semeiotic remained unpublished and survived in manuscript form, some of it finally appearing posthumously in the 8-volume edition of his *Collected Papers,* most of it still awaiting publication to this day.

Saussure does not appear to have been aware of Peirce's founding of semeiotic, and in his programmatic pronouncements concerning the status of language and linguistics he called for a general science of signs which he gave the provisional name *sémiologie.* Saussure was convinced that linguistics stood in direct need of this more general discipline for the proper conduct of inquiry into the nature of language as a sign system. Like Locke, moreover, Saussure accorded language pride of place among human semeiotic systems. Later in the century, the outstanding Danish linguist and theorist of language Louis Hjelmslev was to capture this preeminent status of human speech when he termed it a 'pass-key language,' i.e. a semeiotic system which can encompass any conceivable matter, the content substance of language being capable of including the content substance of all other human sign systems.

Saussure's interpretation of sign structure, particularly of the linguistic sign, stressed the indissoluble linkage of the two components which he called *signifiant* 'signifier' and *signifié* 'signified.' This conception of sign and of its two components appears to constitute a wholesale adoption of a semeiotic theory with roots in Stoic logic and medieval philosophy of language. The Stoics regarded sign as an articulated whole consisting of the signifier (*semainon*) and the signified (*semainomenon*)—the former defined as perceptible (*aistheton*), the latter as intelligible (*noeton*). They systematically distinguished the relation between the signifier and the signified (which Saussure termed *signification*) from denotation (*tynchanon*) or reference, much as Peirce himself did when he called the former the sign's depth and the latter its breadth. The medieval adaptation of the Stoic doctrine, particularly by St. Augustine, utilized Latinized equivalents of Greek terminology: *signum* (sign), *signans* (signifier), and *signatum* (signified). Indeed, medieval logic and the conception of sign of the Schoolmen (Duns Scotus, John of Salisbury, Thomas of Erfurt, and Peter Abelard among others) was a continual wellspring of inspiration and insight for Peirce throughout his life, during which he acquired a thorough knowledge of Scholasticism.

Peirce was not a linguist in the modern sense. He did, however, have many penetrating thoughts on the structure of language which can be found interspersed at numerous points in his writings, particularly on the general topic of semeiotic. When, in 1903, Peirce paused to take stock of the development of the theory of signs from antiquity to the twentieth century, he lamented the great void that followed upon the successes of medieval logic and attributed this neglect to the 'barbarous rage' which had engulfed 'the marvelous acuteness of the Schoolmen,' to the centuries-long detriment of the study of semeiotic. Indeed, Peirce was firmly convinced that had the Middle Ages been followed by periods of achievement of the same high order, such fields as linguistics, for which semeiotic forms a necessary foundation, would be 'in a decidedly more advanced condition than there is much promise that they will have reached at the end of 1950.'

It is tempting to speculate what course the history of linguistics in the twentieth century would have taken had Peirce's seminal writings on semeiotic not remained largely unpublished, hence unknown to Saussure (or to Baudouin de Courtenay). Saussure laid out a program of research in linguistics which subsumed the latter under the general science of signs while explicitly recognizing it as the most important subdiscipline of the wider study. In the middle of the century and a decade after the original Danish publication of *Prolegomena to a Theory of Language,* its author Louis Hjelmslev, as unaware as Saussure before him of Peirce's contributions to the foundations of semeiotic, could still call the field 'practically uncharted territory.'

The first linguist to become aware of Peirce's relevance to the advancement of linguistic theory was Roman Jakobson. It is in the early 1950s that mention of Peirce and brief allusions to his theory of signs crop up in Jakobson's articles and public appearances. The publication of 'Quest for the Essence of Language' in *Diogenes* (1965) marks a milestone in the history of linguistics: while programmatic in purport, it is the first attempt to ground the essential questions of language structure in an explicitly Peircean mode. Jakobson concentrates almost exclusively on Peirce's most famous trichotomy of signs, that of icon, index, and symbol, by which Peirce meant to characterize the mutable relationship ('ground') between the sign and its object. Recasting the sign constituents as signans and signatum to conform to the Saussurian aspect under which Jakobson confronts semiology and semeiotic, he aimed thereby at a kind of trial amalgamation of the European structuralist tradition and the semeiotic legacy of the American founder of pragmatism. There are some definite points of tangency between Saussure and Peirce. Thus, for instance, Saussure originally used the term symbol in the same sense (later abandoned) as Peirce, namely a sign in which the connection between signans and signatum 'consists in its being a rule,' and whose interpretation depends on a convention. Saussure singled out the concept of opposition as the basis for 'the entire mechanism of language.' Peirce, whose scope embraced not just linguistic signs but anything that could be interpreted as a sign because of its action, considered opposition to be the essential dyadic relation. Indeed, for Peirce 'a thing without oppositions *ipso facto* does not exist,' hence it is the study of oppositions which underlies the understanding of the mode of being of things.

There is, however, a capital difference between Saussure and Peirce that is not brought out in Jakobson's comparative discussion. Saussure, as a linguist and founder of structuralism, took his cue from what he perceived to be the structure of language; he therefore emphasized the *dyadic* nature of the sign, its two-sided or dichotomous character as an entity. For Peirce, however, the sign is *triadic*. Semeiosis takes place when the three constituents—sign, object, and interpretant—cooperate in a 'tri-relative influence' that brings the sign into relation with its object, on one hand, and with its interpretant, on the other, 'in such a way as to bring the interpretant into a relation to the object corresponding to its own relation to the object.' The role of the interpretant in Peirce's conception of semeiotic is obviously central; there is nothing strictly comparable in Saussure, with the possible exception of his idea of *valeur linguistique* (linguistic value). In one of the shorter definitions Peirce gives of the interpretant, he calls it 'the proper significate outcome of a sign.' The whole of pragmatism and, therefore, the entire tangled question of the 'meaning' of an intellectual concept is bound up, for Peirce, with the study of interpretants. Indeed, he devoted much of his thought and writing to elaborating a typology of interpretants in the context of what he came to call 'pragmaticism,' in order to dissociate it from the pragmatism of William James.

The question as to how meaning comes about in language thus receives a subtle, ramified, and appropriately complex treatment in the thought of Peirce; in this respect no conceivable construal of Saussure's ideas about signs allows semiology to rival semeiotic in depth or breadth, whatever the object of analysis. The extraneous obstacles which prevented linguists (among others) from reaping the benefits of Peirce's life-long study of signs have for the most part now been removed, and the investigation of language as a semeiotic system ought no longer be regarded, to echo Hjelmslev, as the charting of unknown territory.

Yet the recent history of linguistics can hardly be said to reflect the rapprochement with the wider study of semeiotic that Saussure's program, and those of Hjelmslev and Jakobson after him, invited. The quarter-century hegemony of transformational-generative grammar, particularly in the United States, has had the practical effect of keeping inquiry into language as a system of signs off the agenda of linguistic theory. One of the (unintended) impediments that TG grammar has erected to the pursuit of theory along lines suggested by European structuralists and semeioticians has been its emphasis on language as an activity rather than as a work, to echo the Humboldtian terms borrowed from Greek, *energeia* 'activity' and *ergon* 'work' respectively, in which the question has occasionally been cast by TG proponents themselves.

One of the main rallying points of TG grammar at its inception was an essentially negative one, a reaction to what was perceived as the sterile emphasis on taxonomy for its own sake on the part of the so-called American structuralists (Bloomfield and his followers). Linguistic theory was proclaimed to be advanced directly in the measure of its accounting for the creative or generative capacities of human users of language. Language was not to be viewed as a corpus of ready-made formulae and patterns that speakers of a language learn by rote, but was to be grasped as the activity in which members of a speech community create and re-create speech.

The existence and influence of linguists of all schools on both sides of the Atlantic, whose methodological inclinations predisposed them to regard linguistics as a set of prescriptions for transforming a corpus of texts into a grammar of the language in question, certainly tended to contribute to an impasse in the advancement of theory. This emphasis on language as *ergon* may, indeed, have led to the opposite swing of the pendulum, away from inquiry into the structure of the building-blocks of language (in traditional structural linguistics) and toward its productive potential (in TG grammar), as a means of widening the compass of theory to include usage which had not yet been realized. In effect, this new preoccupation with *energeia* to the neglect of *ergon* meant a narrowing of the concept of patterning in language, since the 'norms of usage' (to reflect the terms propagated by Eugenio Coseriu), comprising what is historically realized and codified in a given language, did not share to the same extent in the dynamic aspect of the 'functional system' of the language. The identification of codedness with unproductiveness, ultimately a tendency to undervalue the patternment of inherited linguistic material in the newly-discovered interests of accounting for the creative possibilities of language use, led to the almost exclusive preoccupation with syntax and syntactic novelty that has continued to characterize the theory and the practice of TG grammarians. Not surprisingly, to the extent that this conception has contributed anything towards moving the enterprise of linguistic theory forward, its successes have chiefly been limited to the investigation of syntactic problems.

The relative freedom enjoyed by the language user in constructing sentences has obscured the complementary restrictedness in selecting the material of which sentences are made. Along the hierarchical scale of units in language, from distinctive features at the phonological level on the bottom to paradigms of sentence and discourse types at the syntactic level on the top, there is a middle ground that is constituted by words and their forms, or morphology. In the tradition of European philology and its structuralist continuation, the study of morphology occupied a position of theoretical and practical importance. In a quite direct sense, recognized from the very beginnings of systematic inquiry into language structure, words are the building blocks of language, and it is their relatively set modes of internal construction that have fostered the perception of language as a work—an *ergon*—in short, a *made object*. Since the primitive element in the make-up of words is the smallest meaningful unit, or morpheme, the relative fixity of the patterning of language has mainly to do with the fixed ways in which morphemes—grammatical and lexical— combine to constitute words and their forms.

While it is clear that language in actual use allows for the production of syntactic arrangements that are novel and the manipulation of meanings that result in semantic innovations (e.g. figural speech), at the core of language structure there is a stock of words and forms that, in their ensemble, are very much akin to a *work of art*. Because language shares with music, literature, and dance an unfolding along the temporal axis that is missing from the plastic arts, it is difficult to speak of it as an object, in the way that made objects—artifacts—are spoken of, due to the immediate simultaneous presence of a physical whole and all of its parts. Works of literature are closer to being physical objects, despite their dependence on time, than languages, and it is indicative of their shared statuses and characteristics that the word 'work' is applied to temporal as well as to atemporal manifestations of art.

Besides the organic connection between literature and language that results from the former being constituted by the latter, the manner in which literature is studied has much to contribute to the proper understanding of the structure of language. The traditional meeting ground of language and literary texts is philology, and although the scientific investigation of language for its own sake may be reckoned to have a millenial history, it is the study of language as an instrument of culture—mainly literature—that has dominated the history of humanistic inquiry throughout the literate world. The preeminence of philology is particularly marked in nineteenth-century Germany, where it was singled out as the paragon example of a *Geisteswissenschaft*, a 'science of man' in contrast to *Naturwissenschaft,* or 'natural science.' The philosopher Wilhelm Dilthey took these terms and developed their conceptual purport by linking them with a methodological dichotomy that has had a great influence ever since, that of *Erklären* 'explanation' and *Verstehen* 'understanding,' introduced originally by the

German historian-philosopher Johann Droysen. On this view, explanation is the aim of the natural sciences, whereas the sciences of man (alias 'history') aspire to understanding. Although ordinary usage tends not to differentiate between the words 'explain' and 'understand,' since practically every explanation contributes to our understanding of things, the effect of this distinction is the inclusion of *intentionality* within the compass of understanding, a consideration that generally finds no place in scientific explanation. Explanation in the natural sciences concentrates on the observation and prediction of events; understanding in the *Geisteswissenschaften* strives to encompass the goals and purposes of an agent, the meaning of signs, and the significance of social institutions or practices.

This nineteenth-century antipositivistic espousal of understanding as a methodology for the sciences of man came to be known under the name of *hermeneutics,* meaning the art of interpretation. With roots in the systematic exegesis of the Bible—a decidedly philological enterprise—hermeneutics was associated particularly with studies in the philosophy of history and the beginnings of sociology as a systematic discipline. Hermeneutics declined after the passage from the scholarly scene of its great German originators and lay dormant in European intellectual life until around the middle of this century, when it revived, particularly through the efforts of the German philosophers Hans-Georg Gadamer, Jürgen Habermas, and Karl-Otto Apel.

Perhaps the most well-known feature of hermeneutic analysis is the 'hermeneutic circle,' by which is meant that the analyst always starts with some pre-knowledge (*Vorverständnis*), from which he works outward by a series of explicative steps, ultimately to loop back upon the starting point, thereby completing the circle. What is important here is that the circle is not vicious in the strict logical sense of circularity; it is more precisely a *spiral,* consisting of organically successive complementary links that enable the analyst to arrive at a grounded and articulated knowledge by a series of mutually-reinforcing interpretations.

Since language is the product of historical accretion, and hermeneutic analysis takes history as a kind of paradigm object of interpretation, language is thus particularly suited to study through hermeneutic method. The pursuit of philological analysis in the wider sense promoted by such nineteenth-century hermeneuticians as August Boeckh (in his famous *Encyclopaedia*) is fundamentally a process of 're-cognition' or re-learning (on the model of Greek *anagignoskein* 'know again, read'). The net result amounts to 'knowledge of what is known,' an increase in understanding or generalized knowledge by reconstruction reminiscent of Plato's concept of *anamnesis*. In the case of language, understanding linguistic structure on this view means the analytical interpretation of the sense of accomplished cognition as embodied in grammatical facts. It is a recovery or a reconstruction of the *coherence* which enables facts to subsist as such.

The introduction of coherence may make hermeneutical analysis appear to be directed merely at uncovering the system underlying the facts, but this is not so. Even the most workmanlike investigation of linguistic structure aims at revealing the system of relations assumed to be immanent in the data. This usually results in a description which is internally consistent and in full compliance with the admonition of Ockham's razor; such as one might, for instance, find in a good grammar book of a language analyzed in that manner, serving the ends of pedagogy and general information. A truly interpretative analysis, however, aspires to an explanatory understanding that goes beyond the cataloguing of linguistic units and the rules of their combination. Its ultimate goal is a re-cognition of the cognized relations embodied by the facts.

This is a task that structuralism, for all its programmatic ambitiousness, has never seriously addressed. It has contented itself with a fundamentally non-hermeneutic approach to linguistic theory, choosing to follow the causal or Galilean model of explanation customary in the natural sciences, rather than the teleological or Aristotelian model of the human sciences. In its adherence to the mathematical ideal-type of a science, linguistics has generally allied itself with the strong positivistic strain that has characterized the methodologies of all academic disciplines, not exempting the humanities.

A reoriented structuralism is not, however, incompatible with hermeneutic analysis. In the case of language, the first step to be taken in this direction is the recognition that *language is a hermeneutic object.* What this means is that, to the extent language is capable of objectification, it is made up of a network of *inferences,* akin to the explanatory hypotheses of a scientific theory. Inherent in the dichotomic structure of the sign—the linking of the signans and the signatum—is a generalization of the type 'If *A* then *B*,' which for linguistic signs in particular implies a kind of rule of the form 'If content *A* then expression *B*.' The relation between sign and object, between signans and signatum, is thus fundamentally an *illative* one ('*A* ergo *B*'), a circumstance masked by the scholastic formula *A liquid stat pro aliquo* so often cited in support of the substitutive role of the signans (expression) in relation to the signatum (content).

Without limiting himself to language, Peirce is quite emphatic in his advocacy of illation as the fundamental relation of logic, hence of semeiotic. The relation between content and expression—and correspondingly between the signatum and the signans of the individual sign—is equivalent in form to the relation between a protasis ('If . . . ') and an apodosis ('then . . . '). 'The copula of equality,' says Peirce, 'ought to be regarded as merely derivative.' Moreover, the relation is asymmetric and transitive, hence dynamic and unidirectional. On this view, the structure of language is a system of inferences whereby content entities are assigned to expression entities through a series of interpretative translations. It follows that at the heart of this system are the *interpretants,* the constituents of sign structure that enable linkages of signantia and signata *to make sense.*

It is through the notion of sense that semeiotic and hermeneutic converge, nowhere more clearly than in the structure of language. If we accept as axiomatic (following Jakobson) the notions that 'all linguistic phenomena . . . act always and solely as signs'; and, furthermore, that 'any linguistic item . . . partakes—each in its own way—in [sic] the cardinal, viz. semantic, tasks of language and *must be interpreted with respect to its significative value*' [emphasis added], then we ought reasonably to expect interpretation to occupy the central position in the structure and theory of grammar. This is precisely the point at which the crucial importance of the *fit* between the theory of the object and the structure of that object transpires. The role allotted to language as a structure—to its very nature and function as a hermeneutic object—demands that the methods of inquiry into language underlying linguistic theory faithfully reflect the principles of organization of language itself.

The essence of hermeneutic is involved in Peirce's definition of meaning as 'the *translation* of a sign into another system of signs' [emphasis added]. Translation is, after all, tantamount to the intercession of an interpretant. A more direct apprehension of the intimate connection between semeiotic and hermeneutic is provided in the Preface to a series of unpublished 'Essays on Meaning' which Peirce drafted in 1909. In discussing what part of Logic should study the 'different sorts of Meanings of signs,' Peirce adduces as a model Aristotle's *De Interpretatione,* originally *Peri hermeneias (On Interpretation),* and suggests that this study 'might be called *hermeneutic, the science of interpretations or Meanings.* Or it might be called *Universal Grammar,* the grammar of signs in general.' Immediately thereafter, Peirce defines a sign as 'anything which represents something else, its *Object,* to any mind that can *Interpret* it so.' The convergence of semeiotic and hermeneutic via the nature of Sign is thus complete.

What remains to be determined is the precise method by which linguistics is to exploit these insights. Jakobson calls Peirce's notion of interpretant 'one of the most ingenious findings and effective devices received from Peirce by semiotics in general and by the analysis of grammatical and lexical meanings in particular.' Given that the 'essence of language' is to be found in the inherent organization of grammar as a system of patterned relationships between sounds and meanings, precisely how are we to proceed in uncovering these relationships? A programmatic subsumption of all linguistic analysis under the rubric of meaning or hermeneutic must be augmented by a method which allows access to *the structure of meaning.*

The habitual colligation of signata with signantia in ready-made linguistic entities of varying breadth and depth (from distinctive features to whole utterances) tends to obscure a pivotal disjunction between the content system and the expression system of language. Although each system forms a structure, the kind of linguistic sign which constitutes the content system is categorically distinct from the kind of sign which constitutes the expression system. The sounds of language that organize themselves into a relational system called a phonology are made up of ultimate units, variously called 'distinctive features,' 'diacritic categories,' or 'diacritic paradigms.' What is of special importance is their status as *signs with a purely diacritic function*. The diacritic signs of a phonological system have the requisite semeiotic structure, being comprised by a sign vehicle or signans realized as a (relational) sound property, and a meaning or signatum, namely its diacritic function. Now, although diacritic signs contract paradigms (oppositions) and combine into syntagms which are simultaneous (i.e. phonemes) or sequential (clusters, syllables, words, etc.) in ways quite analogous to non-diacritic signs, they differ from other linguistic signs in one cardinal respect. Each diacritic sign has the same unique signatum: 'otherness' or 'alterity,' i.e. pure opposition (to all other diacritic signs).

The category to which the signs of the content system belong is fundamentally different from that of the diacritic signs, in that non-diacritic signs always have their own positive signata. The signata of content signs may consist of single content elements or of syntagms of content elements; on the basis of this division into unitary and complex signata, content signs are correspondingly divided into asynthetic and synthetic signs. There exist content signs whose signantia have a direct phonic manifestation (e.g. the different intonation contours associated with the opposition 'interrogative' vs. 'declarative' in many languages), but content signs must typically resort to being represented by complexes of diacritic signs, each with its own signans but devoid of a positive signatum. Content signs for the most part have no material signans; diacritic signs have no individual, positively definable signatum, their signata being strictly synonymous ('otherness'). Content signs, therefore, form oppositions and an entire system of oppositions strictly on the basis of their signata, whereas diacritic signs are opposed and comprise an entire system of oppositions strictly on the basis of their signantia.

The inherent asymmetry between the two articulations of language has a fundamental bearing on the investigation of linguistic structure and on the theory of grammar. Expression and content cannot be compared directly: the structure of language is such that purely diacritic signs possessing no meaning except otherness are used to constitute the material manifestation of content signs (more precisely, their signantia), which do possess a substantive meaning. How is this fundamental disjunction overcome by the structure of language? How is it that grammar actually presents itself as a patterned, coherent arrangement of sounds and meanings?

The answers to these crucial questions form the subject of this book. In anticipation of their greatly amplified treatment in the chapters to follow, it suffices to say here that these questions have never before been posed with the framework for definitive solutions in mind. The full implementation of the requirement of a thorough-going, unified theoretical approach to the problem of form and meaning was manifestly on the agenda of the early European structuralists, particularly the three leading Russian members of the Prague Linguistic Circle, Nikolaj Trubetzkoy, Roman Jakobson, and Sergej Karcevskij. But it remained largely a programmatic desideratum rather than an explicit achievement of structuralism, and the subsequent history of linguistics cannot be said to have made significant advances toward the solution of this all-important problem. (This is true no matter how broadly or narrowly one defines the scope of structural linguistics.)

Contemporary linguistic practice with regard to method has, irrespective of particular doctrines or persuasions, been chiefly oriented towards the description of languages (synchrony, the writing of descriptive grammars) and language states (diachrony), with a pedagogical aim in view more often than not. A concomitant result of this orientation has been the preoccupation of linguists with rule formulation, in concord with the prevailing conception of language as 'rule-governed behavior,' and the presumption that advances in theory are to be identified with the construction of formalisms of maximal generality and abstractness.

With the rise to near-hegemony of TG grammar has come the ascendancy of rules of grammar, not as prescriptive devices but as a means of capturing the systematic (regulative) norms inherent in linguistic behavior. Rules as statements of regularities appear to serve ends that can be considered preliminary to the task of understanding grammar and making sense of it. The hermeneutic treatment of linguistic facts, on the other hand, encompasses a notion of rule that strives to represent the 'tri-relative' bond between signans, signatum, and interpretant. The semeiotic relation between the three elements of a sign must obtain in order for semeiosis to occur: the patterned correspondence between sets of signata and conjugate sets of signantia in language owes its coherence to the sets of interpretants that inhere in every semeiosis. 'Rule' in a semeiotic sense, therefore, is neither causal nor predictive, as it is in the natural sciences. 'Rule' from the hermeneutic standpoint is inherent in 'interpretant,' but the latter concept is much wider and more productive of understanding, given that the object of study is language (or language-like in form).

The exclusion of the concept of rules as descriptive devices from the theory of grammar and its supersedure by the semeiotic notion of interpretant reintroduces questions about the patterned relation between expression and content. We know that the disjunction between expression-form and content-form (to use Hjelmslev's terminology) is overcome by language, which is able to do so because the interpretants on both sides of the sign situation, being directly comparable in kind and function, bridge the hiatus between signantia without signata and signata without signantia. Interpretants are the *agents of mediation* between sign and object, as Peirce himself realized when he equated mediation with representation. The interpretant of the expression sign—of the phonological signantia—can be compared directly to the interpretant of the content sign—the grammatical and lexical signata. Any coherence that emanates from the bond between coordinated signata and signantia in the form of linguistic entities and collocations of entities is, therefore, to be found in the patterned relationship of interpretants.

But what exactly is the interpretant of a linguistic sign? We have ascertained that every sign of language, being the kind of sign that has a 'tri-relative' structure, must have an interpretant. If it is interpretants that mediate between content-form and expression-form, they themselves must be ontologically unitary, whether the domain of their reference is sound or sense. Is there a dimension of language structure which matches the function of the interpretant as agent of mediation in semeiosis, imparting form to meaning?

An answer to these questions can perhaps be traced to the traditions of European structuralism, specifically those of the Prague Linguistic Circle and its most illustrious members, Trubetzkoy and Jakobson. In 1930 Trubetzkoy discovered that the terms of a phonological opposition are not merely polar in phonetic implementation, but that their 'intrinsic content' is 'contraposed.' He identified the unequal evaluation of the terms of a phonological opposition with the presence (or maximum) versus absence (or minimum) of a 'positive mark' and called this conceptual superstructure of the phonological sign 'markedness.' In 1932 Jakobson extended the scope of markedness by applying it to oppositions in grammar, specifically the morphological categories of the Russian verb, and recognized explicitly the inherent asymmetry of markedness relations. Trubetzkoy designated the term of a phonological opposition characterized by the presence (or maximum degree) of a physical (phonetic) quality or mark as the 'marked' member of the opposition, and the term characterized by the absence (or minimal degree) of that quality or mark as the 'unmarked' member. Jakobson's extension of markedness to grammar (and lexis) brought out the fact that members of grammatical and lexical paradigms are not defined individually by their absolute referential scope; rather that whole paradigms, both dichotomic and graded, diagram differences in referential substance with the 'skewed projection' dictated by the asymmetry of such paradigms. The marked term of an opposition has a narrowed referential scope, while the unmarked term is broader in the scope of its application to the field of reference. One part of the referential field must be represented by the unmarked term of an opposition, but the remaining part may be represented by either the marked or the unmarked term. For instance, in the grammatical representation of time, the substantive opposition anteriority vs. non-anteriority to the speech event is rendered by the formal tense opposition 'past' vs. 'non-past,' such that non-anteriority is unambiguously signaled by the non-past—the unmarked member of the opposition—whereas anteriority may be signaled either by the past tense—the marked term of the opposition—or by the non-past (here, the so-called *praesens historicum*). In this example it is clear that the contradictory opposites of the referential category of time are so rendered grammatically that one member of the opposition of tense includes the other member. This broader scope of the unmarked member is similarly reflected in lexical oppositions such as English *man* vs. *woman,* where the former is the generic (unmarked) designation of humankind, while the latter is reserved for the designation of only a subset of the referential field.

It can be seen that the concept of markedness facilitates the unitary conception of the structure of phonology, grammar, and lexis—in short, of language. This unitary conception is at the center of the long-standing supposition (stemming from the work of Jakobson and Hjelmslev in the 1930s) that different levels of language structure are governed by identical principles of organization, which is to say that the levels are *isomorphous.* The isomorphism is mirrored in part by the formal identity of the definition of markedness as it pertains to the diverse elements of both the expression system and the content system. Despite differences stemming from the disparity in focus—the phonic level of signantia in the case of expression and the semantic level of signata, in the case of content—all instances of the marked term share a narrowed specification and a circumscription of scope vis-à-vis their unmarked counterparts. In phonology, the marked term of an opposition constrains or narrows a certain (negative or positive) relational sound property which is relatively (and polarly) unconstrained and uncircumscribed in the corresponding unmarked term. In grammar and lexis, the narrowed definition affects a conceptual item, delimiting the referential scope of the marked term vis-à-vis the relatively unnarrowed scope of the unmarked term.

The Prague School concept of markedness is largely confined to linguistics and the study of language structure, despite some inklings as to its applicability to other areas of human behavior. Its fundamental role as a semeiotic universal is adumbrated somewhat more sweepingly (if inchoately) by Saussure's famous dictum that 'language is a system of pure values.' Unfortunately, Saussure failed to integrate his notion of linguistic value with his sign theory, and the subsequent development of European structuralism, both before-and after the Second World War, does not include a ramified appreciation of the relationship between markedness and value. (An awareness of Peirce and of his semeiotic would no doubt have facilitated the progress in understanding grammar that is now finally emerging, owing to the wider dissemination of Peirce's philosophical writings).

Indeed, the idea can now be advanced with some confidence that markedness is a species of interpretant, fully compatible in its own way with the system of interpretants established by Peirce (see chapter 1 herein). One of Peirce's (many) definitions of sign is 'an object which is in relation to its object on the one hand and to an interpretant on the other in such a way as to bring the interpretant into a relation to the object corresponding to its own relation to the object.' If by signification is meant the action of a sign whereby the interpretant is brought into relation with the object of the sign, it is understandable why Peirce saw the sign's 'essential significant character [as] the character of causing the interpretation of its object.' The being of the sign, therefore, consists in its causing an interpretation; in other words, in causing an *evaluation* of the relationship between sign and object.

The evaluative or axiological dimension of the sign's connection with a system of interpretants is implied by Peirce's discussion of semeiotic but has not been clearly perceived. The interpretants of linguistic signs are values—markedness values. While markedness is subject to grading, degrees of markedness are expressible exclusively in terms of just two values, 'marked' and 'unmarked,' which imply each other but are fundamentally asymmetric. The asymmetry of the linguistic sign in its paradigmatic dimension of markedness emerges in its syntagmatic dimension as ranking or hierarchy. Thus the relation between signans and signatum which gives rise to signification always comports some measure of *significance* or value. If this were not true, sign relations would not conform to a pattern because there would be no overarching principle of order.

'Every single constituent of any linguistic system,' writes Jakobson, 'is built on an opposition of two logical contradictories: the presence of an attribute ("markedness") in contraposition to its absence ("unmarkedness"). The entire network of language displays a hierarchical arrangement that within each level of the system follows the same dichotomous principle of marked terms superposed on the corresponding unmarked terms.' While this formulation faithfully reflects the original Prague School understanding of markedness as being associated with attributes or marks, and thereby with substance, the status of markedness as an interpretant points to its proper place in the form of language. Markedness is a matter of *conceptual complexity* and as such is to a significant extent independent of the substance of language. Conceptual complexity is tantamount to (grades of) value. Thus every linguistic opposition, besides consisting of a signans/signatum duple, has an evaluative superstructure defined by the two polar values, marked and unmarked. These values constitute inherent semeiotic definientia of a given opposition's terms. The scope of markedness as the dominant principle of conceptualization is not limited by language: it inheres in the patterning of all human semeiotic systems, hence in all of human culture. Its asymmetric character, moreover, is clearly rooted in biological and neurophysiological isomorphisms, namely the structure of the genetic code and the lateralization of the brain. The mental capacity of human beings is defined by the universal principle that there is no conceptualization without evaluation: the integration of concepts into paradigms and syntagms necessarily involves grading and ranking, i.e. markedness.

The concept of markedness can be advanced materially beyond its programmatic proclamation as the universal semeiotic principle underlying the organization of linguistic structure. One of the chief tasks set out in the chapters to follow is the aggrandizement of the Prague School notion of markedness to embrace discoveries of its nature and workings made in the last fifteen years or so. The access to the principles of organization governing linguistic structure provided by markedness also affords a way of returning to the question posed at the very beginning of this Introduction, that of *physei* vs. *thesei*.

Jakobson's identification of the 'essence' of language with the fact that the system of signantia may diagram relations in the corresponding system of signata, and that these expression/content mapping relations pervade the entirety of language, establish language in part as what mathematicians call an 'automorphism,' i.e. as a structure defined by relations of symmetry between its parts. To the extent that such symmetry or congruence is manifest in language, it is an affirmation of the 'naturalist' (*physei*) position. Language conforms to nature by the fact that it diagrammatizes content in expression.

The veracity of the *physei*-as-diagrammatization position is directly ascertainable from a consideration of the relations in a synchronic grammar. This does not mean, however, that mapping relations are irrelevant to the problem of language change, more specifically to the assumption that change is to a large extent motivated rather than arbitrary, just as relations in the structure of the linguistic sign itself. Such relations of semeiotic congruence are undoubtedly involved in the teleology of function characteristic of linguistic change, although they are typically covert and not accessible to direct observation by the grammarian while in statu nascendi. Indeed, covert patterns of correspondence determine tendencies of development, so that the drift of a language can be explicated as a gradual actualization in its surface forms of virtual patterns, patterns that are established over time as part of the linguistic competence of speakers. It is these patterns that constitute the functional system or the productive center of language, in contradistinction to its norms or unproductive periphery, and determine which deviations from the received grammar will be accepted, which rejected. The dynamics of language follows a trajectory of maximizing the patterns of diagrammatization and minimizing or ultimately eliminating those that are devoid of such semeiotic basis. This understanding of the telos of linguistic change brings synchrony and diachrony into an inalienable structural relation: change is thereby conceived as an aspect of continuity.

The presumption underlying all contemporary inquiry into language —that it is a system—also entails the search for patterns of coherence among linguistic facts. The semeiotic perspective on language structure consonant with Peirce's fundamental discoveries of the nature of signs is informed by three cardinal interconnected tenets. First, there exist semeiotic universals—principles of organization—which govern the patterning of linguistic data. Second, the patterning is coherent, which is to say that the genuinely structured or motivated sets of facts—the functional system or structure sensu stricto, as distinct from the norm-governed adstructure—are explicable and to be understood as cohesions or correlations between expression-form and content-form. Third, the patterning of form/meaning correlations owes its coherence to a mediating interpretative component of semeiosis or 'structural cement' that binds the facts together and allows them to subsist systematically alongside each other. This component, corresponding in all essential details to Peirce's interpretant, is markedness.

Why are certain specific expressions associated with certain specific contents? This utterly basic question has, remarkably, never been posed in the history of linguistics, perhaps because it seemed absurd to ask why a fact can be a fact. But that is precisely what needs to be inquired into so as to arrive at a truly explanatory theory of grammar, a theory of language facts that satisfies the requirements of the hermeneutic understanding of a hermeneutic object.

The semeiotic values that enable sounds and meanings to cohere in a pattern are markedness values. The search for principles of organization, for coherence in language structure, is thus an investigation of the ways in which markedness values arrange themselves in language, giving this most important of all forms of semeiosis its status as a system.

No linguistic entity is without its markedness value, since every linguistic entity participates in a network of oppositions whose nature and significance is directly determined by markedness. Language is a system of signs, a semeiotic; therefore all such entities are signs and contribute as parts to the whole that is a semeiotic system. While heretofore such stock items of linguistic description as stems and suffixes, including their positional shapes or alternants, have been looked upon simply as artifacts which facilitate an economical, internally consistent statement of distributional facts, now these entities must be viewed as having semeiotic values—markedness values—which vary coherently and uniformly with contexts and the values of contexts.

There is thus at the core of structure a coherence of facts, which resides in the patterned cooccurrence of contexts and units accompanied by a coordination of their markedness values. The circularity inherent, furthermore, in manifestations of coherence must not be viewed as a defect: quite the contrary, it is of the very nature of language as a hermeneutic object. To conceive of facts as cohering with other facts, as contexts do with units, is to recognize circularity as a definiens of coherence. The search for 'independent motivation' in linguistic explanations is actually a distorting imitation of the Galilean mode of the natural sciences. The notion of coherence consonant with the Aristotelian mode appropriate to hermeneutic conceptualization entails circularity as a virtue, owing to its immanence in the structure of language. Both the theory of grammar and the method of analysis leading to the proper understanding of linguistic facts cannot dispense with circularity for the simple reason that it is of the essence of language.

Linguistic facts must be recognized for what they are, the actual variations of language rather than the 'underlying forms' or 'deep structures' posited by contemporary practitioners. A theory of grammar which places the matter of *the sense of grammatical alternation* at the center of its agenda considers variations of form associated with variations of meaning to be its proper explananda. It substitutes for the question 'How does one get from deep to surface structure?' the question 'Why are the surface facts of grammar as they are?' Seeking the answer to such a radical question presupposes the belief that 'surface' variations—the actual stuff of language—do not vary haphazardly, but organize themselves into a semeiotic, a system of signs. Surface variants and alternations are thus seen not as mere agglomerations of data to be systematized by the linguist's intervention and appeal to formalisms at a putatively deeper (hence 'truer') level of linguistic reality, but as entering directly into a pattern of semeiotic relations with each other.

Transposing the theoretical enterprise of linguistics to another dimension, away from the mechanistic and scientistic impasse in which it has been mired in the last quarter-century, means formulating a theory of grammar that puts fundamentally different questions to its data and frames them in a fundamentally different mode, one defined by the nature of language as a hermeneutic object. The replacement of causal explanation by hermeneutic understanding as the province of theory entails the jettisoning of conceptions of language structure and linguistic method that result in the prevailing self-confinement to goals that are fundamentally (if unwittingly) non-explanatory. The pursuit by TG grammarians of a 'complete scientific description of the language' corresponding to 'a fluent speaker's knowledge of his language' expressed in the construction of rule formalisms is, therefore, fundamentally irrelevant for linguistic theory: a theory of grammar is not a theory of knowledge but a theory of *habit,* in the sense imparted to the word and the concept by Peirce's pragmaticism (see chapter 1). Explanation aspiring to hermeneutic understanding must focus on why the data of language cohere as signs, not on mechanisms by which grammatical forms can be derived by the judicious choice and application of rules (ad hoc or not). This requirement once and for all removes predictability-via-rules from the agenda of theory.

The entire recent history of linguistics demonstrates with great clarity the feasibility of forcing data into a proliferating number of mutually-compatible formalized configurations or notational variants. It is characteristic that these frameworks, and the schools with their adherents that they represent, take no cognizance of the principle (laid down by Jakobson among others) that *all* linguistic entities participate above all in the semantic tasks of language and must be interpreted in terms of their significative value. It is obvious, on the other hand, that even the interests of a purely descriptive linguistics are ill-served by an attitude toward language that ignores its status as a semeiotic.

The grammarian writing a description of a particular language must accept the burden of showing how the various grammatical rules he formulates stand with respect to their semeiotic function. Since linguistic rules are such that one entity or structure is transformed into another entity or structure in a given context, they thereby purport to act as an interpretant which gives a means of representation (signans) to an object of representation (signatum). If this is so, the grammar writer cannot limit his task to formulating rules that merely register generalizations about the distribution of entities in texts, or which transform structures of one kind into structures of the same kind without any change in information or function. A linguistic description which lays claim to being the faithful account of a speaker's language competence cannot evade the responsibility of explicitly characterizing the semeiotic status—the 'significative value'— of all the primitive elements and all the effects wrought on them by the rules formulated to encompass them.

It is a plain fact that the mainstream of linguistic practice has failed to conceive its tasks in terms of this responsibility. In so doing, linguists have ignored the fundamental truth that language is a semeiotic. It is with the amelioration of this fundamental disability of linguistic theory and method in mind that the present work is offered.

PART ONE

Theoretical Prolegomena

I

Peirce's Semeiotic

Peirce's theory of signs, or semeiotic, is intended by him to apply, in the most general manner possible, to everything capable of being a sign, which is to say everything that can be interpreted—by a feeling, an action, or a thought. His 'general Semeiotic' (H 118) articulates a compass for the analysis of signs which is as large as the universe itself, for, according to Peirce, 'all this universe is perfused with signs, if it is not composed exclusively of signs' (5.448n). If anything is a sign, as long as it is capable of being correctly interpreted, then all subjects whatever are capable of being regarded from the semeiotic point of view. Exactly this attitude charac- terizes the entire span of Peirce's working life, as he recalls in a letter of 1908 to Lady Welby:

> Know that from the day when at the age of 12 or 13 I took up, in my elder brother's room a copy of Whately's "*Logic*," and asked him what Logic was, and getting some simple answer, flung myself on the floor and buried myself in it, it has never been in my power to study anything,—mathematics, ethics, metaphysics, gravitation, thermodynamics, optics, chemistry, comparative anatomy, astronomy, psychology, phonetics, economics, the history of science, whist, men and women, wine, metrology, except as a study of semeiotic. (H 85-6).

In considering Peirce's theory, therefore, one would do the greatest justice to the topic by taking seriously the very broad view of sign and semeiosis corresponding to Peirce's although he himself (in the same letter to Lady Welby) 'despair[ed] of making [his] own broader conception understood' (H 81). Nor is the effect of signs in the universe limited as a matter of principle to that on human minds. Notwithstanding the potentially all-encompassing domain of sign and semeiotic, it is clear that

Peirce, as a matter of actual practice, emphasizes human language and its use as the epitomical application of his concepts: 'all thought whatsoever is a sign, and is mostly of the nature of language' (5.421). By treating language as a sign system, Peirce manifests in a fundamental way the pervasive and continuing influence of medieval logic, particularly ideas connected with the notion of Speculative Grammar in the Middle Ages. (This is a tradition that loses its place in the history of linguistics for all practical purposes until its resuscitation at the end of the nineteenth century.)

1. Speculative Grammar

The mention of Speculative Grammar is not fortuitous. As one of the first modern philosophers to return to the Schoolmen for insight and inspiration, Peirce acquainted himself particularly deeply with the writings of Duns Scotus and even dubbed himself a 'Scotistic realist.' From the *Grammatica Speculativa* commonly misattributed to Duns Scotus (actually written by Thomas of Erfurt) in the editions of Peirce's time, Peirce took over the name for the most important of the three subdivisions of Logic within his architectonic of sciences, namely Speculative Grammar, Critic (or Critical Logic), and Methodeutic (or Speculative Rhetoric). The first is defined by Peirce as 'the general theory of the nature and meanings of signs, whether they be icons, indices, or symbols'; the second 'classifies arguments and determines the validity and degree of force of each kind'; the third 'studies the methods that ought to be pursued in the investigation, in the exposition, and in the application of truth' (1.191).

Without exploring the question whether Peirce's notion of logic is coextensive with semeiotic or subsumed by it (Fisch 1978:51-3), it is clear that he conceived logic as a study of 'the general necessary laws of signs' (2.93). Consequently, his conception of sign in all its ramifications is intimately connected with Speculative Grammar in the first instance, as the primary and most fundamental of his three divisions of logic. In fact, one of Peirce's many definitions of a sign—'something which stands to somebody for something in some respect or capacity' (2.228)—contains the three elements (i.e. in some *respect* for *something* to *somebody*) on which the tripartition of logic hinges (Feibleman 1970:88). Speculative Grammar, having a particularly broad scope, can be seen as Peirce's version of a theory of assertion (cf. Brock 1975), with which semeiotic has an intimate connection, since Peirce conceived of thought as being assertory in nature while consisting of signs. It is important to keep in mind Peirce's adherence to Plato's position 'that thinking always proceeds in the form of a dialogue—a dialogue between different phases of the *ego*—so that, being dialogical, it is essentially composed of signs, as its matter' (4.6). Speculative Grammar is not just an inquiry into 'the general conditions to which thought or signs of any kind must conform in order to assert anything' (2.206); it appears to be intended to encompass, furthermore, theories of propositional truth, meaning, and cognition (Brock 1975:128; cf. 2.206).

The relation between signs and cognition is a particularly crucial one, for Peirce clearly intends his semeiotic to be a theory of cognition. By the latter phrase (equivalent in most senses to epistemology) Peirce means the very same Speculative Grammar, 'or analysis of the nature of assertion' (3.432), which aims at explaining the 'possibility of knowledge.' The circle is now complete: semeiotic, speculative grammar, cognition, assertion. Strictly speaking, it is not complete unless assertion is understood to imply meaning, since meaning inheres in semeiotic. But assertion, for Peirce, does involve meaning: the phrase 'to assert anything' is clearly used by him as equivalent to the phrase 'to mean anything' (Brock 1975:129). Speculative Grammar, which is the same as pure grammar, says Peirce in another connection, is called upon to investigate what must be true of the signs used by 'every scientific intelligence in order that they may embody any *meaning*' (2.229).

The relation of meaning, and through it of cognition, to semeiotic and assertion transpires from the central role of the proposition. Signs, according to Peirce, are inherently linked to the proposition: 'no sign of a thing or kind of thing—the ideas of signs to which concepts belong—can arise except in a proposition' (4.583). Since to assert and to mean are equivalent, signs divorced from the context of propositionalizing and asserting are ipso facto not cognitively meaningful (Brock 1975:129-30).

2. The Categories

Logic studies signs, and it does so in three ways: in respect of the general conditions whereby they have meaning, in respect of the conditions of their truth, and in respect of the conditions whereby their meaning is transferred to other signs (NE 4:331). Speculative Grammar is thus a member of a triad, one of many such triads that permeate the entirety of Peirce's thought. More than that, triads are said to be reflective of the structure of phenomena and of ideas about them. In fact, Peirce admits that his Formal Logic is a 'Kantian step of transferring the conceptions of logic to metaphysics' (loc. cit.). The tripartition of logic is not just a classificatory convenience, but in the very nature of the sign relation itself. And the study of logic, including modes of inference (also fundamentally three, about which more below, section 4), seemed to Peirce inevitably to abut in three recurrent ideas, corresponding in form to the sign relation, wherein 'the Sign, in general is the third member of a triad; first a thing as a thing; second a thing as reacting with another thing; and third a thing as representing another to a third' (loc. cit.). In their most general and purest form these three ideas are called *categories* by Peirce, and he proposes to call their study *Phenomenology* or *Phaneroscopy* (also *Ideoscopy*), the latter two names being of Peirce's own invention. The categories themselves Peirce called by new names, too: Firstness, Secondness, Thirdness—in order to distinguish his conception from that of predecessors (such as Aristotle, Kant, and Hegel). What is subsumed by each of these categories is called a First, a Second, and a Third, respectively.

Peirce defines the categories as follows (8.328):

> Firstness is the mode of being of that which is such as it is, positively and without reference to anything else.

> Secondness is the mode of being of that which is such as it is, with respect to a second but regardless of any third.

> Thirdness is the mode of being of that which is such as it is, in bringing a second and third into relation to each other.

Recognizing the excessive generality and vagueness of these terms, Peirce repeatedly refashions and amplifies his definitions of them, as in these extended examples:

> *Firstness* may be defined as . . . the mode in which anything would be for itself, irrespective of anything else, so that it would not make any difference though nothing else existed, or ever had existed, or could exist. Now this mode of being can only be apprehended as a mode of feeling. For there is no other mode of being which we can conceive as having no relation to the possibility of anything else. In the second place, the First must be without parts. For a part of an object is something other than the object itself. Remembering these points, you will perceive that any color, say *magenta*, has and is a positive mode of feeling, irrespective of every other. Because, firstness is all that it is, for itself, irrespective of anything else, when viewed *from without* (and therefore no longer in the original fullness of firstness) the firstnesses are all the different possible sense-qualities, embracing endless varieties of which all we can feel are but minute fragments. Each of these is just as simple as any other. It is impossible for a sense-quality to be otherwise than absolutely simple. It is only complex to the eye of comparison, not in itself. (NE 4:332)

> A *Secondness* may be defined as a modification of the being of one subject, which modification is *ipso facto* a mode of being of quite a distinct subject, or, more accurately, secondness is that in each of two absolutely severed and remote subjects which pairs it with the other, not for my mind nor for, or by, any mediating subject or circumstance whatsoever, but in those two subjects alone; so that it would be just the same if nothing else existed, or ever had existed, or could exist. You see that this Secondness in each subject must be

secondary to the inward Firstness of that subject and does not supersede that
firstness in the least. For were it to do so, the two subjects would, insofar,
become one. Now it is precisely their twoness all the time that is most essential
to their secondness. But though the secondness is secondary to the firstness, it
constitutes no limitation upon the firstness. The two subjects are in no degree
one; nor does the secondness belong to them taken together. There are two
Secondnesses, one for each subject; but these are only aspects of one
Pairedness which belongs to one subject in one way and to the other in another
way. But this pairedness is nothing different from the secondness. It is not
mediated or brought about; and consequently it is not of a comprehensible
nature, but is absolutely blind. The aspect of it present to each subject has no
possible *rationale*. In their *essence,* the two subjects are not paired; for in its
essence anything is what it is, while its secondness is that of it which is another.
The secondness, therefore, is an accidental circumstance. It is that a blind
reaction takes place between the two subjects. It is that which we experience
when our will meets with resistance, or when something obtrudes itself upon
sense. Imagine a magenta color to feel itself and nothing else. Now while it
slumbers in its magenta-ness let it suddenly be metamorphosed into pea green.
Its experience at the moment of transformation will be secondness. (NE 4:332-
3)

The idea of *Thirdness* is more readily understood. It is a modification of the
being of one subject which is the mode of a second so far as it is a modification
of a third. It might be called an inherent reason. That dormitive power of
opium by virtue of which the patient sleeps is more than a mere word. It
denotes, however indistinctly, some reason or regularity by virtue of which the
opium acts so. Every law, or general rule, expresses a thirdness; because it
induces one fact to cause another. Now such a proposition as, Enoch is a man,
expresses a firstness. There is no reason for it; such is Enoch's nature,   that is
all. On the other hand the result that Enoch dies like other men, as result or
effect, expresses a Secondness. The necessity of the conclusion is just the brute
force of this Secondness. In Deduction, then, Firstness by the operation of
Thirdness brings forth Secondness. Next consider an Induction. The people
born in the last census-year may be considered as a sample of Americans. That
these objects should be Americans has no reason except that that was the
condition of my taking them into consideration. There is Firstness. Now the
Census tells me that about half those people were males. And that this was a
necessary result is almost guaranteed by the number of persons included in the
sample. There, then, I assume to be Secondness. Hence we infer the *reason* to
be that there is some virtue, or occult regularity, operating to make one half of
all American births male. There is Thirdness. Thus, Firstness and Secondness
following have risen to Thirdness. (NE 4:333)

Firstness is the categorial rubric under which are entered the common
characteristics of freshness, life, freedom, immediacy, feeling, quality,
vivacity, and independence (1.302-3, 1.337, 1.357, 6.32); of being or being-
in-itself (1.356, 1.329); and of mere potentiality (1.328). The idea of a

character or quality best summarizes these in the abstract. Although an indefinite aggregate of individual things may resemble one another through a common trait or quality, and may be contrasted with all individuals devoid of this same trait or quality, the trait or quality can be abstracted from the things which have it or lack it, i.e. be isolated and considered in itself apart from the individual things which share or fail to share in it. No matter how disparate and haphazard a collection of entities may be, there will always be some abstractable quality, even if it is nothing more than a peculiar flavor of oddity or strangeness. A quality thus abstracted can be regarded in itself, as an undifferentiated unity. The name Firstness appears to have suggested itself to Peirce partly with this consideration in mind.

An important dimension of Peirce's first category goes beyond quality while encompassing it. The here and now character of a concrete quality (for instance, the color or hardness of an object actually being examined by a mineralogist) is not an instance of Firstness. Rather, Firstness is the *possibility* that some quality may be abstracted or isolated, which would then render it fit to be considered as a unity without parts or elements, without explanatory antecedents or causal consequents. It is the independence of Firstness that allows Peirce to associate it most closely with ideas of freedom, spontaneity, and originality.

Once the spatio-temporal locus of anything under consideration is invoked, however, factors such as effort, resistance, and force come into play, which necessitate dependence, such as is not to be found in Firstness. Secondness, says Peirce, 'is the experience of effort, prescinded from the idea of a purpose' (H 25). Since 'generally speaking genuine secondness consists in one thing acting upon another,—brute action' (H 26), the main idea of Secondness is that of opposition and raw existence, set off from other ideas by the very same opposition and by contrast. Whatever exists either acts to exert some force on something else external to it; or it is the patient, as it were, of the force exerted upon it by things external to itself. Accordingly, there can be said to be two types of Secondness, active and passive. Secondness confronts us whether we wish it or not; it is a datum, a singular *this,* which Peirce occasionally refers to as a *haecceity*. The hard facts of experience, such as are meant when one speaks of experience teaching us this or that, are examples of Secondness. Similarly, mere contiguity, as in pointing to an object, or mere proximity between objects, without any description or classification accompanying the act or state, manifest Secondness. Dyadic relations are frequently adduced by Peirce as involving the idea of Secondness. Most prominent among Seconds are varieties of limits, boundaries, or termini, wherein something confronts its negation. The category of Secondness is found in action, resistance, facticity, dependence, relation, compulsion, effect, reality, and result (1.337, 1.356, 1.358).

Secondness is inadequate, however, to cover the *mental* element, the status of two things when they are combined or mediated by some third thing. The crucial role of the binding element is stressed by Peirce in a whole variety of ways; one of the most direct is as follows:

> Three ideas are basic: those of something, other, and third, or middle. For suppose anything, and there is at once the idea of something. But this something cannot have any distinct property, unless it be opposed to something else. Nor can this opposition exist without the opposites are connected through some *medium*.

> In this mathematical proposition (for such it is shown to be) you have all logic and all metaphysics in a nut-shell. (MS 915:1)

Thirdness is the word Peirce uses corresponding to the Kantian and Hegelian synthesis. This category inheres in mediation, synthesis, living, continuity, process, moderation, learning, memory, inference, representation, intelligence, intelligibility, generality, infinity, diffusion, growth, and conduct (1.337, 1.340, 1.356, 1.359, 1.361, 1.362, 1.366, 6.32). Three ways of classifying this category might be particularly apposite.

First, mediation: any two things connected by some third thing. A node, meeting point, or intersection of three lines exemplify Thirdness. In Peirce's scheme, the middle term of a syllogism is a Third. So is a sign, in that it mediates between the object it stands for and the interpretant to which it represents the object. Peirce habitually speaks of Thirds as entities connecting two others.

Second, rule: any principle, function, or law which translates or transforms one thing into another is a Third. Any activity to which thought and understanding are essential exemplifies Thirdness. Action and change which are uniform, regular, and amenable to description in terms of general laws exhibit Thirdness. One of Peirce's favorite and important examples of Thirdness is habit (about which more below); so are reasoning, language, and inquiry.

Third, growth: laws themselves change and develop in accordance with higher-order or supervening laws. With respect to human conduct, such changes are subject to criticism and self-control. For Peirce, evolution is bound up with a whole hierarchy of laws, lower levels subsumed by higher levels, thus making changes within the hierarchy conform to the pattern imposed by superordinate laws. The orderly changes involved in growth are subject to a leading principle which applies the categories to themselves. Using active and passive forms as classifiers, Seconds divide into two varieties, the active member subdividing once again; and Thirds go through a process of fission in a similar manner. The beginnings of this process can be represented by Figure 1 (Savan 1976:8).

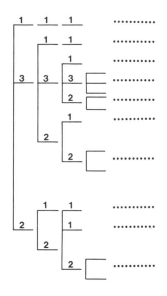

FIGURE 1. Thirdness Divided

The categories are not individual things but general aspects of everything that presents itself for perception or cognition—in short, everything that can be known. The hierarchical structure of the inter-relationships between the categories is a direct reflection of their definitions. Thirds are more complicated than Seconds, which are more complicated than Firsts. The compounding of categories reveals some instances to be fuller or purer than others, and Peirce calls the less complete or impure combinations *degenerate,* using the word in its mathematical (unpejorative) sense (3.359). Thus the passive member of a pair of Seconds is a degenerate case of Secondness. The third member in a triplet of Thirds is a complete or genuine Third, while the first and second members are degenerate in different degrees; and so on.

Applying the so-called 'rhematic' form of presentation which Peirce himself favored, the basic structure of the categories is as in Figure 2 (Esposito 1980:163).

3. Signs and Semeiosis

'The essential function of a sign is to render inefficient relations efficient,—not to set them into action, but to establish a habit or general rule whereby they will act on occasion' (H 31). In this formulation of 1904, the role of the categories in Peirce's semeiotic is not made explicit, but it is

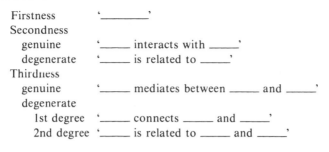

Firstness   '_____'
Secondness
  genuine   '_____ interacts with _____'
  degenerate   '_____ is related to _____'
Thirdness
  genuine   '_____ mediates between _____ and _____'
  degenerate
    1st degree   '_____ connects _____ and _____'
    2nd degree   '_____ is related to _____ and _____'

FIGURE 2

clear from the context that his entire system of signs is pervaded by the categories. The prime example of Thirdness, adduced by Peirce himself, is that of a sign: 'In its genuine form Thirdness is the triadic relation existing between a sign, its object, and the interpreting thought, itself a sign, considered as constituting the mode of being of a sign' (H 31). It is not enough to say that the categories play an important role in Peirce's semeiotic: they are absolutely vital to it. All of its definitions, subdivisions, and workings are governed by applications of the theory of categories.

The first such application comes with the most basic classification of signs, a trichotomy embodying the three ways in which signs may be divided, i.e. according to: (1) 'their modes of being as *Entia,* in themselves' (L 67:35), that is to say 'their own material nature' (H 32); (2) their relations to their objects; and (3) 'the mode of their appeal to their interpretants' (L 67:35).

A. Signs in themselves

A sign considered in itself is the ground on which the object it stands for is interpreted by the sign into which the original sign is translated or transformed. A ground is the particular respect in which the sign represents its object; not all respects are equally relevant (2.228). The ground is not the same as the sign-vehicle, since the latter may have many characteristics, most of which will be irrelevant to its specific functioning as a sign. Thus a road sign directing travellers to a specific location may be made of a certain kind of material, may be this or that color or shape, but the only thing essential to its functioning will be the place name and an arrow or mileage indicator (if these are mentioned).

The trichotomous divisions dictated by the theory of categories leads Peirce to a trichotomy of grounds, i.e. of signs considered as they are in themselves. These he calls *qualisigns, sinsigns,* and *legisigns.* A qualisign is variously defined by Peirce as 'an indefinite possibility' (L 67:36), 'a quality which is a Sign' (2.244), and 'a sign . . . of the nature of an appearance' (H 32). What is important is the quality as such: a qualisign signifies through its abstractable quality only, without any supervening fact or connection. The red light that signals motorists to stop is not a qualisign because it is encompassed by a rule of traffic safety that is dependent on convention. But a swatch of red cloth used to identify the color of curtains made from it is completely direct in its signification: it is the color alone that is relevant. Wherever a quality is a sign that is to be imitated, replicated, copied, mimicked, or otherwise reproduced, we have the action of a qualisign.

Although what comes to mind first in discussing quality may be simple sensory qualities such as color, sound, or odor, fidelity to Peirce's ideas requires a much broader concept. Any character which can be abstracted as a Firstness and regarded as a unity is suitable for inclusion under Peirce's definition of a qualisign. Abstracted from its individual occurrence and shared by more than one individual, a quality or complexus of qualities comes to be designated by adjectives which refer to such composite objects as geographical landscapes ('Mediterranean,' 'Alpine,' 'Tropical') or human personalities ('Churchillian,' 'Chaplinesque').

Qualisigns are indispensable ingredients of any and all communicative acts. Only this species of sign is capable of communicating the peculiar character of a taste, odor, or sound. Even words, apart from their cognitive meanings, may have affective nuances conveyed by their sounds alone. Every sign must convey some information about the quality of its object; to that extent, therefore, every sign must involve a qualisign.

A Second corresponding to a qualisign as a First is the sinsign, a name fashioned by Peirce on the model of *sim*ul, *sem*el, *sin*gular, *sim*plex, etc., and defined as 'an actual existent thing or event which is a sign' (2.245). This species of sign is by definition connected to direct experience. Essential to a sinsign's status is its singularity as an encountered thing or occurrence, that which makes it a sign. A clue which establishes the particularity of some object or event is a sinsign. A signal, such as a sound, color, shape, or odor, which elicits a particular response in a particular context is a sinsign—so long as there is a direct dependence on the circumstances of its occurrence. The red stop signal ceases to have the meaning that it does if it is just a red light hanging from a porch window or is set up anywhere but on a roadway. Words that are utilized in a ritualized or performative context (such as that of oath-taking, contracts, marriages, promising, apologizing, etc.) are sinsigns, since it is the concrete circumstances in which they occur that make them the kind of sign that they are.

Owing to the determinative character of the categories, every sinsign (as a Second) must comprise a qualisign (i.e., a First) as part of its structure. The relationship is, of course, ranked: without a First there can be no Second (or Third).

The Third in the particular case of signs considered in themselves is a legisign—'a law that is a Sign' (2.246). A sign does not become a legisign just because it has some general or law-like character. Only if it is the law that gives the sign its character as a sign does the law become a sign. The most important system of legisigns is language, and each of the constituent elements of a natural language are legisigns. Any particular instantiation of one or an aggregate of these elements is, according to Peirce, a replica of a legisign—i.e., a Second, or sinsign, whose characteristics and the method of its interpretation apart from the circumstances of its occurrence are defined by a covering legisign. The distinction between a legisign and its replica is also known as the Type-Token distinction (Savan 1976:13). Legisigns are, of course, not limited to natural language. Regularities of behavior such as customs or conventions generally are legisigns, as are patterns of physical phenomena like the regular association with rain of air pressure, wind, and cloud formation; or the symptoms regularly mani- festing themselves as signs of an illness or syndrome.

Qualisigns, sinsigns, and legisigns thus make up the first triad of sign types. While each member of the triad is treated by Peirce as separate from the other two, it is important to stress the limited nature of their separateness and, what is more, to emphasize their inherent connectedness both structurally and empirically. It follows from Peirce's view that only qualities can be qualisigns (cf. Savan 1976:14). In order to be able to regard qualities as signs, they must be abstracted as possibilities from their actual occurrences bounded by space and time. Moreover, the two other constituents of sign structure, object and interpretant, must in the case of qualities remain virtual, potential, or possible (something which Peirce consistently recognized). To the extent that qualisigns are distinct from sinsigns, they are a non-occurrent sign.

The same sort of dependency condition defines the relation between sinsigns and legisigns. Sinsigns always occur, to some degree, as replicas of legisigns; qualisigns cannot be manifested apart from their occurrence in sinsigns. Therefore, semeiosis turns out to be multiaspectual. The tri- chotomy of grounds on which a sign is a sign presents a graded continuum in which the boundaries distinguishing its members are ontologically precise but empirically approximate.

B. Signs, objects, and their relation

Peirce's concept of sign encompasses three terms: sign, object, and interpretant. These are determined by the three categories in such a way as to render sign a First, object a Second, and interpretant a Third. Since the object of a sign is its Second, the relation between them is a Secondness. In conformity with the distinction made earlier between active and passive forms of Secondness, objects will differ depending on whether sign action is directed outward or is confined within the sign itself. Accordingly, two types of objects are distinguished by Peirce, active or *dynamic* objects, and passive or *immediate* objects. Each of these two types is further subdivided by the trichotomy of categories, as is the relation between sign and dynamic object. Altogether these subdivisions yield three new trichotomies.

Peirce defines the object of a sign as 'that with which [the sign] presupposes an acquaintance in order to convey some further information concerning it' (2.231). 'The Object as cognized in the Sign and therefore an Idea' (NE 3:843 = 8.183) is called the Immediate Object, whereas 'the Object as it is regardless of any particular aspect of it, the Object in such relations as unlimited and final study would show it to be' (loc. cit.) is called the Dynamical Object. The two types of objects correspond to two ways in which the world is regarded semeiotically. 'The immediate object is the world, or some part of it, as the sign represents it to be, while the dynamic object is the world—or the relevant portion of it—that will actually determine the success or failure of any given interpretant of the sign' (Short 1981:214).

If the real is that towards which representation tends, then the immediate and dynamic objects can be regarded as beginning and end points along a semeiotic continuum defined by their relative independence of being represented in the sign. Peirce puts this in terms of experiential knowledge of the world needed in order that signs be interpreted:

> We must distinguish between the Immediate Object,—i.e. the Object as represented in the sign,—and the Real (no, because perhaps the Object is altogether fictive, I must choose a different term, therefore), say rather the Dynamical Object, which, from the nature of things, the Sign *cannot* express, which it can only *indicate* and leave the interpreter to find out by *collateral experience*. (8.314)

By 'collateral experience' or 'collateral observation' Peirce means 'previous acquaintance with what the sign denotes' (NE 3:841). The dynamic object is (generally) a real thing; it is the object of the sign 'in itself' (8.333), 'the really efficient but not immediately present Object' (8.343), 'the Object as it is regardless of any particular aspect of it, the Object in such relations as unlimited and final study would show it to be' (NE 3:842). The immediate object of a sign is the dynamic object as the sign presents and expresses it: there is a distinction between the two, but no difference except insofar as the sign either misrepresents or does not fully represent its object.

'A sign is something by knowing which we know something more' (H 31-2). Semeiosis thus involves the addition of information to a body of preexistent knowledge. The information specifically conveyed by a given sign must, on Peirce's view, presuppose prior and independent information, which the sign extends. 'Collateral experience' is another designation for information obtained through the action of prior and independent signs.

Within a loose but familiar understanding of 'information,' knowledge presupposed in interpreting sign action can be identified with the *context* of the sign (Savan 1976:16). It is Peirce's position that 'no sign can be understood . . . unless the interpreter has "collateral acquaintance" with every Object of it' (NE 3:843).

All signs have dynamic objects, even though not all dynamic objects are semeiotically true or valid, and do not answer to the immediate object (some signs represent their objects falsely). A weather vane still points on a windless day, though there be no wind direction signified; 'unicorn' has no real referent. But each such sign signifies something and comports instructions within its signification as to whether its immediate object is real or not (Short 1981:217). The reality towards which such a sign points is the dynamic object independent of the sign itself. In the case of the weather vane, it is the velocity of the circumambient air; in the case of 'unicorn'— the world insofar as it may or may not be specified as including animals of this description. Collateral observation of such dynamic objects leads to the conclusion that 'there is nothing in them that answers to the immediate object of the sign' (Short 1981:217). As with qualisigns and iconic signs generally, there is a tendency for immediate and dynamic object to blend as an embodied possibility; such is the nature of the objects of mimicked sounds and colors in animal communication, as well as the context-bound objects of such purely relational linguistic units as conjunctions and prepositions.

There are (as expected) three kinds of dynamic objects. First, the object may be a quality; Peirce calls this species of object a *Possible* (H 83), and the sign corresponding to it an *Abstractive*. The name Possible is more apposite than Quality because Peirce wishes to include among Firsts not just simple sensory qualities but abstract mathematical objects and complex physical notions (such as mass) as well.

Included among the second sort of dynamic object are occurrences, existent entities, and facts having to do with entities and events bounded by space and time. For signs of these objects Peirce proposes the name *Concretives* (H 84); and objects themselves fall under the class of *Existents* (H 82). Concretive signs are exemplified by linguistic expressions such as substantives designating occurrences and events, by mechanical devices such as barometers, by bodily symptoms of certain illnesses, fossil signs of past sociological realia, etc.

The third and final class of dynamic objects encompasses laws, habits, continua, and whatever is expressible in a universal proposition; Peirce calls these *Necessitants,* and the signs corresponding to them *Collectives.* Examples of collectives are to be found among linguistic signs of tendencies, propensities, and dispositions to act regularly in certain ways. Despite the name, Peirce does not consider this species of dynamic object as being correlated with signs of individual collections, each the totality of the individuals collected. Since he conceives necessitants to be expressed by the subjunctive conditional ('what would be if . . .'), and therefore as laws which cannot be exhausted by the sum of their occurrences, this sort of sign is always something more than the sum of its replicas. Mankind is a necessitant in virtue of being more than any one man or woman, more than the collective total of all human beings that have lived in the past, are living in the present, or will live in the future.

Dynamic objects are Seconds that act on signs in such a way that the latter react or resist the action of the former. There is an externality inherent in this aspect of semeiosis, since what is at stake here is reference and referents (in the sense of Frege, Russell, and Quine), as distinct from the way in which the object is represented internally, in the sign itself. Peirce's very broad conception of sign, object, and their relation identifies the latter as the immediate object of a sign, i.e., that in the sign which corresponds to the action of the dynamic object. The trichotomy of immediate objects makes reference, in the same way as dynamic objects, to possibles, existents, and necessitants. If the immediate object is a possible, its sign is a *Descriptive*. If the immediate object is an existent, its sign is a *Designative*. And if it is a necessitant, its sign is a *Copulant*.

There is a connection between Peirce's concept of immediate object and his theory of perception, involving a human percipient-interpreter and, therefore, mental representation. Where the sign is addressed to a human interpreter, the immediate object is the dynamic object as it is initially perceived. Peirce calls this the *percipuum,* i.e., the immediate object of a sign whose interpretant is mental. This is the element that is immediately present on any specific occasion of interpretation by the mind apperceiving the sign—apart from any critical appraisal or reflection or judgement. The locus of critical interpretation is the interpretant, whereas the object of the sign (both immediate and dynamic) function as prior conditions of signification and as a context establishing part of the conditions whereby interpretation can proceed.

The context of Peirce's notion of immediate object can be better grasped by rehearsing an example which he himself cites (cf. Savan 1976:21-2):

> Two men are standing on the seashore looking out to sea. One of them says to the other, "That vessel there carries no freight at all, but only passengers." Now, if the other, himself, sees no vessel, the first information he derives from the remark has for its Object the part of the sea that he does see, and informs him that a person with sharper eyes than his, or more trained in looking for such things, can see a vessel there; and then, that vessel having been thus introduced to his acquaintance, he is prepared to receive the information about it that it carries passengers exclusively. But the sentence as a whole has,

for the person supposed, no other Object than that with which it finds him already acquainted. (2.232)

Assuming a true report on the part of the speaker, the dynamic object of his remark is the ship, but the immediate object differs for the two interlocutors. Peirce focusses on the recipient of the information; for him the immediate object is the part of the sea with which he has prior acquaintance and now perceives. The linguistic information serves as the basis for a grounded relation between the immediate object and the dynamic object—the ship.

Peirce's notion of immediate object excludes conceiving it as a collection of sense data, no matter how complex, since he regards sensory qualities to be abstractions from the very outset, 'prescinded' from the perceptual object by the action of intellection and inference. In the example cited, the immediate object is that portion of the water and that aspect of the actual situation with which the percipient subject is factually acquainted. The entire situation, together with its constituent parts, is governed here (as elsewhere) by the gradience of the categories (Savan 1976:22). The *hic et nunc* nature of the situation as a whole comes under the compass of Secondness. In line with the hierarchical determinacy of the categories, Secondness includes all the colors, sounds, and odors of the sea, as well as the state of the water (calm or turbulent); all these qualities are Firsts and instances of Firstness. A more generalized knowledge of the sea, finally, involves Thirdness: an acquaintance with general patterns, uniformities, continuities, and tendencies. The potential typology of immediate objects in this example, then, encompasses a blend of possibles, existents, and necessitants associated with designative, descriptive, and copulant signs, respectively.

Sign and object having been considered in themselves, it is now their relation that needs illumination. This relation must be of a sort that any further signs, which interpret or translate the original sign, may come to stand for the same object as the original. Peirce recognized a trichotomy of mutable relations between sign and object which he termed *icon, index,* and *symbol.* This is the most well-known of Peirce's trichotomies, and the one he himself most frequently used. When the relation between sign and object is one of likeness, resemblance, or similarity it is an iconic relation. A sign is an icon if it resembles its object, and if the quality or character grounding the resemblance inheres in the sign irrespective of the actual existence or non-existence of its object. The relation between sign and object is indexical when it is defined by a spatio-temporal (factual or existential) contiguity between them. A sign is an index if both its constituents do now exist or did exist in the past, and the sign is related to its object through the dynamic action of the latter on the former. The relation obtaining between sign and object is symbolic when it depends on a convention or a habit (acquired or inborn). A sign is a symbol if both its constituents are laws (necessitants or Thirds), and are related to each other by a law or general rule. To summarize: the relation between sign and object may be one of iconic resemblance (such as a portrait and the person portrayed), of indexical contiguity and dynamic interaction (smoke and fire), or of symbolic law (a habit, such as an item of language).

Peirce's own words delineating and exemplifying the trichotomy of relations between sign and object are particularly useful in grasping not only their individual purport but their hierarchical interconnectedness as well:

> An icon is a representamen [= sign] of what it represents and for the mind that interprets it as such, by virtue of its being an immediate image, that is to say by virtue of characters which belong to it in itself as a sensible object, and which it would possess just the same were there no object in nature that it resembled, and though it never were interpreted as a sign. It is of the nature of an appearance, and as such, strictly speaking, exists only in consciousness, although for convenience in ordinary parlance and when extreme precision is not called for, we extend the term *icon* to the outward objects which excite in consciousness the image itself. A geometrical diagram is a good example of an icon. A pure icon can convey no positive or factual information; for it affords no assurance that there is any such thing in nature. But it is of the utmost value for enabling its interpreter to study what would be the character of such an object in case any such did exist. Geometry sufficiently illustrates that. (4.447)

> Of signs there are two different degenerate forms. But though I give them this disparaging name, they are of the greatest utility, and serve purposes that genuine signs could not. The more degenerate of the two forms (as I look upon it) is the *icon*. This is defined as a sign of which the character that fits it to become a sign of the sort that it is, is simply inherent in it as a quality of it. For example, a geometrical figure drawn on paper may be an *icon* of a triangle or other geometrical form. If one meets a man whose language one does not know and resorts to imitative sounds and gestures, these approach the character of an icon. The reason that they are not pure icons is that the purpose of them is emphasized. A pure icon is independent of any purpose. It serves as a sign solely and simply by exhibiting the quality it serves to signify. The relation to its object is a degenerate relation. It asserts nothing. If it conveys information, it is only in the sense in which the object that it is used to represent may be said to convey information. An *icon* can only be a fragment of a completer sign. (NE 4:241-2)

> Of a completely opposite nature is the kind of representamen [= sign] termed an *index*. This is a real thing or fact which is a sign of its object by virtue of being connected with it as a matter of fact and also by forcibly intruding upon the mind, quite regardless of its being interpreted as a sign. It may simply serve

to identify its object and assure us of its existence and presence. But very often the nature of the factual connection of the index with its object is such as to excite in consciousness an image of some features of the object, and in that way affords evidence from which positive assurance as to truth of fact may be drawn. A photograph, for example, not only excites an image, has an appearance, but, owing to its optical connexion with the object, is evidence that that appearance corresponds to a reality. (4.447)

The other form of degenerate sign is to be termed an *index*. It is defined as a sign which is fit to serve as such by virtue of being in a real reaction with its object. For example, a weather-cock is such a sign. It is fit to be taken as an index of the wind for the reason that it is physically connected with the wind. A weather-cock conveys information; but this it does because in facing the very quarter from which the wind blows, it resembles the wind in this respect, and thus has an icon connected with it. In this respect, it is not a pure index. A pure index simply forces attention to the object with which it reacts and puts the interpreter into mediate reaction with that object, but conveys no information. As an example, take an exclamation "Oh!" The letters attached to a geometrical figure are another case. Absolutely unexceptionable examples of degenerate forms must not be expected. All that is possible is to give examples which tend sufficiently in towards those forms to make the mean suggest what is meant. It is remarkable that while neither a pure icon nor a pure index can assert anything, an index which forces something to be an *icon,* as a weather-cock does, or which forces us to regard it as an *icon,* as the legend under a portrait does, does make an assertion, and forms a *proposition.* (NE 4:242)

A Symbol is a law, or regularity of the indefinite future. Its Interpretant must be of the same description; and so must be also the complete immediate Object, or meaning. But a law necessarily governs, or is "embodied in" individuals, and prescribes some of their qualities. Consequently, a constituent of a Symbol may be an Index, and a constituent may be an Icon. . . . Thus, while the complete object of a symbol, that is to say, its meaning, is of the nature of a law, it must *denote* an individual, and must *signify* a character. (2.293)

A symbol is a representamen [= sign] whose special significance or fitness to represent just what it does represent lies in nothing but the very fact of there being a habit, disposition, or other effective general rule that it will be so interpreted. (4.447)

An icon has such being as belongs to past experience. It exists only as an image in the mind. An index has the being of present experience. The being of a symbol consists in the real fact that something surely will be experienced if certain conditions be satisfied. Namely, it will influence the thought and conduct of its interpreter. (4.447)

The value of an icon consists in its exhibiting the features of a state of things regarded as if it were purely imaginary. The value of an index is that it assures us of positive fact. The value of a symbol is that it serves to make thought and conduct rational and enables us to predict the future. (4.448)

The symbol, by the very definition of it, has an interpretant in view. Its very meaning is intended. Indeed, a purpose is precisely the interpretant of a symbol. (NE 4:244)

A symbol is essentially a purpose, that is to say, is a representation that seeks to make itself definite, or seeks to produce an interpretant more definite than itself. For its whole signification consists in its determining an interpretant; so that it is from its interpretant that it derives the actuality of its signification. (NE 4:261)

Peirce summarizes his trichotomy of the relations between sign and object in Figure 3 (NE 4:243).

Since the various semeiotic trichotomies are structurally inter-connected in semeiosis, signs considered in themselves and in their relation to objects form synthetic combinations. Thus any qualisign is an icon, although the converse does not hold. Icons can be sinsigns and legisigns as well as qualisigns. Strictly speaking, iconic qualisigns are only a possibility. Actually existing or occurring qualities, if they are signs, are sinsigns, and Peirce terms such iconic sinsigns *hypoicons* (2.276), which he subdivides into a triad reflecting the 'mode of Firstness of which they partake' (2.277):

Those which partake of simple qualities, or First Firstnesses, are *images;* those which represent the relations, mainly dyadic, or so regarded, of the parts of one thing by analogous relations in their own parts, are *diagrams;* those which

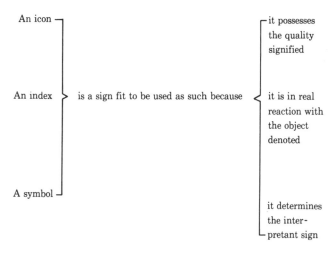

FIGURE 3

represent the representative character of a representamen [= sign] by representing a parallelism in something else, are *metaphors*. (2.277)

At the core of the notion of iconic signs is similarity or resemblance, and Peirce recognizes the impossibility of giving a formal account or analysis of resemblance. Indeed, he explicitly categorizes statements of the form *x* resembles *y* as hypotheses, and thereby subsumes resemblance under Thirdness, i.e., as subject to a rational rule—itself subject to change and emendation in the light of further evidence rationally evaluated.

Sinsigns and legisigns encompass qualities, and if they resemble their objects owing to some quality of the sign, sinsigns and legisigns fall under the class of icons. Examples of iconic sinsigns are color chips or swatches as signs of colors of paint or cloth, animal signaling behavior (courtship, nest building, combat among birds, etc.), and an individual instance of a geometrical figure or diagram (2.255).

Indexical sinsigns, on the other hand, direct attention to their objects or isolate them instead of exhibiting them the way iconic signs do. A spontaneous cry, to use Peirce's example (2.256), draws our attention to its source by affecting our instinctual or conditioned reflexes. A weathercock (2.257) points out the direction of the wind; in so doing, of course, this sign necessarily involves an icon of the wind's direction, and in this case it is the actual direction of the wind rather than a mere possibility. Here we see the inclusion relations obtaining between the sign types and defining thereby the hierarchical nature of sign complexes.

The blending of several sign types within a sign complexus as a whole is a cardinal feature of semeiosis. Since every sinsign, for instance, involves the action of external forces upon it (Secondness), regardless of any specific interpretation, every sinsign is therefore an index. Since every sign must have a qualitative aspect, there is nothing to prevent sinsigns from functioning as icons. Indexical sinsigns are best fitted to establish the existence of their objects; inevitably, however, their mode of semeiosis will include an icon. The condensation track in a cloud chamber is an index of the existence of certain subatomic particles, but it is also an icon of the direction of their movement, not to speak of a whole set of physical characteristics (cf. Savan 1976:25).

Indexical sinsigns are always specific cases rather than general types. Indexical legisigns, however, are never singular individuals but are types or laws, whose existence is to be inferred from their replicas or instantiations, susceptible of individual action and reaction. Expressions of different types of emotion such as pain, joy, anger, or fear are indexical legisigns so long as they conform to a common pattern of exhibiting them. Each individual expressive act contains attributes that are singularly tied to specific times and places, and so the indexes involved are also sinsigns (Savan 1976:27).

A type of index which is especially relevant to a discussion of semeiosis in language is the pronoun, particularly the demonstrative kind. Peirce regards words like 'this,' 'that,' 'here,' and 'now' as indexes, although they fit the definition of an index only in an attenuated sense ('a sign which refers to the Object that it denotes by virtue of being really affected by that Object'; 2.248). Words of this sort are characterized by a number of properties, however, which legitimate their categorization as indexes. Thus each individual occurrence of a demonstrative pronoun delineates a specific context of that occurrence, and its object contracts a relation to the sign because of some property of the context which is unique to that context. Peirce clarifies his conception in the following passage:

> An *index* represents an object by virtue of its connection with it. It makes no difference whether the connection is natural, or artificial, or merely mental. There is, however, an important distinction between two classes of indices. Namely, some merely stand for things or individual quasi-things with which the interpreting mind is already acquainted, while others may be used to ascertain facts. Of the former class, which may be termed *designations,* personal, demonstrative, and relative pronouns, proper names, the letters attached to a geometrical figure, and the ordinary letters of algebra are examples. They act to force the attention of the thing intended. Designations are absolutely indispensable both to communication and to thought. No assertion has any meaning unless there is some designation to show whether the universe of reality or what universe of fiction is referred to. (8.368, fn. 23)

The relation between sign and object in the species of sign Peirce calls index is one of existent fact, independent of whether the fact is known, recognized, or interpreted; 'an *index* is a sign which would, at once, lose the character which makes it a sign if its object were removed, but would not lose that character if there were no interpretant' (2.304). Herein lies the crucial difference between icons and indices, on one hand, and symbols, on the other. A number of further passages (NE 4:235-63) make it emphatically clear that there are no symbols without interpretation (cf. the earlier quotations):

> There is an infallible criterion for distinguishing between an index and an icon. Namely, although an index, like any other sign, only functions as a sign when it is interpreted, yet though it never happened to be interpreted, it remains equally fitted to be the very sign that would be if interpreted. A symbol, on the other hand, that should not be interpreted, would either not be a sign at all, or would only be a sign in an utterly different way. (NE 4:256)

> A symbol is distinguished as a sign which becomes such by virtue of determining its interpretant. (NE 4:260)

> A symbol is something which has the power of reproducing itself, and that

essentially, since it is constituted a symbol only by the interpretation. (NE 4:260)

> Now it is of the essential nature of a symbol that it determines an interpretant, which is itself a symbol. A symbol, therefore, produces an endless series of interpretants. (NE 4:261)

A symbol is a sign which is related to its object by virtue of a law, rule, or habit. Sign and object in symbolic relations are, moreover, themselves laws or habits, making all symbols legisigns (but not vice versa; cf. Savan 1976:29, Short 1982). Accordingly, all words are also legisigns, although the indexical relation predominates over the symbolic in deictic words such as pronouns. The symbolic aspect of words is dominant in concepts, propositions, and arguments; in fact, when Peirce speaks of symbols, it is generally with such linguistic items in mind.

The conventionality of legisigns comes to the fore in examples drawn from human language, but Peirce also explicitly provides in his semeiotic for natural legisigns; as when he defines a symbol to be 'a Sign which is constituted a sign merely or mainly by the fact that it is used and understood as such, whether the habit is natural or conventional' (2.307). Replicas of natural legisigns occur, for instance, in animal display, as when the bright colors of male birds' plummage attracts their female counterparts (Short 1982). Natural legisigns of this sort differ from conventional ones in the degree to which instinct—the evolutively accrued disposition to use and to interpret such signs—has rigidified into fixed roles and patterns. The conventional legisigns of human language demand of its users that they be able to alternate habitually and with ease between the roles of sign-producer and sign-interpreter. In certain cases of animals, the line dividing the dichotomy cannot be crossed: the male bird produces the display, the female reacts (on occasion) in the appropriate manner.

C. Interpretants

The legisign (or type) subsumes an expansible set of replicas (or tokens); although no finite collection of replicas can exhaust the set, the legisign exists in virtue of the individual occurrences and properties of its replicas. In the case of a legisign of natural language, like the English word *man,* its object is mankind, even though individual replicas of the word refer indexically as signs to individual human beings (cf. Savan 1976:29). Since the word *man* is a collective sign and its object a necessitant (as we saw earlier), a question arises concerning the manner or mode of relating the collective legisign *man* with the general class of humans.

Peirce answers this crucial question by appeal to the most important part of his semeiotic, the theory of the *interpretant,* upon which many other parts of his philosophy depend, none more so than his pragmaticism. The word *man* must be interpreted—have an interpretant—in order to be the sign of its object. Any word, for that matter any symbol, is constituted a sign by being related to its object via its interpretant.

Peirce's conception of the interpretant (a term he coined) is complex and variegated, its content shifting with the context in which Peirce speaks of it. The most frequent ingredient in defining interpretant is 'the proper significate outcome of a sign' (5.473) or its 'proper significate effects' (5.475). At other points, he talks of interpretants as the '*cognition produced in the mind*' (1.372), 'the idea to which [the sign] gives rise' (1.339); and more schematically:

> That determination of which the immediate cause, or determinant, is the Sign, and of which the mediate cause is the Object may be termed the *Interpretant.* (6.347)

Implicit in this definition is Peirce's insistence that signification is a triadic relation, in which the interpretant is the third relatum (sign being the first, object the second) and hence a Third. The role of the interpretant is, in fact, indispensable to what a sign is and to the nature of its action:

> A sign therefore is an object which is in relation to its object on the one hand and to an interpretant on the other in such a way as to bring the interpretant into a relation to the object corresponding to its own relation to the object. I might say 'similar to its own' for a correspondence consists in a similarity; but perhaps correspondence is narrower. (H 32)

Peirce held that essential to all semeiosis is the triadic production of interpretants (not necessarily of signs; cf. Short 1981:206-7; Fisch 1978:41, fn. 6). He makes the crucial distinction between dyadic (dynamic) action and triadic (intelligent) action, without at all restricting intelligence or semeiosis to the human variety (5.472-472). Dyadic action is exemplified by all process in which one effect follows upon another in a purely additive way, as in the example of the action of temperature on the mercury in a thermometer (Fitzgerald 1964:73). If each rise in degree is considered an effect, it is clear that each increment is produced independent of its predecessor and its successor. Triadic production, on the other hand, involves the production of one thing *as a means* to another, which is to say that (for Peirce) all triadic action is teleological, particularly semeiosis. The definitions of interpretant adduced above (cf. also 2.274) all hinge on the proper understanding of triadic relations, which underlie semeiosis.

A triadic relation is a relation with three terms, for example: *A* gives *B* to *C; B* is between *A* and *C; A* prefers *B* to *C*. Some triadic relations can be reduced to combinations of dyadic relations, for example: *A* moved from *B* to *C* could be reduced to *A* left *B* and *A* arrived at *C* (Savan 1976:31). According to Peirce, however, a genuine triadic relation is not susceptible of reduction without remainder to a conjunction of dyadic relations. All relations involving mind, cognition, and intelligence are genuinely triadic relations, for on Peirce's view all such relations are ultimately semeiotic, as all thought is in signs, and the sign relation (sign-object-interpretant) is the epitomically genuine triadic relation.

Interpretants are thus the key ingredient of thought as a semeiotic process; but they are not by any means limited to the context of mental representation. Feelings and actions can also be identified with interpretants.

Peirce's conception of sign, moreover, being extremely broad in several respects, renders the interpretant an inalienable factor of semeiosis regardless of the presence of any (human) interpreter. Each sign has the potentiality of being interpreted as such, even though it may not initially be recognized as a sign. A sign's potential interpretant need not, finally, be an entity limited to formation in the human mind, although the intellectualistic thrust of Peirce's semeiotic is unmistakable. The response of animals to what are commonly understood as signs is an example of non-human interpretation (cf. Short 1981:201); Peirce even encompasses the 'habit-taking' of plants, not to speak of non-living objects like water in a river bed (5.492). For Peirce, indeed, human mind is a special case of semeiosis, rather than semeiosis being a special instance of mind (Short 1981:203).

Despite this very broad framework, Peirce's own thinking about semeiotic (as reflected in his writings) is concentrated on signs in the narrow sense, i.e., on signs whose interpretant is itself a sign, in short—mental signs. The difficulty of successfully promulgating a semeiotic that goes beyond consciousness was acknowledged by Peirce in a letter to Lady Welby of 1908:

> I define a Sign as anything which is so determined by something else, called its Object, and so determines an effect upon a person, which effect I call its Interpretant, that the latter is thereby mediately determined by the former. My insertion of 'upon a person' is a sop to Cerberus, because I despair of making my own broader conception understood. (H 80-1)

To summarize, three conditions must be met in order for something to be an interpretant in the narrow sense of sign. It must be an effect in the mind of the interpreter. It must be the result of triadic sign production, i.e., it must have been produced with a purpose, by a sign. Finally, it must bear the same relation to the object as does the sign itself (cf. Fitzgerald 1964:75). In a more generalized sense, all signs are interpretants of some other sign, and any sign is constituted an interpretant 'if (1) it instantiates a general habit (or rule) of transforming an antecedent sign into a consequent sign, and (2) signifies its object through some antecedent sign of that object' (Savan 1976:36).

The most salient points concerning Peirce's notion of interpretant, to be kept in mind before approaching his classification of interpretants, are the following (cf. Savan 1976:32-6):

1. The triad of constituents making up the sign—sign, object, and interpretant—are defined circularly, with reference to each other, so that each is defined only in terms of the other two. This is not a vicious circularity; quite the contrary, the mutual ontological dependency of the three constituents on each other is a reflection of the structure of semeiosis.

2. Every interpretant is at least potentially a sign, and stands in the same relation to its object as does the sign of which it is the interpretant. In terms of the medieval semeiotic formula *aliquid stat pro aliquo,* the interpretant is substitutable for a sign with a shared object.

3. Every sign is at least potentially an interpretant of some other sign, to which it is related through their shared object. In terms of antecedent and consequent, every sign is at least potentially the interpretant of an antecedent sign, and is interpreted by some consequent sign, which stands to the first as its interpretant.

4. Sign and interpretant are distinguished from each other by the fact that the interpretant is determined by the sign, whereas the converse does not usually hold true. Peirce uses the word 'determined' to mean something like 'delimited,' glossing it (at NE 3:839) by 'specialized' and German *bestimmt.*

5. The interpretant stands for its object in three ways. First, it stands for its antecedent sign, and thereby also for the object of its antecedent sign. The latter, however, itself stands for its object via yet another antecedent sign, and so on, in a potentially infinite series. Resorting to a modern terminology that postdates Peirce, the interpretant *signifies* its object; and this object can be termed the *signified object* (Savan 1976:33). Accordingly, *man* is the interpretant of *homme:* the English word stands for its signified object by standing for the antecedent sign in French that is its equivalent (cf. 1.553). The potential circle of antecedent signs could be expanded by adducing further equivalents in other languages, all of which would share the same object.

Second, the interpretant signifies its dynamic object by making a direct reference to the actually existing circumstances, or context, of the sign. In Peirce's scheme, any actually occurring sign bears an indexical relation to its dynamic object, and knowledge of this relation cannot be derived from the sign itself, but rather through collateral experience or information (as mentioned earlier above).

The interpretant affirms the identity of the signified object and the dynamic object, representing them to be one and the same.

The threefold relation of the interpretant to its object, which encompasses the significative, the referential (dynamic), and the identifying functions, is to be found in Peirce's original definition of interpretant (going back to his 1867 paper, "On a New List of Categories"): '*a mediating representation which represents the relate to be a representation of the same correlate which this mediating representation itself represents*' (1.553).

6. Every interpretant is at the same time at least potentially a sign to some further interpretant which shares its object. There is thus no first or last interpretant; each interpretant of an object has a predecessor and a successor, both of which are also interpretants. Peirce's conception of semeiosis accounts in this way for the obvious overlap and interrelatedness of meaning and of the entities constituting it. Any given interpretant, isolated for the purposes of analysis, actually has its semeiotic locus in a multidimensional continuum of signs, objects, and interpretants.

7. The interpretant is at least potentially in a mediating relation between an antecedent and a consequent sign, which is to say that it provides a means of comparing and relating members of these two potentially infinite classes of signs. Peirce considers mediation to be tantamount to a general rule, which he variously calls a leading principle, guiding principle, rule of inference, or rule of illative transformation (cf. Savan 1976:33). This general rule is itself a legisign. An interpretant thus mediates, on the one hand, between its antecedent sign and their common object by providing further and more determinate signs of that object; and, on the other, by providing the means whereby an antecedent sign can be translated or transformed into its consequent interpretant.

8. A particular species of interpretant, called the ultimate logical interpretant (about which more below, section 4), is a habit. Although the other kinds of interpretant (energetic, emotional, and verbal logical interpretants) are not habits, some of them may be formed in accordance with and as determined by habit.

It follows from the status of ultimate logical interpretants as habits that they may also be legisigns. Qualisigns and sinsigns lack the generality of pattern, law, and continuity that Peirce reserves for Thirds, of which habits are a paramount example. Although habits are embodied in individual occurrences, their essential definiens is an ability to span a whole series of individual occurrences: occurrences, insists Peirce, are Seconds and 'exist,' while habits are 'real.' Similarly, legisigns find their embodiment ('exist') in concrete sign situations, i.e., in sinsigns that subsume a qualisign.

D. Classes of interpretants

Peirce's theory of the interpretant comprehends a sixfold classification of interpretants: more precisely, two trichotomies—immediate/dynamic/final and emotional/energetic/logical—which intersect, yielding nine types (Short MS). The class of logical interpretants, furthermore, is subject to qualification by the distinction between ultimate and non-ultimate interpretants, affecting immediate logical, dynamic logical, and final logical interpretants. The total number of types is thus twelve. This is the picture that can be reconstructed, at any rate, from Peirce's mature writings of ca. 1904 to 1909 (but with clearly traceable roots in his papers of the 1860s and 1870s).

The first trichotomy of interpretants contains the types Peirce labels *emotional, energetic,* and *logical.* Several quotations aid in showing their content from different but complementary angles:

> A sign mediates between the *interpretant* sign and its object. Taking sign in its broadest sense, its interpretant is not necessarily a sign. Any concept is a sign, of course . . . . But we may take a sign in so broad a sense that the interpretant of it is not a thought, but an action or experience, or we may even so enlarge the meaning of sign that its interpretant is a mere quality of feeling. (H 31)

> A Sign has an Object and an Interpretant, the latter being that which the Sign produces in the Quasi-mind that is the Interpreter by determining the latter to a feeling, to an exertion, or to a Sign, which determination is the Interpretant. (4.536)

> The first proper significate effect of a sign is the feeling produced by it. There is almost always a feeling which we come to interpret as evidence that we comprehend the proper effect of the sign, although the foundation of truth in this is frequently very slight. This 'emotional interpretant,' as I call it, may amount to much more than that feeling of recognition; and in some cases, it is the only proper significate effect that the sign produces. Thus, the performance of a piece of concerted music is a sign. It conveys, and is intended to convey, the composer's musical ideas; but these usually consist merely in a series of feelings. If a sign produces any further proper significate effect, it will do so through the mediation of the emotional interpretant, and such further effect will always involve an effort. I call it the energetic interpretant. The effort may be a muscular one, as it is in the case of the command to ground arms; but it is much more usually an exertion upon the Inner World, a mental effort. It never can be the meaning of an intellectual concept, since it is a single act, [while] such a concept is of a general nature. But what further kind of effect can there be? (5.475)

> In advance of ascertaining the nature of this effect, it will be convenient to adopt a designation for it, and I will call it the *logical interpretant,* without as yet determining whether this term shall extend to anything beside the meaning of a general concept, though certainly closely related to that, or not. Shall we say that this effect may be a thought, that is to say, a mental sign? No doubt, it may be so; only, if this sign be of an intellectual kind—as it would have to be—it must itself have a logical interpretant; so that it cannot be the *ultimate* logical interpretant of the concept. (5.476)

The emotional interpretant, which Peirce describes as 'a mere quality of feeling,' is the qualitative effect of that sign. Since every semeiotic effect of a sign has at least a qualitative aspect, and must include a qualisign which bears an iconic relationship to its object, any sign which has an actual interpretant must have at least an emotional interpretant. As with all of the Peircean trichotomies, there is a hierarchical dependency between the three types determined by the three categories. Accordingly, sinsigns may have energetic interpretants as well as emotional interpretants, and legisigns may have all three types, but qualisigns may only have emotional interpretants. In Peirce's example of 'a piece of concerted music,' the immediate interpretant is the quality of the sounds that are repeated with every performance, while the feelings aroused thereby in the audience are the musical signs' emotional interpretant.

Words and propositions also have emotional interpretants, if nothing more than the feeling of familiarity or unfamiliarity, whether such words or propositions have any emotive (affective) value or not. A word in one's native language (let alone a foreign one) whose meaning is grasped in but the most inchoate manner may still partake of what Peirce regards as the 'first and lowest grade of clearness' (Savan 1976:43).

The Second, in relation to which the emotional interpretant is a First, is the energetic interpretant. This is the mode of interpretation of a sign involving an act in which some energy is expended. The energetic interpretant may engage the external world and thereby be defined by muscular exertion; or it may consist in the energy associated with the inner world of images, with their manipulation and exploration (characteristic of the dialogic process of thought). For Peirce, the energetic interpretant is applicable to the workings of the mind because he conceives of imagination and intellection as involving the same sort of resistance to manipulation as physical objects that act upon us or resist our action upon them. The self-identity of fancies, images, and thoughts may differ in degree of intensity from that of physical objects in the outer world, but Peirce insists that the experimental aspect or aspect of play associated with such ingredients of cogitation are semeiotically of a kind. His avowed source in regarding thought and reasoning to proceed by means of observation and experiment is mathematical and scientific theory formation (cf. 3.560).

Some examples of energetic interpretants are the grounding of arms by soldiers in response to a command; the fulfillment of promises, as well as the (guilty) acts which ensue from failing to keep a promise; mourning, celebration, prayers, thanksgiving, all sorts of rituals and ceremonies (Savan 1976:44). These are the effects of the signs which stand to them as semeiotic causes. Peirce holds that all legisigns have—via their replicas which are sinsigns—an action of the imagination or a muscular effort as their energetic interpretants.

The true purport of this position is revealed by considering the hierarchically supervening semeiotic entity of interpretation, the logical interpretant. Peirce groups all thoughts, concepts, and elements of the understanding actually produced by a sign under this rubric that is a Third. To carry on the cogitative process in the broad sense is to make inferences, conceive the consequences of certain premises, and be guided in the direction one's thoughts take by some general rule. In Peirce's words, 'thought is a thread of melody running through the succession of our sensations' (5.395). To think, to conceive, and to understand is made up of more than just one single event or occurrence, although the whole process is unitary. Continuing with Peirce's musical metaphor, while a single tone is complete unto itself at any given time, and regardless of the whole of which it may be a part, a melody 'consists in an orderliness in the succession of sounds which strike the ear at different times; and to perceive it there must be some continuity of consciousness which makes the events of a lapse of time present to us' (5.395).

The logical interpretant, then, is a general rule, and is of the nature of a conjecture or hypothesis (as will become clearer below). The rule is not a verbal expression, but rather a habit of action which has a verbal analogue or correspondent. There is an illative or inferential form to the verbal correspondent of a habit which states that 'if certain actions are performed upon objects answering to a certain description, results of a general kind will be observable' (Savan 1976:45). The actions can (as we have seen) be of a muscular sort, or be the effort attendant upon cogitation. In either case, they are semeiotic instantiations of a rule; such semeiotic effects also react with the rule, inducing possible modifications of the rule, shaping future results, and enabling rational conduct based on reasonable predictability to proceed. The sets of actions which fulfill the rule are energetic interpretants that replicate logical interpretants. The overarching patterns of habit are future-directed, being potentially repeatable without end, whereas emotional and energetic interpretants are necessarily bounded by time, being past- and present-oriented, respectively.

The shifts in meaning that accompany changes in the relation between speaker and referent in the case of words such as *uncle, father,* or *Mr. President* are generally characteristic of signs, variously named dependent on their relations to their various interpretants. When the sign's frame of reference is its emotional interpretant, Peirce suggests the term *Sympathetic;* when the frame is its energetic interpretant, the term *Percussive;* and in the context of the logical interpretant, the term *Usual* (8.370; cf. Savan 1976:45). Examined in the light of these semeiotic distinctions, qualisigns, as Firsts, can only be sympathetic; sinsigns, as Seconds, can be sympathetic or percussive; and only legisigns, as Thirds, can be usual.

The first of Peirce's trichotomy of interpretants makes broad reference to qualities, actions, and thoughts. Peirce makes it clear, however, that there are Firstnesses of Firstness, of Secondness, and of Thirdness (1.530-534). So that when he writes that 'the Immediate Interpretant consists in the *Quality* of the Impression that a sign is fit to produce' (8.315), meaning 'this quality is a quality *of* the "impression" that would interpret the sign' (Short MS:14), then the immediate interpretant is a Firstness of an emotional interpretant, an energetic interpretant, or a logical interpretant.

The immediate interpretant is the first type in the second of Peirce's two trichotomies of interpretants, the second and third types being the dynamic and the final interpretant. In his own words:

> My Immediate Interpretant is implied in the fact that each Sign must have its peculiar Interpretability before it gets any Interpreter. My Dynamical Interpretant is that which is experienced in each act of Interpretation and is different in each from that of any other; and the Final Interpretant is the one Interpretative result to which every Interpreter is destined to come if the Sign is sufficiently considered. The Immediate Interpretant is an abstraction, consisting in a Possibility. The Dynamical Interpretant is a single actual event. The Final Interpretant is that toward which the actual tends. (H 111)

> The Dynamical Interpretant is whatever interpretation any mind actually makes of a sign. This interpretant derives its character from the Dyadic category, the category of Action. This has two aspects, the Active and the Passive, which are not merely opposite aspects but make relative contrasts between different influences of this Category as More Active and More Passive. . . . When an imagination, a day-dream fires a young man's ambition or any other active passion, that is a more Active variety of his Dynamical Interpretation of the dream. When a novelty excites his surprise,—and the scepticism that goes along with surprise,—this is a more Passive variety of Dynamical Interpretant. I am not speaking of the *feelings* of passion or of surprise as *qualities*. For those *qualities* are no part of the dynamic Interpretants. (8.315)

> The Final Interpretant does not consist in the way in which any mind does act but in the way in which every mind would act. That is, it consists in a truth which might be expressed in a conditional proposition of this type: 'If so and so were to happen to any mind this sign would determine that mind to such and such *conduct*.' By 'conduct' I mean *action* under an intention of self-control. No event that occurs to any mind, no action of any mind can constitute the truth of that conditional proposition. The Immediate Interpretant consists in the *Quality* of the Impression that a sign is fit to produce, not [in] any actual reaction. Thus the Immediate and Final Interpretants seem to me absolutely distinct from the Dynamical Interpretant and from each other. (8.315)

The dynamic interpretant is the actual semeiotic effect of a sign; the final interpretant is the effect that the sign would produce if it were allowed the time and the circumstances fully and finally to satisfy the conditions imposed upon it by the norm governing it; and the immediate interpretant is the effect of the sign as the sign itself presents it, without engaging the world of 'collateral observation,' defined by Peirce as 'previous acquaintance with what the sign denotes' (NE 3:841). The immediate interpretant requires an acquaintance with the system of signs; the final interpretant requires at least some amount of collateral experience. The semeiotic system of which a given sign is a member determines its interpretability (= immediate interpretant). Indeed, this type of semeiotic effect is tantamount to 'the interpretant as it is revealed in the right understanding of the Sign itself, and is ordinarily called the *meaning* of the sign' (4.536); again, 'it is all that is explicit in the sign itself apart from its context and circumstances of utterance' (5.473). The explicit content of the sign is 'so much of the effect of a Sign as would enable a person to say whether or not the Sign was applicable to anything concerning which that person had sufficient acquaintance' (H 110). The aspect of critical reflection or analysis of the sign's effect is absent from the immediate interpretant, although it is implied teleologically by the nature of semeiosis; in Peirce's words, the immediate interpretant is 'the total unanalyzed effect that the Sign is calculated to produce, or naturally might be expected to produce; and I have been accustomed to identify this with the effect the sign first produces or may produce upon a mind, without any reflection upon it' (H 110).

The categories would provide that immediate interpretants be subdivisible into a trichotomy, and Peirce does in fact offer a rather tentative description of what the latter might look like (cf. Savan 1976:40-42). The Firstness of an immediate interpretant is a qualitative possibility, much like the lowest grade of clarity or inchoate ratiocination attendant upon the automatic understanding and use of words—a feeling of familiarity, absence of hesitancy, or what Peirce calls 'a subjective feeling of mastery' (5.389). For example, a qualisign such as a note in a piece of music can take only the most rudimentary form of immediate interpretant: 'a quality which is a sign is able to convey to its interpretant nothing more than a qualitative resemblance to the interpreted sign' (Savan 1976:41). Resemblance of a qualisign to its object is (as was pointed out earlier) of the nature of a hypothesis; the same relationship obtains between a qualisign and its immediate interpretant. Indeed, Peirce calls signs considered with reference to their immediate interpretants *Hypothetic* (8.369).

The Secondness of an immediate interpretant has to do with the significant information transmitted by the sign as it pertains to some occurrence or existent entity. This second variety of immediate interpretant serves to make explicit the interpretability of the sign as designating an occurrence, or as predicable of some subject—without identifying the subject or providing a rule whereby the subject can be selected. For example, an arrow used as a signpost on a roadway has an immediate interpretant—the direction in which the head points, without regard to the specific location of the signpost. Even though the arrow is a sinsign, indexically related to its object, nothing but the directionality of the head is semeiotically relevant to its interpretant. This sort of sign, where the external circumstances of its signification have no bearing on its immediate interpretant, is called *Categorical* by Peirce (8.369).

The category of Thirdness, as it applies to the trichotomous structure of this immediate interpretant, is engaged when the sign communicates information about a universal set of instances—in other words, when the immediate interpretant is a law or rule. Peirce exemplifies this aspect by propositions such as 'Burnt child shuns fire' (5.473) or 'Stones fall' which are universalistic in purport, and proposes that a sign considered in relation to its law-like immediate interpretant be termed a *Relative* (8.369). A legisign may be either hypothetic, relative, or categorical, but a qualisign can only be a hypothetic and a sinsign either hypothetic or categorical (Savan 1976:42).

Moving now to the dynamic interpretant, recall that Peirce characterizes each such interpretant as different from every other (H 111). To the extent that a dynamic interpretant is an actualization of the possibility represented by a hierarchically correspondent immediate interpretant, it is still the case that possibilities are invariably vague, and that each actualization of a given possibility renders the latter definite in a different way (Short MS:8).

In the same way that the immediate interpretant is the Firstness of each of the other three types of interpretant (emotional, energetic, logical), the dynamic interpretant is a Second ('every actual interpretation is dyadic'—8.315). However, every such interpretant is one of three kinds: the occurrence of a feeling (emotional interpretant), of an action (energetic interpretant), or of a new thought or a new habit or action (logical interpretant) (cf. Short MS:15).

Dynamic interpretants are formed on the basis of increasing collateral experience; they cumulatively actualize the corresponding immediate interpretant, including in this process the correction of errors that might have been made and detected in previous interpretants, as well as the addition of new information to what was deposited in these earlier interpretants.

Each sign only has one immediate interpretant, but any finite number of dynamic interpretants, beginning with zero. Peirce's theory of interpretants argues that semeiosis is teleological, that interpretation is shaped by a normative goal toward which it tends at all times. Dynamic interpretants, being finite bounded events, bring semeiosis to a terminus. A simple additive sequence of actions without cumulation into a pattern of habit remains, according to Peirce, at the level of dead Secondness. It is powerless to register the significance of a sign, or to be the sign of some object by signifying yet another sign of the same object. For this reason, Peirce concludes, there must be principles, norms, and laws that guide the interpretation of signs beyond the endless mechanical repetition of identical patterns of behavior.

The full semeiotic effect of a sign, under the condition that its purposed or intended goal is achieved in the indefinite future, is what Peirce means by the Final (or Normal) Interpretant (cf. Savan 1976:49). This type of interpretant is a Third, a standard embodied in the interpretation a sign would receive under ideal conditions. While certain kinds of signs are capable of having a number of dynamic interpretants, Peirce can be interpreted as maintaining that the final (otherwise called 'Destinate' or 'Intended') interpretant is unique for each sign—like the immediate interpretant (cf. Short 1981:214). The final interpretant, again in common with the immediate interpretant, does not need to be actualized; from this standpoint, as Thirds and Firsts, respectively, these types of interpretant differ from the dynamic interpretant, in that the latter necessarily represents an actualization of the immediate interpretant of the sign in question. The final interpretant is what the dynamic interpretant would turn out to be when 'sufficiently considered.'

To summarize and consolidate the account of the second trichotomy of interpretants so far:

> First, the idea of an immediate interpretant presupposes that of a ground of interpretation: the significance of a sign is its immediate interpretant and this is its grounded interpretability, which the sign possesses regardless of whether it is actually interpreted. Second, the idea of a final interpretant presupposes that of a goal of interpretation. For, apart from such a goal, 'consideration' of a sign would not lead the interpreter to any 'destined' conclusion: regardless of the amount of consideration made, any conclusion would remain just as good. But if each sign has a unique final interpretant, then each is the sign that it is in relation not only to a ground but also to a goal of interpretation. It is clear, then, that Peirce conceived of semeiosis as a teleological process and of signs as being what their potential role in semeiosis makes them to be. (Short 1981:214)

The teleological nature of semeiosis entails the Peircean position that sign interpretation is a self-corrective process (cf. Short MS:22). What this means is that at some point in the process the interpretant, or the sign as interpreted in a given interpretant, can be tested. This point is reached when there is an interpretant that is related to the dynamic object of a sign, not via yet another interpretant, but in a more direct manner. The test and demonstration of the directness of this relation comes with the establishment of general laws—logical interpretants—that inhere in habits of action and of expectation. These habits are subject to continuous testing and revision in the light of experience, with the ultimate result that would accurately mirror the generality of laws. For Peirce, 'the real and living logical conclusion *is* that habit; the verbal formulation merely expresses it' (5.491). This is, in capsule form, a statement of Peirce's pragmaticism (about which more will be said below).

The importance of purpose and intentionality in semeiosis is stressed in the conception of final interpretant because this type of interpretant is defined as 'the full semeiotic effect of a sign if its purpose or intention were to be achieved' (Savan 1976:49). The purpose that a sign may fulfill furnishes Peirce with an opportunity to expand his trichotomous classification to final interpretants (8.372; cf. Savan 1976:49-50, Lieb 1953:52). The first of the three types of purpose is the standard or norm by which qualities are evaluated. With respect to ends toward which signs tend, this type of sign is called *Gratific* by Peirce, reflecting his notion of one end as a qualitative ideal admirable in itself (something akin to Greek *kalos*). It is an aesthetic interpretant, in that this first type of purpose has as its goal the production of qualities of feeling which are admirable in some degree, correlative with signs of intrinsically admirable qualities. An illustration to which Peirce himself recurs is the musical sign. It is gratific because it is a sign whose qualitative final interpretant 'is a quality of intrinsic admirableness' (Savan 1976:50). From the standpoint of semeiosis, music is a sign whose emotional interpretant is the occurrence of specific qualities of feeling; but it is the goal or purpose of the sign to bring the composition to life, to invest its emotional interpretants with a living power. There is, however, a norm or law which acts as a standard of excellence in shaping the listener's response—that is to say, in directing the creation of emotional interpretants and evaluating their degree of success in meeting criteria of aesthetic goodness.

The second type of sign with respect to final interpretants is what Peirce terms *Practical,* by which he means a sign whose purpose is the direction of conduct, and whose final interpretants are therefore ethical. Examples of a practical sign are commands, some kinds of promises, ceremonies, etc.; and the signals and releasers of some types of animal behavior (Savan 1976:50).

The third type of sign in this trichotomy 'according to the Purpose of the Eventual [= Final] Interpretant' is meant to produce 'self-control' (8.372), and the following quotation from Peirce is helpful in understanding why he chose to call it *Pragmatistic:*

> Every man exercises more or less control over himself by means of modifying his own habits; and the way in which he goes to work to bring this effect about in those cases in which circumstances will not permit him to practice reiterations of the desired kind of conduct in the outer world shows that he is

well-acquainted with the important principle that reiterations in the inner world—fancied reiterations—if well-intensified by direct effort, produce habits, just as do reiterations in the outer world; and these habits will have power to influence actual behaviour in the outer world; especially, if each reiteration be accompanied by a peculiar strong effort that is usually likened to issuing a command to one's future self. (5.487)

In the hierarchy of signs relative to their final interpretants, the highest or ultimate purpose is reached in the dominance of critical control over habits and beliefs. The leading principles of logic are just such critical norms by which the validity of inferences made on the basis of semeiotic relations is evaluated. Peirce regards deliberate self-criticism to be the outstanding feature of interpretants whose signs are pragmatistic:

> The habit conjoined with the motive and the conditions has the action for its energetic interpretant; but action cannot be a logical interpretant, because it lacks generality. The concept which is a logical interpretant is only imperfectly so. It somewhat partakes of the nature of a verbal definition, and is as inferior to the habit, and much in the same way, as a verbal definition is inferior to the real definition. The deliberately formed, self-analyzing habit—self-analyzing because formed by the aid of analysis of the exercises that nourished it—is the living definition, the veritable and final logical interpretant. Consequently, the most perfect account of a concept that words can convey will consist in a description of the habit which that concept is calculated to produce. (5.491)

A further trichotomy of signs involves the relation of the sign to its final interpretant: corresponding to the traditional triad of term, proposition, and argument, Peirce proposes the names *Rheme* (alternatively *Seme*), *Dicent* (or *Dicisign* or *Pheme*), and *Argument* (or *Delome*). The differences between these types are glossed briefly (at 8.373): 'As to the Nature of the Influence of the Sign: Semes, like a simple sign; Phemes, with antecedent and consequent; Delome, with antecedent, consequent, and principle of sequence.' Somewhat more fully, they are defined by Peirce as follows:

> A *Rheme* is a Sign which, for its Interpretant, is a Sign of qualitative Possibility, that is, is understood as representing such and such a kind of possible Object. Any Rheme, perhaps, will afford some information; but it is not interpreted as doing so. (2.250)

> A *Dicent Sign* is a Sign, which, for its Interpretant, is a Sign of actual existence. It cannot, therefore, be an Icon, which affords no ground for an interpretation of it as referring to actual existence. A Dicisign necessarily involves, as a part of it, a Rheme, to describe the fact which it is interpreted as indicating. But this is a peculiar kind of Rheme; and while it is essential to the Dicisign, it by no means constitutes it. (2.251)

An *Argument* is a Sign which, for its Interpretant, is a Sign of law. Or we may say that a Rheme is a sign which is understood to represent its object in its characters merely; that a Dicisign is a sign which is understood to represent its object in respect to actual existence; and that an Argument is a Sign which is understood to represent its Object in its character as a Sign. (2.252)

A rheme is any sign that is not true nor false, like almost any single word except 'yes' or 'no,' which are almost peculiar to modern languages.... A dicent is not an assertion, but is a sign capable of being asserted.... Holding, then, that a Dicent does not assert, I naturally hold that an Argument need not be actually submitted or urged. I therefore define an argument as a sign which is interpreted in its signified interpretant not as a Sign of the interpretant (the conclusion) [for that would be to urge or submit it] but *as if* it were a Sign of the Interpretant or perhaps as if it were a Sign of the state of the universe to which it refers, in which the premisses are taken for granted. I define a dicent as a sign represented in its signified interpretant *as if it were* in a Real Relation to its Object. (Or as being so, if it is asserted.) A rheme is defined as a sign which is represented in its signified interpretant as *if it were* a character or mark (or as being so). (H 34)

Peirce holds that while terms, propositions, and arguments are traditionally said to differ by degrees of complexity, the distinction that separates them from one another 'is by no means a difference of complexity, and does not so much consist in structure as in the services they are severally intended to perform' (4.572). The structural differences between semes, phemes, and delomes pertain to the 'services they are severally intended to perform' rather than to the signs themselves; in other words, the focal point of this trichotomy is the influence the sign exerts on its final interpretant (Short 1982).

Another way of putting this action of sign on interpretant is to place the emphasis on the mode of appeal of the sign rather than on what is signified. The manner of appeal or influence is brought out in yet another set of definitions:

By a *Seme,* I shall mean anything which serves for any purpose as a substitute for an object of which it is, in some sense, a representative or Sign. The logical Term, which is a class-name, is a Seme. By a *Pheme* I mean a Sign which is equivalent to grammatical sentence, whether it be Interrogative, Imperative, or Assertory. In any case, such a Sign is intended to have some sort of compulsive effect on the Interpreter of it. As the third member of the triplet, I sometimes use the word *Delome* (pronounced deeloam, from [Greek] *déloma*), though *Argument* would answer well enough. It is a Sign which has the Form of tending to act upon the Interpreter through his own self-control, representing a process of change in thoughts or signs, as if to induce this change in the Interpreter. (4.538)

A rheme is a sign whose final interpretant represents it to be 'some quality which *might* be embodied in a possibly existing object' (Savan 1976:51); a qualisign must be a rheme, since its final interpretant can only represent it as the presence of a sign of quality whose instantiation depends on some possible occurrence or entity. An indexical sinsign may be a rheme; for example, the laughter that is indexically related to its object, but interpreted as signifying the quality of happiness itself, as in the phrase *happy laughter* (Savan 1976:51). Indexical legisigns which are rhemes can be found in the use of demonstratives like *here* and *now*. This use illustrates the point that some rhemes compel attention (Short 1982). They serve this end, but in such a way as to emphasize the possibility of something, even if the object of attention is an actuality. The final interpretant of a rhematic sign interprets the sign as presenting qualities or possibilities, predicable of some individual.

A dicent is a sign which is interpreted by its final interpretant 'as proposing some information about an existent' (Savan 1976:51). It signifies existence or fact by imposing itself upon the interpreter, by means of its own compulsive character (Short 1982). A dicent is capable of being true or false:

> A weathercock is an example of a dicent indexical sinsign. It is interpreted as a sign of the wind and it informs the interpreter of the direction in which the wind is blowing. A portrait painting with the names of subject and artist is interpreted as a sign of both subject and painter, informing the interpreter of the qualities of both. The song of a nightingale is a dicent indexical sinsign if it is interpreted as providing information concerning the song of the individual bird. If it is interpreted as providing information concerning the species it is a legisign. (Savan 1976:52)

An argument, for Peirce, is not the process or mechanism by which valid conclusions are regularly derived from stipulated premises. Instead, argument or delome is a sign which is interpreted by its final interpretant as a law, rule, or principle. Only symbolic legisigns qualify as arguments; sinsigns and qualisigns by themselves are incapable of being interpreted as arguments. In the case of a syllogism, arguments in the Peircean sense result only when the interpreter himself can determine that a valid conclusion follows from the premises with which he is supplied: 'the peculiar syntax or other remarks by which we know an argument to be one signify only through the appeal they make to the interpreter to go through a process of inference himself' (Short 1982:301).

E. Assurance of interpretation

Semeiosis in the fullest sense necessarily involves genuine triadic relations, says Peirce, and his favorite example of that kind of relation is that of giving: 'A gives B to C.' The sign classes and types discussed above all hinge, however, on relations which are either monadic or dyadic. Signs classified according to each of their three major constituents considered in themselves (sign, object, interpretant) are monadic. The three semeiotic relations—sign to dynamic object, sign to dynamic interpretant, and sign to final interpretant—are all dyadic. But Peirce's unwavering position on semeiotic relations is that no combination of monads and/or dyads is capable of constituting a genuine triadic relation. At the same time, it is only the genuine triadic relation obtaining between sign, object, and interpretant that enables signs to *offer assurance* to the interpretant that the object for which it stands is simultaneously identical with the object of the sign the interpretant interprets (Savan 1976:53).

The act of giving suits Peirce as an example of triadicity because it necessarily comports the recognition of a law or principle whereby the right or authority of possession is transferred from one subject to another—over and above the simple physical movement of the item given. Without the accompanying intentionality (on both sides) the physical movement would be devoid of meaning (cf. Savan 1976:42). There would be two dyadic relations—between the donor and the object, on one hand, and the recipient and the object, on the other—but no mediation, hence no notion of giving.

In the same way, if the relation between object and sign is dyadic, and the sign is dyadically related to its interpretant, the interpretant's status as a sign of the same object as the original sign could just as well be fortuitous. Indeed, the interpretant could easily turn out to be a sign of a different object, as is often the case when one hears an unfamiliar or partly familiar language and attempts to guess at the meaning of the utterances; the chances of being wrong might be just as great as those of being right.

Peirce assumes for semeiosis that the chances of guessing right are significantly greater than guessing wrong in the long run, and he attributes human progress to man's inherent ability to frame correct hypotheses. As far as the semeiotic relation is concerned, this capacity for making correct inferences, in scientific endeavors as in ordinary life, must rest, argues Peirce, on the Assurance of the Utterance (using Utterance as synonymous with Sign; Savan 1976:53).

There are three types of assurance, dictated by the categories. First, the interpretant may be assured of its connection with sign and object *by instinct*. By using this word Peirce intends certain fundamental natural capacities that transcend particularities of species, geographic locus, and accumulated experience; ones that allow knowledge and communication to proceed:

Nature is a far vaster and less clearly arranged repertory of facts than a census report; and if men had not come to it with special aptitudes for guessing right, it may well be doubted whether in the ten or twenty thousand years that they may have existed their greatest mind would have attained the amount of knowledge which is actually possessed by the lowest idiot. But, in point of fact, not man merely, but all animals derive by inheritance (presumably by natural selection) two classes of ideas which adapt them to their environment. In the first place, they all have from birth some notions, however crude and concrete, of force, matter, space, and time; and, in the next place, they have some notion of what sort of objects their fellow-beings are, and how they will act on given occasions. . . . Man has thus far not attained to any knowledge that is not in a wide sense either mechanical or anthropological in its nature, and it may be reasonably presumed that he never will. (2.753)

Side by side, then, with the well established proposition that all knowledge is based on experience, and that science is only advanced by the experimental verifications of theories, we have to place this other equally important truth, that all human knowledge, up to the highest flights of science, is but the development of our inborn animal instincts. (2.754)

Assurance by instinct for Peirce means a 'qualitative affinity, a subconscious linkage of Firstness, which enables the interpretant to interpret the sign as evidence of the character of its object correctly' (Savan 1976:55). The quality of the object has the capacity to arouse a sympathetic response in the interpretant of the sign, and a responsive reciprocity is established between sign and interpretant. When children learn to use and understand speech sounds, for instance, there must be the assurance furnished by self-control. The correctness of sign interpretation is assured when one is able to control and modify one's feelings, actions, and thoughts through that interpretation.

The second type of assurance in Peirce's final trichotomy is the *assurance of experience*. The characteristics of the object ascribed to it by its sign must pass the test of experience; otherwise the interpretant cannot be assured that such an object really exists. The process of semeiotic mediation of sign, object, and interpretant being virtually without termination, there must be some collateral information or experience, argues Peirce, that verifies the fact that sign and interpretant stand for the same object. What allows the identification of a common object to occur is 'an insistent environment common to all three terms' (Savan 1976:55) of the semeiotic triad. The most important feature of experience insofar as assuring an interpretant is concerned is its hard, brute, insistent nature, which prevents it from being manipulated and distorted by whim, caprice, and fancy. Action, thought, and communication all depend on taking the givenness and autonomy of facts into account. The interpretant is assured of its existence by a 'collision with an obdurate object' (Savan 1976:55).

The third and last type of assurance is that of *Form*. There must be a unity of form that assures the interpretants of signs when the latter are laws and necessitants. This type of assurance affects judgements of the most mundane kind—for instance, regarding the color, weight, hardness, etc. of ordinary objects:

> Although Peirce is most interested in assurance of form as it is found in scientific reasoning, humble and everyday examples abound. To say of any object—an apple, for example—that it is red implies an elementary law, the law, namely, that under standard conditions of vision, lighting, etc., the apple would in the future look red. Even to say that the apple *looks* red now, says Peirce, is to imply the law that it would continue in the immediate future to look red. . . . We reason that the apple is red, and if it is red then it will look red at various times in the future. We thus infer the formal conclusion that the apple looks red at such and such times, and the conclusion is verified by observation. *Assurance by form* thus enters into the interpretants of the most ordinary everyday signs, because these signs, their objects, and their interpretants are laws. (Savan 1976:57).

Although Peirce himself proposes no names for the three types of sign that assure their interpretants by instinct, experience, and form, they can be called (following the suggestion in Savan 1976:57), respectively, *Presentiments, Empirical Signs,* and *Formal Signs.*

F. Summary of sign types

The several semeiotic trichotomies discussed above can be summarized (cf. Lieb 1953:51-5) utilizing the principle of triadic division which Peirce employed in conformity with the categories. The three types Peirce himself explored most thoroughly and their categorial varieties are shown in Figure 4 (adapted from Anttila 1977a:227).

The combination of varieties of sign are restricted by the hierarchical nature of the categories. In Peirce's words, 'it is evident that a Possible can determine nothing but a Possible, it is equally so that a Necessitant can be determined by nothing but a Necessitant' (H 84). Given these restrictions, the three trichotomies above provide for 10 (rather than 27) classes of sign combinations:

1. Qualisigns
2. Iconic sinsigns
3. Iconic legisigns
4. *Vestiges,* or Rhematic Indexical Sinsigns
5. *Proper names,* or Rhematic Indexical Legisigns
6. Rhematic Symbols
7. Dicent sinsigns (as a portrait with a legend)

	FIRST	SECOND	THIRD	
1	qualisign (tone)	sinsign (token)	legisign (type)	sign in relation to itself
2	icon	index	symbol	sign in relation to object
3	rheme	dicent	argument	sign in relation to interpretant
	sign as possibility	sign as actuality	sign as rule or law	

FIGURE 4

  8. Dicent Indexical Legisigns
  9. *Propositions,* or Dicent symbols
10. Arguments   (H 35-6)

Ten additional trichotomous divisions result upon the recognition that a sign has two objects (dynamic and immediate) and three basic interpretants (immediate, dynamic, final). Peirce first divides signs according to (1) their own nature, (2) the nature of their immediate objects, then according to their relation to (3) their dynamic objects, (4) their final, (5) dynamic, and (6) their immediate interpretants (H 32-5). Each of these divisions is a triad; in each of the last three cases, the triadic subdivision into sign types is conjugate with the tripartition of the respective interpretant into emotional, energetic, and logical subtypes (Short MS:13). The expansion into ten trichotomies ('the ten respects according to which the chief divisions of signs are determined') is described by Peirce as follows:

   1st, According to the Mode of Apprehension of the Sign itself,
   2nd, According to the Mode of Presentation of the Immediate Object,
   3rd, According to the Mode of Being of the Dynamical Object,
   4th, According to the Relation of the Sign to its Dynamical Object,
   5th, According to the Mode of Presentation of the Immediate Interpretant,
   6th, According to the Mode of Being of the Dynamical Interpretant,
   7th, According to the Relation of the Sign to the Dynamical Interpretant,
   8th, According to the Nature of the Normal [= Final] Interpretant,
   9th, According to the Relation of the Sign to the Normal Interpretant,
 10th, According to the Triadic Relation of the Sign to its Dynamical Object
      and to its Normal Interpretant.

                                             (H.344)

Translated into the terms utilized in the discussion above, the ten trichotomies appear in catalogue as follows (cf. Lieb 1953:52):

1. *Signs in Themselves*
   a. Qualisigns
   b. Sinsigns
   c. Legisigns

2. *Immediate Objects in Themselves*
   a. Descriptives
   b. Designatives
   c. Copulants

3. *Dynamic Objects in Themselves*
   a. Abstractives
   b. Concretives
   c. Collectives

4. *Relation of Signs to their Dynamic Objects*
   a. Icons
   b. Indexes
   c. Symbols

5. *Immediate Interpretants in Themselves*
   a. Hypotheticals
   b. Categoricals
   c. Relatives

6. *Dynamic Interpretants in Themselves*
   a. Sympathetics
   b. Percussives
   c. Usuals

7. *Relation of Signs to their Dynamic Interpretants*
   a. Suggestives
   b. Imperatives
   c. Indicatives

8. *Final Interpretants in Themselves*
   a. Gratifics
   b. Practicals
   c. Pragmatistics

9. *Relation of Signs to Final Interpretants*
   a. Rhemes
   b. Dicents
   c. Arguments

10. *Assurances of Interpretants by Signs*
    a. Assurance by Instinct
    b. Assurance by Experience
    c. Assurance by Form

4. Pragmaticism, Habit, Abduction

Peirce was the founder of pragmatism; he was also the inventor of the name for the doctrine that was popularly associated from its beginnings with William James and others, rather than with its originator (cf. 5.412, 5.414). Finding his conception of pragmatism ('a method of ascertaining the meanings, not of all ideas, but only of what I call "intellectual concepts," that is to say, of those upon the structure of which, arguments concerning objective fact may hinge'; 5.467) to have been distorted by those who took it up, Peirce came to call his more strictly defined doctrine 'pragmaticism,' a name he deemed 'ugly enough to be safe from kidnappers' (5.414).

The connection between pragmaticism and semeiotic is fundamental. Peirce's pragmaticism is a theory of meaning that is intimately dependent on his sign theory, itself a theory of cognition (cf. Fitzgerald 1964). For Peirce, 'the problem of what the "meaning" of an intellectual concept is can only be solved by the study of the interpretants, or proper significate effects, of signs' (5.475). But the study of interpretants necessarily comports the investigation of 'habits':

> I do not deny that a concept, or general mental sign, may be a logical interpretant; only, it cannot be the ultimate logical interpretant, precisely because, being a sign, it has itself a logical interpretant. It partakes somewhat of the nature of a verbal definition, and is very inferior to the living definition that grows up in the habit. Consequently, the most perfect account that we can give of a concept will consist in a description of the habit that it will produce. (NE 3:493-4)

Peirce's notion of habit, central to both his pragmaticism and his semeiotic, has a much broader purport that is commonly associated with the word. For him,

> It denotes such a specialization, original or acquired, of the nature of a man, or an animal, or a vine, or a crystallizable chemical substance, or anything else, that he or it will behave, or always tend to behave, in a way describable in general terms upon every occasion (or upon a considerable proportion of the occasions) that may present itself of a generally describable character. (5.538)

The role of habit in semeiosis is brought out by Peirce's understanding of sign interpretation as 'an essentially teleological, hence, self-corrective process' (Short MS:22). This means that interpretants can be put to the test; more precisely, that logical interpretants which purport to embody and to represent general laws of nature are testable in their hypostasis as habits of expectation or habits of action. This is what Peirce intended in saying, therefore, that 'the real and living logical conclusion *is* that habit; the verbal formulation merely expresses it' (5.491).

Peirce's pragmaticism rests in part on differentiating between final and ultimate logical interpretants (Short MS, 1981). The final logical interpretant is the true interpretation of a sign; the ultimate logical interpretant is the meaning of any logical interpretant, irrespective of its truth or falsity (Short MS:22). Every logical interpretant—whether it be immediate, dynamic, or final—must have its ultimate form. Verbal logical interpretants are penultimate to an interpretation of them that are habits, ultimate logical interpretants. Given the teleological essence of semeiosis, every genuine interpretant must be testable; furthermore, only habits and, through them, the verbal logical interpretants they interpret are testable and self-correctable.

The difference between meaningfulness and meaninglessness, on this view, comes down to the distinction between verbal formulas that have ultimate interpretants—i.e., are testable—and those that do not (Short MS:23). The mere translation or conversion of one verbal formula into another does not constitute testability. Final logical interpretants could not come into being without ultimate logical interpretants: final interpretation depends crucially on the testing of habits. At the same time, final and ultimate interpretants cannot be collapsed:

> Final logical interpretants need not be ultimate, though they must be interpretable by ultimate interpretants. To suppose that every final logical interpretant must be ultimate is to suppose that the aim of theory is practice. Instead, the point of pragmatism is that practice is the test of theory even when theory is sought for its own sake. The final logical interpretant sought in disinterested inquiry would be enjoyed in its verbal form. For it is in that form that it *represents* reality to us. But to be final, it would have to be capable of surviving testing in its ultimate form. (Short MS:23)

Peirce's own reasoning in identifying habit and 'habit-change' with the ultimate logical interpretant is instructive for an understanding of the semeiotic grounding of pragmaticism:

> In advance of ascertaining the nature of this [significate] effect, it will be convenient to adopt a designation for it, and I will call it the *logical interpretant,* without as yet determining whether this term shall extend to anything beside the meaning of a general concept, though certainly closely related to that, or not. Shall we say that this effect may be a thought, that is to say, a mental sign? No doubt, it may be so; only, if this sign be of an intellectual kind—as it would have to be—it must itself have a logical interpretant; so that it cannot be the *ultimate* logical interpretant of the concept. It can be proved that the only mental effect that can be so produced and that is not a sign but is of a general application is a *habit-change;* meaning by a habit-change a modification of a person's tendencies toward action, resulting from previous experience or from previous exertions of his will or acts, or from a complexus of both kinds of cause. (5.476)

> I ask myself, since we have already seen that the logical interpretant is general in its possibilities of reference (i.e., refers or is related to whatever there may be of a certain description), what categories of mental facts there be that are of general reference. I can find only these four: conceptions, desires (including hopes, fears, etc.), expectations, and habits. I trust I have made no important omission. Now it is no explanation of the nature of the logical interpretant (which, we already know, is a concept) to say that it is a concept. This objection applies also to desire and expectation, as explanations of the same interpretant; since neither of these is general otherwise than through connection with a concept. Besides, as to desire, it would be easy to show (were it worth the space), that the logical interpretant is an effect of the energetic interpretant, in the sense in which the latter is the effect of the emotional interpretant. Desire, however, is cause, not effect, of effort. As to expectation, it is excluded by the fact that it is not conditional. For that which might be mistaken for a conditional expectation is nothing but a judgment that, under certain conditions, there would be an expectation: there is no conditionality in

the expectation itself, such as there is in the logical interpretant after it is actually produced. Therefore, there remains only habit, as the essence of the logical interpretant. (5.486)

Peirce conceives of habits as Thirds, and it is their status as generals that allows them to be called 'the essence of the logical interpretant.' Habits are tendencies to act in this or that manner under specifiable conditions; they are thus at one remove from the realm of the here and now, or Secondness. Habits govern—in the manner of leading principles—activities, which are Seconds, within the class of existent individuals, and this regulative relation has built into it the attainment of some goal.

Habits are, in Peirce's scheme, also the products of experimentation, much in the manner of scientific inquiry, though this form of testing need not be muscular: habits can be developed merely by the repeated exercise of thought, which Peirce calls 'reiterations in the inner world . . . likened to issuing a command to one's future self' (5.487). Indeed, Peirce restricts his brand of pragmatism to intellectual concepts, that is to say to meaning as intellectual purport (5.402, n. 3). This restriction stems in part from the fact that only intellectual signs have interpretants that are Thirds (Fitzgerald 1964:147). Another reason for it is Peirce's colligation of pragmaticism with his theory of inquiry, specifically his doctrine of *abduction,* or inferences that are based on signs allowing conclusions to be drawn from them.

The process of thought underlying all inquiry in which an explanatory hypothesis is formed—such is the content of abduction (also called retroduction or hypothesis by Peirce, and occasionally confused with induction by his interpreters). In terms of syllogism, abduction states that something is the case and is, therefore, the only fallible mode of reasoning as compared to the other two modes, deduction and induction, given the premisses. Peirce describes all three modes as follows:

> Abduction is the process of forming an explanatory hypothesis. It is the only logical operation which introduces any new idea; for induction does nothing but determine a value, and deduction merely evolves the necessary consequences of a pure hypothesis.
>
> Deduction proves that something *must* be; Induction shows that something *actually is* operative; Abduction merely suggests that something *may be*.
>
> Its only justification is that from its suggestion deduction can draw a prediction which can be tested by induction, and that, if we are ever to learn anything or to understand phenomena at all, it must be by abduction that this is to be brought about.
>
> No reason whatsoever can be given for it, as far as I can discover; and it needs no reason, since it merely offers suggestions. (5.171)

Abduction and interpretation are inextricably bound up with one another, which is to say that the formation of interpretants proceeds by series of abductive inferences whose character is affected by repeated testing and experimentation. Peirce himself explains pragmaticism as a theory of meaning that is tantamount to the logic of abduction:

> If you carefully consider the questions of pragmatism you will see that it is nothing else than the question of the logic of abduction. That is, pragmatism proposes a certain maxim which, if sound, must render needless any further rule as to the admissibility of hypotheses to rank as hypotheses, that is to say, as explanations of phenomena held as hopeful suggestions; and, furthermore, this is *all* that the maxim of pragmatism really pretends to do, at least so far as it is confined to logic, and is not understood as a proposition in psychology. For the maxim of pragmatism is that a conception can have no logical effect or import differing from that of a second conception except so far as, taken in connection with other conceptions and intentions, it might conceivably modify our practical conduct differently from that second conception.... Thus, the maxim of pragmatism, if true, fully *covers* the entire logic of abduction.... if pragmatism is the doctrine that every conception is a conception of conceivable practical effects, it makes conception reach far beyond the practical. It allows any flight of the imagination, provided this imagination ultimately alights upon a possible practical effect; and thus many hypotheses may seem at first glance to be excluded by the pragmatical maxim that are not really so excluded. (5.196)

The role of semeiotic in pragmaticism includes inference as a leading principle: the circle consisting of sign, interpretant, and habit is held together by the pragmatic maxim and the logic of abduction (cf. 8.191).

All that remains to be fitted into this conception is the perceptual component, which Peirce does by relating abduction and perception in a systematically grounded way:

> Abductive inference shades into perceptual judgment without any sharp line of demarcation between them; or, in other words, our first premisses, the perceptual judgments, are to be regarded as an extreme case of abductive inferences, from which they differ in being absolutely beyond criticism. The abductive suggestion comes to us like a flash. It is an act of *insight,* although of extremely fallible insight. It is true that the different elements of the hypothesis were in our minds before; but it is the idea of putting together what we had never before dreamed of putting together which flashes the new suggestion before our contemplation. (5.181)

The comparison between the formation of explanatory hypotheses and perception is effected through the systematic tangency of abduction and what Peirce refers to consistently as the 'perceptual judgment' (cf. Reilly 1970:46-55): this is a mental proposition connected with the sense experience of the person forming the judgment—or as Peirce puts it, 'a judgment asserting in propositional form what a character of a percept directly present to the mind is' (5.54). Pragmatic meaning originates in the perceptual judgment, and Peirce adduces the Aristotelian dictum *Nihil est in intellectu quod non prius fuerit in sensu* (5.181) to ground his position. This act of mind working on the data supplied by the senses is the premiss behind all critical thinking and mental control, although 'it itself is not subject to control or criticism, since there is no meaning beyond it which could serve as a norm of criticism' (Reilly 1970:46-7).

The meaning units predicated of the perceived objects are general, and this fact connects abduction with perceptual judgments: both contain general elements. Moreover, the two are systematically similar in that both are beyond the control of reason and criticism in the first instance. Perceptual judgments are 'forced upon [our] acquaintance, and that by a process which [we are] utterly unable to control and consequently [are] unable to criticize' (5.157). Abductive inferences or explanatory hypotheses are, in origin, products of the imagination, flashes of insight not subject to the influence of the critical faculty or reason and chosen for further testing and examination by an instinct independent of deliberate control.

Ultimately, however, the two part company with respect to their subjection to the control of the rational faculty. Abduction, born of instinct and imagination, comes under the compass of reason, since it undergoes testing as to its validity. Perceptual judgments, on the other hand, escape the corrective influence of criticism: 'we cannot form the least conception of what it would be to deny the perceptual judgment' (5.186).

Both are interpretative, in that they each abstract or represent only some part of the knowable features of objects without exhausting their meaning. On Peirce's view, however, perceptual judgments, though indubitable at the moment of formation, may come to be doubted subsequently—on the basis of later, conflicting perceptual judgments. They are thus indubitable in one sense but eminently fallible nonetheless. Abduction, on the other hand, is fallible and subject to error *by definition,* since it asserts that something may be the case—tentatively and subject to revision.

The process of interpretation, of furnishing successions of interpretants that are increasingly refined in reflecting the purport of the signs and objects to which they are connected, is grounded in experience: 'every general element of every hypothesis, however wild or sophisticated it may be [is] given somewhere in perception, . . . every general *form* of putting concepts together is, in its elements, given in perception' (5.186). In terms of abductive reasoning this entails, for Peirce, the position that the abductive conclusion is necessarily suggestive by its premisses (5.189). But the interpretation abduction furnishes is eminently fallible nonetheless, since it only goes so far as to assert that the conclusion drawn is a systematic possibility contained in the premisses on which it is based.

Pragmaticism, or the pragmatic maxim of meaning, pertains fundamentally to this point by limiting the admissibility of hypotheses; in fact, 'a hypothesis may be judged admissible if it is in accord with the pragmatic maxim' (Reilly 1970:54). Interpretants arising as abductive inferences are verifiable. Pragmaticism imposes a limit on the free play of imagination whenever the goal is interpretation of phenomena. Peirce's own focus in this enterprise is scientific inquiry, but the purport of his conception clearly extends its scope to embrace all activity that involves interpretation.

5. Conclusion

It can now be seen that Peirce's philosophical enterprise is a thoroughly semeiotic one. His pragmaticism is a theory of meaning and converges with his semeiotic, which is a theory of cognition. To study meaning is to study signs; to study the consequences of the pragmatic maxim is to study interpretants.

Moreover, for Peirce, 'all thought whatsoever is a sign, and is mostly of the nature of language' (5.421). One of Peirce's greatest achievements is his extension of the concept of sign to language. Since linguistic units are all legisigns, of which symbols are the most prominent class, the semeiotic study of language and its structure comports the thorough investigation of the way in which symbols—which hierarchically include icons and indexes—fulfill their function, a process to be interpreted as a matter of law or habit. At the heart of semeiosis is the teleology of function encompassed in the formula 'a sign is not a sign unless it translates itself into another sign in which it is more fully developed' (5.594). The process of translation is tantamount to interpretation, to rendering successively more determinate the epitomical vagueness that inheres in the very ontology of a symbol (NE 4:261).

Apologizing to his reader for being unable to answer all questions arising from his conception, Peirce excuses himself by admitting: 'I am, as far as I know, a pioneer, or rather a backwoodsman, in the work of clearing and opening up what I call *semiotic*, . . . and I find the field too vast, the labor too great, for a first-comer. I am accordingly, obliged to confine myself to the most important questions' (5.488). His keen insight into language and its structure notwithstanding, Peirce the scientist and philosopher devoted himself to the foundations of his larger subject while expressing admiration for 'the vast and splendidly developed science of linguistics' (1.271). Indeed, from the very beginnings of his semeiotic to its most mature culmination after close to fifty years of study, Peirce steadfastly adhered to a conception of signs that identified them essentially with 'the same general structure as words' (6.338). Peirce's theory of signs, therefore, is intended as a conscious adumbration of a theory of grammar.

II

Sketch of a Peircean
Theory of Grammar

A semeiotic theory of grammar, taking grammar in the broad sense of the entirety of linguistic structure, begins with an account of the signs of language. The triadic structure of signs in general is nowhere better epitomized than in human language, the example par excellence of semeiosis.

Corresponding to Peirce's fundamental tripartition into Sign, Object, and Interpretant, all linguistic entities are *signa* (signs) comprised by (1) a material or perceptible *signans*, (2) an intelligible or translatable *signatum*, and (3) an *interpretant* (rule) governing the relation between signans and signatum. Since signantia are the means of expression by which the signata, or content entities, are communicated, the interpretant of a linguistic sign turns out to be the *form of the content*. That is to say, the interpretant is at once the embodiment of the relation between signans and signatum and its content form (to use the Hjelmslevian term). The interpretant has no material or perceptible shape of its own apart from the signans to which it stands as its evaluative correlate vis-à-vis the conjugate signatum. The absence of corporality in an interpretant of a linguistic sign is totally expected, since *all* interpretants, qua values, inhere totally in the conceptual side of phenomena, that is to say in their *order,* for which there is never a direct physical manifestation. While an integral and inexcludable aspect of semeiosis, order—whatever its guise—is always the product of the imposition of mind.

The recognition, following Peirce, that linguistic signs, like all other signs, have not just a material and a translatable part but a rule of relation between these two parts necessarily situates any given sign in a context, or what for language signs is, at the most fundamental level of semeiosis, a *minimal paradigm* defined by the two terms of an opposition. For although analysis habitually isolates signs, the structure of semeiosis necessarily articulates a 'horizontal dimension' in addition to the 'vertical dimension' defined by signans and signatum considered in and of themselves. As soon as the interpretant is invoked, it becomes necessary to transcend the individual sign which analysis has isolated for ease of exposition and to encompass the 'other' sign (the 'horizontal dimension') with which the first is paired virtually. The nature of this pairing, indeed, is not a simple juxtaposition: it is the dyadic one of *opposition,* as Peirce himself insisted ('A thing without oppositions *ipso facto* does not exist'; 1.457).

The association, therefore, of a particular signans with a particular signatum (or set of signata) results in *signification;* but the interpretant always introduces into signification an additional dimension—that of evaluation or *significance.* The relational nature of the interpretant is brought out by its bifocal reference: first, to the particular signans-signatum duple it interprets; second, to the latter's oppositional counterpart—also a signans-signatum duple with its own interpretant. Without the linking up, in a systematic way, of the interpretants associated with the terms of oppositions there would be no order in the relations between signs, hence neither semeiotic nor semeiosis. To say that language is a system, on this view, is thus tantamount to saying that linguistic elements and their combinations are related to each other in an ordered manner.

It thus emerges as an axiom of the theory of grammar adumbrated by Peircean semeiotic that interpretants are inalienable parts of linguistic signs. Since Peirce's writings remained unknown to the founders of structural linguistics, it is not surprising to find this most important aspect of the sign to be all but totally absent from discussions and analyses of language data carried out by even those linguists (like Hjelmslev) who were aware of the status of language as a fundamentally semeiotic system. The sole quasi-exception, possibly prefigured by Saussure's notion of *valeur linguistique,* is the concept of markedness which originated in the Prague Linguistic Circle—more properly, in the work of the two leading Russian members, Trubetzkoy and Jakobson (Greenberg 1966:11, fn. 3; see now Jakobson and Pomorska 1980:93-8).

Trubetzkoy first conceived of markedness (according to the testimony of Jakobson and Waugh 1979:90-1, commenting on Trubetzkoy 1975:162 f.) to account for what he called the 'intrinsic content' of the terms of phonological oppositions. In his original terminology, Trubetzkoy used the Russian word *priznak* and then German *Merkmal* (cf. French *marque*) to designate a phonological 'mark' of 'any entity opposed to its absence' (Jakobson 1974:37). He distinguished this concept from that rendered by

Russian *različitel'noe svojstvo* and German *distinktive* [Schall] *Eigenschaft* (loc. cit.; cf. Jakobson 1971:386), which comes out as English *distinctive feature* (cf. French *propriété distinctive,* later *trait distinctif* under the influence of English usage).

Jakobson (1974:38) explains the 'conceptual and terminological discrimination' between mark and feature via an illustration which can be repeated with profit here. The phonological opposition between long and short in vowels is implemented as a difference in relative duration, or vocalic quantity. Quantity functions, says Jakobson, as the distinctive feature of the long/short opposition: 'the mark of this feature is length opposed to shortness, viz. to the lack of prolongability' (loc. cit.). The two terms of the opposition are 'provided,' he continues, with the 'attributes' named by G *merkmalhaft* (*merkmalhaltig, merkmaltragend*) vs. *merkmallos,* R *priznakovyj* vs. *bespriznakovyj,* F *marqué* vs. *non-marqué,* and E *marked* vs. *unmarked.* 'Thus the *principium divisionis* of long and short vowels, or, in other words, the distinctive feature of the "quantitative" opposition, bifurcates into the "marked feature" of longs and the "unmarked feature" of shorts' (loc. cit.).

Trubetzkoy's 'intrinsic content,' or markedness, as applied to phonological oppositions was extended by Jakobson to grammatical and lexical categories (1932), achieving thereby the requisite unitary approach to linguistic phenomena demanded by the evidence of systematic structure in language, and of the isomorphism between its various levels. What had been one of the cardinal assumptions of structuralism thus became a demonstrable principle of the organization of language. This first explicit application of the notion of isomorphism to language structure was followed by the first recognition (Hjelmslev 1938) of the pervasiveness and perfectness of the analogy between the structure of the expression plane and that of the content plane (Andersen MS:14).

Although it was Saussure who first among modern linguists qualified language as a system of signs, his *sémiologie* stressed the dyadic nature of the linguistic sign; and it is clear that Saussure remained ignorant of Peirce's semeiotic, with its crucial emphasis on the interpretant and the latter's paramount role in the sign's triadic structure. Trubetzkoy and Jakobson, apparently without realizing it, were taking linguistic theory in the direction of a triadic understanding of the sign with their notion of markedness, but they too (like the rest of linguistic scholarship) remained unaware of Peirce and could not profit by his fundamental insights.

As will become manifest from the discussion in this chapter, markedness and interpretant are synonymous where the structure of the linguistic sign is concerned. More precisely, the former is a species of the latter, a kind of logical interpretant, subject to division and related to its dynamic instances in the ways outlined in chapter 1.

In understanding markedness as a species of interpretant (cf. Shapiro 1981) it is important to bear in mind the differences inherent in the kinds of examples of linguistic data to which the terms have been applied. As is evident from several illustrative examples adduced in the preceding chapter, students of semeiotic often recur to lexical items in discussing interpretants. Thus E *man* is said to be an interpretant of F *homme* and vice versa. By extension, intra-linguistic synonymy would also qualify as mutually interpretative, so that, for example, *bachelor* and *unmarried man* could be seen as interpretants of one another.

Besides the looseness evident, however, in the application of interpretant to such examples, it is clear that language has levels other than the purely lexical, and interpretants are part of every linguistic sign, not just lexical signs. The isomorphism of the content and expression systems of natural languages, to the extent that it embraces the grammatical fabric of language, must make reference to a conception of interpretant which is ramified enough to serve the ends of the totality of the system of signs. In this more comprehensive role, markedness as a particular kind of interpretant is both the appropriate term and the explanatory universal affecting the structure of all of human semeiotic systems, not just language (cf. Jakobson & Waugh, 92; Andersen 1972:45, n. 23).

1. The Two Basic Subsystems of Language

Language is made up of two fundamental types of signs, on the basis of which it is subdivided into two systems, the expression system (sounds) and the content system (meanings). The expression system encompasses all of the phonological signs, phonic elements and their combinations, which serve as vehicles for the physical (sensible, perceptible) manifestation of human speech. The content system, a structure constituted by the semantic categories, encompasses all of the grammatical and lexical signs. These content signs enter into oppositions constituted by semantic features, their signata. This 'twofold articulation' of language has become a commonplace of structural linguistics, but the precise semeiotic relation between the two planes needs to be emphasized (following Jakobson 1939/1962 and Andersen 1979) in any theory of grammar that aspires to the explanatory understanding of linguistic phenomena. It will in fact be seen that the structure of the expression system 'presents a clear mirror image of the content system of language' (Andersen 1979:377).

The expression system—the phonology—is unique among all human semeiotic systems: the signs of this system are identified solely on the basis of their signantia, owing to the fact that their signata are strictly synonymous (Jakobson 1939/1962). All phonological signs that are purely diacritic, i.e., that serve the strictly linguistic ends of a phonology and are differentiated from physiognomic and pragmatic signs (Andersen 1979: 377; more about these below), have the same signatum—'otherness' or 'alterity' (Jakobson 1939/1962). These diacritic signs making up the core of any phonology have the function of differentiating the signantia of the content system. The central place of this function of diacritic signs transpires from the fact that content signs have, for the most part, no signantia of their own apart from those of the diacritic system. With the exception of such cases of direct expression of grammatical meaning as the opposition between declarative and interrogative sentences expressed by a simple difference in intonation contours (rising vs. falling, respectively, in English and many other languages) or the rendering of the opposition exact vs. approximate in Russian by word order (e.g. *pjat'čelovek* 'five people' vs. *čelovek pjat'* 'ca. five people'), meanings can be expressed in language only by recourse to units of sound which have no positive meaning of their own. Each signatum of a phonological signans is definable only as 'otherness,' which is to say that its meaning is equal to its diacritic function. There is thus a fundamental asymmetry between content signs and diacritic signs. The former typically have no signantia of their own and must resort to those of the expression system; the latter all have no individual, positively definable signatum and are, therefore, strictly synonymous via their shared signatum of otherness. Content signs form oppositions, which make up the system of meanings in language, strictly on the basis of their signata; diacritic signs, on the other hand, form oppositions, which make up the system of sounds in language, strictly on the basis of their signantia (cf. Andersen MS:20).

2. The System of Phonological Signs

As was mentioned above, the phonology of a natural language contains phonic signs other than the diacritic signs of the expression system proper whose function is the differentiation of the signantia of the signs comprising the content system. Those elements which convey information about a speaker's age, sex, or specific identity—called physiognomic signs by Bühler (1934:286)—are indexes because they are 'established by an existential relation between a *signans* token and the speaker, and not by conventional rules' (Andersen 1979:377). They are not part of language sensu stricto, being particularized byproducts of the physical realization of speech, or phonetic sinsigns with a purely indexical function and an object (signatum) that are aspects of the utterer of the sign himself.

Besides physiognomic signs, there is a class of phonic elements that, while still not part of the class of diacritic signs, do belong to the expression system of language. These are what have been called pragmatic signs

(Andersen 1979:377), although Peirce's own usage would be better served by the related term practical sign (see chapter 1), i.e., the sort of sign whose interpretant is a Second considered in itself. Such signs are indexical symbols interpretable by reference to aspects of the total communicative system (Andersen 1974:18-9; 54, fn. 1). This system (as delineated in Jakobson 1960:352f., cf. 1980:81-92) comprises the several constituents of the total communicative context in which speech is situated, and the parallel functions defined by these constituents: the (a) emotive, (b) conative, (c) referential, (d) poetic, (e) phatic, and (f) metalingual functions. The phonological signs signal, correspondingly, (a) the speaker's attitude toward or personal involvement in the speech event, or (b) his attitude towards the addressee and evaluation of the latter's involvement, or (c) his evaluation of the content of his message; or these signs serve to (d) (re)present the message as an aesthetic object, or (e) establish or maintain communicative contact, or (f) disambiguate or gloss the structure of the code in which the message is communicated (cf. Andersen 1979:377, minus the metalingual function).

The signantia of the diacritic signs that form one part of the bipartite core of the phonological expression system are the familiar (Jakobsonian) distinctive feature terms, such as +nasal, —nasal, +voiced, —voiced, etc. These terms are each signs and as such enter into oppositions—i.e., binary paradigms—and a system of oppositions defined exclusively by their signantia, their sign vehicles. The signantia are realized phonetically as differences between sounds, and the paradigms to which they belong are defined by a coordinated set of audio-perceptual parameters (Andersen 1979:378). The diacritic signs themselves have no positive phonetic values. Owing to the relative and negative character of distinctive feature oppositions, these signs 'can be realized with appreciably different concrete manifestations in different contexts and by different speakers' (loc. cit.). The phonetic parameters associated systematically with the diacritic signs that constitute the ultimate units of phonology organize themselves into diacritic categories (Andersen 1978:11, fn. 4), so that, for example, the diacritic signs +voice or —voice are associated with the diacritic category voicing.

Saying that diacritic signs—specifically, each phonological term and its opposite—form binary paradigms means that the relation between them is one of mutual exclusivity: one term is in praesentia while the other is in absentia, and vice versa. This relation is what keeps the two signs distinct from each other. The definition of phonological paradigms via the signantia of diacritic signs is expressed in terms of the latter's audio-perceptual parameters, and it is this distinctness that is presupposed in qualifying the signatum of all diacritic signs as 'phonemic otherness.'

The semeiotic relevance of distinctness-within-opposition in phonological paradigms is that the relation between the opposed signs is one of asymmetry. Whether or not the phonetic realization of the two signs of a diacritic paradigm is strictly dichotomous (privative) or is graded, the relation between them is not one of equipollence but of polarity. The signantia of diacritic signs are expressed as polar specifications of the diacritic categories in question, as plus or minus the given opposition. This asymmetry is the primary semeiotic relation holding between the signs; secondarily, and owing to the binariness of the paradigm, there is also a relation of symmetry between them (cf. Andersen 1974:892). Each of the two relations has its consequences for the sound pattern of any language.

Paradigmatic asymmetry is another, more general characterization of the strictly relational content of diacritic signs. One of the two signs in a paradigm is more narrowly defined than the other. The first is the marked, the second the unmarked member of the paradigm. 'More narrowly defined' means *of greater conceptual complexity,* so that the marked sign is conceptually more complex than its unmarked counterpart. In Trubetzkoy's original formulation, markedness was associated with aspects of phonetic substance such as the presence of a specific articulatory effort connected with the production of the marked term of a phonological opposition. Understood in a semeiotic light as the interpretant of the diacritic sign, markedness can now be properly seen as belonging to linguistic form rather than to substance, of which it is largely independent while being systematically interrelated with it (Andersen 1974:893).

That the two interpretants of the signs of the minimal paradigm differ in value, one having the opposite value from the other, transpires from the ontological status of opposition in general. Whereas in mathematics and logic opposition may not entail differences in value of the opposed terms, in human semeiosis it does so without fail: perhaps in consonance with biological and neurophysiological factors (such as brain lateralization), it appears that human beings are unable to integrate signs into paradigms (and syntagms, as will be clear below) except by grading and ranking them (cf. Andersen 1974b:44). All conceptualization necessarily involves evaluation.

It is the evaluative focus of markedness that confirms its independence of substance and its primarily conceptual (formal) focus. The paradigmatic asymmetry of oppositions in the content system, and the syntagmatic asymmetry evident in both the expression and the content systems, are all of a piece; they could not be compared and integrated with phonological markedness were it not for the uniformity inherent in all manifestations of markedness (cf. Greenberg 1966:56f., Andersen 1979:379).

Whereas in grammar and in lexis there can be either asynthetic or synthetic signata—that is to say, a grammatical or lexical morpheme may have one signatum or more than one, respectively—diacritic signs not only have only one signatum (are exclusively asynthetic) but, conversely, can only appear as one of a set of signantia (cf. Andersen 1973:769). That is what is meant by the statement that 'terms of phonological oppositions do not occur in isolation, but are obligatorily combined into syntagms of various extents' (Andersen 1974a:892). No signans of a diacritic sign can occur singly; each such sign requires a synthetic domain in which it is joined by other, co-occurrent signantia. These simultaneous syntagms, the smallest simultaneous sign complexes realizable in language, are what is known under the conventional name phoneme.

Contrary to their long-standing (mis)characterization as mere 'bundles of distinctive features' (as in Jakobson & Waugh, 25, only the latest in a long series going back to Bloomfield 1933:79), phonemes are organized into hierarchical structures; their immediate constituents—the diacritic signs—enter into relations of subordination (rank order). In this respect phonemes are in full conformity with the chief principles of organization of their isomorphous counterparts in grammar and lexis. However, unlike the latter signs, in whose structure hypotaxis (subordination) and parataxis (coordination) may coexist as possibilities, the constituents of diacritic syntagms may only occur as hypotactic structures in which rank order is determinative in assigning relative importance to any pair or set of signs (Andersen 1979:379).

Phonemes are hierarchical structures, and this means that the entire inventory of phonemes is itself an overarching hierarchic structure. The ranking of diacritic signs in the simultaneous syntagm is the syntagmatic counterpart—the asymmetry—of markedness, since markedness is the asymmetry (as we saw) of paradigmatic relations. Although markedness relations and ranking relations are both universally constitutive principles of organization of all languages, it appears that 'ranking to a much larger extent than markedness is a purely conceptual operation, independent of linguistic substance, and hence rank relations are determined on a language particular basis' (Andersen 1979:379; cf. 1973, 1974, 1975, 1978).

The relations which characterize the hierarchy of diacritic signs in phonology—the phonological interpretants—are immanent in the sound system and must be realized in speech in order to attain the level of actual palpability. The set of regulative modes of their systematic realization in speech chains can be expressed in the form of illative transformations, conventionally known as rules. These rules are tantamount to principles of structural organization, a definition of their function which extends beyond the bounds of phonology to embrace all of language. The interpretative nature of such rules or principles transpires from the fact that, as interpretants do generally, they assign a means of representation to an object of representation (cf. Andersen MS: 5, 8 et passim). In this respect such rules conform perfectly to the illative or inferential form of explanatory hypotheses, of the sort characteristically present in scientific theories and all generalizations typically involved in learning-about-the-world. Moreover, they replicate the illative relation holding between the signatum and the signans of a sign. In exactly the same way that signification results from the patterned conjunction of signata and signantia via the mediation of the all-important Third, the interpretant, so all of linguistic content is rendered manifest in the structure of language by series of interpretants that have the form 'If content A, then expression B.'

The realization of diacritic signantia in speech is the function of an interpretant or 'realization' system, which

> serves to transform a phonemic representation, couched in the oppositive, negative, and relative terms of diacritic signs into a phonetic representation with sufficiently specific phonetic detail to be realized—though still couched in relative terms. The output of the realization system is merged with (superimposed on or modified by) the expression elements of the content system and of the pragmatic phonic signs. (Andersen 1979:380)

It would be wrong to take this characterization in a way which would have rules 'apply' to 'outputs' in the mechanistic sense which has permeated contemporary linguistic methodology. In the hermeneutic theory of grammar being set forth here, rules are signs of mediation which relate the 'underlying' structure to that of actual speech. No mutational force should be attached to rules of this kind, and the word 'transform' must be understood in a strictly relational sense, as a handy synonym for the Peircean 'translate'—as in his definition of meaning: 'the translation of a sign into another system of signs' (4.127).

There are several aspects to the translation of diacritic signs into the directly observable phonetic data of speech. If we adhere to the common usage of linguists and continue to call such translations rules, the primary function of the rules is the translation or transformation of the system of diacritic signs, 'representations couched in purely oppositive terms' (Andersen 1979:378), into phonetic representations realized as differences in sound. Implementation rules (as they have been called; see Andersen 1979) of this type fulfill, therefore, a phonetic function: the assignment of phonetic properties to diacritic signs. The ensemble of such properties constitutes many of the physical details of the pronunciation of a given language or dialect, which are recognizable as differences contributing to the differentiation of varieties of speech. These include the so-called 'low-level' features (also termed allophonic or 'redundant') which despite their lesser significance vis-à-vis the diacritic system have important functions in communication. Among the latter is what Trubetzkoy called the 'sociative function' (1958: 46 f., cit. Andersen MS:27), by which allophonic features serve as indexes of immediately contiguous diacritic signs in the speech chain.

Secondarily, there exist two kinds of implementation rules which discharge functions other than the purely phonetic, and these have been called neutralization and variation rules (Andersen 1973:785). Neutralization rules suspend oppositions. They are reductive of communicative information in the sense that they remove the possibility that one member of an opposition of diacritic signs will appear in a particular context. In Russian, for instance, in position before pause and before sonorants or voiceless obstruents (true consonants), the signs +*voiced* and —*voiced* which otherwise differentiate, say, *rod* 'clan, gender' from *rot* 'mouth,' cease to be opposed: the two words are realized identically with the final voiceless obstruent *t*. The suspension of an opposition—a relation on the paradigmatic level—effected by a neutralization is mirrored on the syntagmatic level by the removal of the possibility of contrast between two forms differing only in their manifestation of the two terms of a phonological opposition; this mirroring relationship between opposition and contrast exemplifies the polarity principles of linguistic structure (Jakobson & Halle 1971:15). Neutralization in grammar as a whole (not just phonology) is an important semeiotic process, about which more will be said below. At this point, note should be taken of the fact that it deals exclusively with diacritic signs, i.e., with those signs that have the capability of distinguishing the signantia of content signs.

Variation rules, on the other hand, 'assign allophonic features in complementary distribution' (Andersen MS:28); they flesh out, as it were, the simultaneous syntagm that constitutes the phoneme with non-phonemic signs, so that 'different values for a given phonetic parameter occur in complementary distribution' (Andersen 1979:380). For example, vowels in Russian are specified as (occur with the relative phonetic value of) [+ front] before palatalized consonants, but as [— front] before unpalatalized consonants and before pause; hence the characteristic and completely predictable (non-diacritic) fronting of /e/ in words like *šest'* 'six' as opposed to *šest* 'stake.' This species of complementation is an important heuristic clue in linguistics—not to speak of the process of language acquisition—since it allows the linguist (and learner) to discover which features are diacritic (phonemic) and which are not. In the Russian example, the complementary distribution of relatively more and less fronted vowels shows that fronting is not phonemic in this language.

The semeiotic nature of the relation between the system of diacritic signs and their manifestation in speech via rules/interpretants was first discovered by Andersen (1966) and is summarized succinctly in the following statement (1979:380):

As they apply to diacritic signs implementation rules do not assign positive phonetic values to individual diacritic signs, but rather render paradigmatic oppositions as relative phonetic differences, which remain constant despite contextual variation. Since these rules transform one kind of relation (phonemic oppositions in the diacritic system) into another kind of relation (phonetic differences in realization), they establish diagrammatic signs.

In terms of the kinds of function that rules may fulfill, and remembering that, in Peirce's semeiotic scheme, diagram is a species of icon, implementation rules which do more than simply specify or constate allophonic particulars can be said to have an *iconic function* (Andersen 1966). Of course, the phonetic function of such rules is no less iconic or semeiotic than that of neutralization and variation rules. For if we understand the relation between interpretative rule and diacritic sign to be essentially one of form to substance, then its diagrammatic nature is presupposed in the very notions of these terms: 'the relation between a form and the stuff formed by it is of necessity diagrammatic' (Andersen MS:28). When fulfilling no more than a phonetic function, implementation rules are still instruments of mediation or representation between relations of one kind and relations of another, since even in this role they translate phonemic oppositions into phonetic differences. That is to say, rules of this sort still deal with relative terms rather than with phonetic absolutes.

Given Peirce's tripartition of the relation between a Sign and its Object into Icon, Index, and Symbol, it becomes apparent that the several types of phonological rules discussed so far conform to one or another of these three species of sign. The implementation rules are (as we saw) diagrams, a kind of icon. Rules which deal with signs that make reference to immediately contiguous diacritic signs (Trubetzkoy's 'sociative' function) are themselves indexes. And the 'pragmatic' signs discussed earlier—that is to say, the phonic signs which refer to one or another aspect of the total speech situation (speaker, addressee, referential context, message, communicative contact, and code)—are (indexical) symbols (cf. Andersen 1979:377).

The role of symbolic semeiosis in phonology is not limited, however, to pragmatic signs.

> Besides implementation rules, a realization system comprises a set of *adaptive* rules, whose function is to adjust the speaker's pronunciation to the norm of his speech community in accordance with his status and roles. Unlike implementation rules, which diagram relations in the diacritic system, adaptive rules produce phonic signs which symbolize the speaker's relation to his speech community. (Andersen 1979:381; cf. 1973:773, 781 f.)

Because all interpretants represent the relation of Sign and Object, giving significance to signification, it is not surprising that implementation rules are diagrammatic. Indeed, were this not so, no learner of a language would have access to the relations defining the diacritic system, and the language would be neither learnable nor perpetuable. With respect to linguistic change, the implementation rules are teleologically consistent with the defining relations of the system, which is to say that changes affecting these rules can be counted as genuinely evolutive whereas adaptive changes reflected by adaptive rules can do no more than symbolize the speaker's relation to his speech community (Andersen 1973a:785-6). Being coordinate with evolutive change, implementation rules are at the center of the phonological system whereas adaptive rules, lacking the intrinsic structural motivation of implementation rules, are at its periphery and consequently subject to gradual elimination over time. In this respect, adaptive rules are like morphophonemic rules (see chapter 4), that is to say they are relatively unproductive (cf. Andersen 1973a:782). Adaptive rules may differ from morphophonemic ones, however, in representing 'simultaneous and sequential phonetic feature values which are not provided for in the phonological structure' (loc. cit.). Their essentially ad hoc nature almost inevitably portends their elimination from the language.

There is a more specific semeiotic conditioning involved in what has been characterized as the iconic function or diagrammatic character of implementation rules, which makes the systematic purport of the interpretant system more palpable (to both linguist and learner alike). Variation rules (as was said) translate the relations of the diacritic system into phonetic differences in their realization, in accordance with the principle of complementation. But the 'relations' between diacritic signs, and the particularity (cf. Andersen 1973:769, fn. 5) within individual signs between signantia and signata (despite the latter's synonymousness), are more than the abstraction associated with this word: they are markedness relations. Hence the diagram produced by phonological interpretants at the syntagmatic level are in fact supplemented by a further diagram, in which equivalence in markedness (the paradigmatic level) is reflected as 'relations of contiguity in phonetic realizations' (Andersen 1979:381). Complementary phonetic entities are thus correlated with specific contexts.

Perhaps the most fruitful and important discovery in recent phonological research has been that phenomena of the kind subsumed by variation rules conform to a universally valid semeiotic principle, which has been called markedness assimilation (Andersen 1968:175, 1972:44-5). According to this principle (which, as a matter of fact, extends beyond phonology to embrace all human semeiosis; see below), the normally unmarked value for a given feature occurs in an unmarked (simultaneous or sequential) context, and the normally marked value in the marked context.

In conventional phonological terms, the discovery of markedness assimilation has a direct effect on the understanding of what assimilation means. Since markedness is a formal semeiotic universal, explanations couched in its terms make reference to conceptual entities, rather than to physical (phonetic) factors. Assimilation is thereby 1) taken out of the oftentimes capricious realm of articulatory 'accomodations' and the putative propensities of speech organs (à la Martinet 1955); and 2) aligned with completely parallel processes in grammar and lexis, where a physical basis is excluded by the very nature of the matter.

The first examples of markedness assimilation (offered in Andersen 1968) were limited to the distribution of allophonic features in complementary simultaneous contexts. For instance, the Japanese rule (cf. Andersen 1972:44) which assigns a [+ strident] realization (the normally marked value for that feature in abrupt obstruents) to dental stops before [+ diffuse] vowels (i.e., the normally marked value for that feature in vowels) is recognized as a markedness assimilation rule: [č] and [c] are marked for stridency, as are [i] and [u] for diffuseness. The [— strident], i.e. [U strident], realizations occur—complementarily—before vowels which are [— diffuse], i.e., [U diffuse].

The common parlance of linguistics makes it easy to fall into the habit of speaking of such relations between sounds and contexts as mutational, as if there were a 'change' in the synchronic grammar of Japanese (restating what was obviously true of historical Japanese) whereby dental stops were permuted to strident affricates before diffuse (high) vowels. But the theory of grammar being sketched here ought to prevent the analyst from falling into such a methodological trap: what is central in the Japanese case is the *alternation* of the sounds in certain contexts. It is true that one particular alternant may be less narrowly defined, hence basic and unmarked. But the point is that the structural coherence of the phonological system at any stage of its development is reflected precisely in the patterned cooccurrence of units and contexts, in the relational correspondences of interpretants. The distribution of strident affricates before diffuse vowels and dental stops before nondiffuse vowels represents, in a Peircean diagram, the *semeiotic equivalence* of phonetically disparate units, on the one hand, and their respective coherence with the marked/unmarked semeiotic values of the context, on the other.

Since its promulgation more than a decade ago, it has become clear that markedness assimilation is far from being limited to the status of 'the effect of a universal constraint on the combination and concatenation of phonetic features' (Andersen 1972:44). Markedness assimilation is the principle of structure governing a whole spectrum of phenomena in language. In phonology, it extends to diacritic (phonemic) signs as well as to non-diacritic. Thus, in positions of neutralization the realization of a neutralized opposition is determined by the sequential context. Trubetzkoy (1936) had thought that it was normal for the unmarked member of an opposition to appear in positions of neutralization, and he was at a loss to explain the exceptional cases of the appearance of the marked member. For example, in Russian, obstruents are realized as [+ voiced] (the marked value) before voiced obstruents, but as [— voiced] in other positions of neutralization—before voiceless obstruents, and before word boundaries followed by segments unmarked for voicing (vowels, sonorants, and voiceless obstruents) or by pause. In cases of neutralization where the marked value appeared—voiced obstruent before voiced—Trubetzkoy did not perceive the essential parallelism between this apparently aberrant result and what he considered normal because he made a basic distinction between 'externally' and 'internally' conditioned neutralization, i.e., between assimilation explicable by the sequential context and neutralization (as before pause in the Russian case) not so explicable. The absence of sound associated with pause is, of course, only a special variety of context, and as a 'zero sign' is conventionally identified with the unmarked value (Jakobson 1939; but cf. Shapiro 1972:357).

What is important semeiotically about neutralization is the relation between the representative sound (or form) manifested in positions of neutralization and the system of units to which markedness as an interpretant makes reference. Specifically, while a rule of the Russian type which eliminates the possibility of contrast between voiced and voiceless obstruents before pause 'does not have any positive output' (Andersen 1979:381), the very fact that a particular diacritic paradigm is neutralized 'may diagram its rank in the hierarchy of diacritic signs' (loc. cit.). An example of this is the phenomenon of vowel harmony, of which different types may be said to reflect differences in rank between the diacritic categories involved in vowel systems (Jakobson 1971:108-9).

Positions of neutralization are also linked with variation in the sense that 'neutralization rules provide contexts in which variation rules may assign diagrammatic representations of the markedness values of diacritic paradigms' (Andersen 1979:381). More concretely, a variation rule seen against the background of markedness assimilation may tell both the learner and the analyst which category is diacritic or distinctive in a language, which non-diacritic or redundant. A good illustration of this role of markedness assimilation is furnished by the relation between syllable peaks and contiguous obstruents in English, as it bears on the problems of quantity in vowels and the phonological status of tenuis and media consonants, respectively (cf. Andersen 1979: 380-1). In English, syllable peaks are [— long] before tense obstruents but are [+ long] before lax obstruents, before sonorants, and in final position: hence *beet* is [bit], but *bead, bean,* and *bee* are [bi:d bi:n bi:]. The complementary distribution of the short and long vowel realizations is a sign (as was mentioned earlier) of the non-diacritic status of quantity in English. Beyond that, however, the assumption that the relevant tenues and mediae are distinguished by tenseness and not by voicing enables the variation rule *to make sense* as a case of markedness assimilation, since tense obstruents are marked relative to the unmarked lax obstruents. The shorter realization of /i/ in *beet* [bit] understood as an abridgement of syllable peaks before the [M tense] obstruent /t/ makes the variation coherent: the narrowly defined (marked) context of a contiguous tense obstruent is congruent with the marked (shorter) syllable peak. If voicing had been assumed to be the diacritic category involved, no markedness assimilation could be appealed to, since voiceless obstruents are [U voice] relative to the [M voice] status of voiced obstruents. An additional piece of evidence in support of this interpretation is the asymmetry of the contexts (Andersen 1979:381): since abridged vowels occur only in one context (that of tense obstruents), whereas unabridged vowels occur in all other contexts (before lax obstruents, before sonorants, and finally), the first context is itself the more narrowly defined of the two, and the coherence of markedness values is complete. Parenthetically, Trubetzkoy's claim (1969:147) that 'it is impossible to say whether in English a correlation of tension or a correlation of voice is present' thus turns out to be groundless. Naturally, the resolution of what he perceived to be irresolvable hinges on the admission of circularity into the coherence of structure and the concomitant methodological devaluation of 'independent motivation.' The mutual dependency of the elements of the solution—the shorter realizations of the syllable peaks seen as abridgements rather than the longer ones as prolongations, the role of markedness assimilation, and the status of protensity as the relevant diacritic category—all cohere *as an ensemble* of conditions informing the phenomena in question. This sort of coherence, where units and contexts are evaluated in tandem, in a mutually dependent manner, *is of the essence of linguistic structure,* and will be recognized as such time and time again in this book (see especially chapter 3).

Implementation rules are diagrammatic: they make manifest in speech the relations that characterize the phonological structure of a language. But it is obvious that there are also pronunciations which reflect rules lacking the intrinsic, structural motivation of implementation rules. Thus, for example, New Yorkers, for whom *beard, bared,* and *bad* are strictly homonymous in spontaneous speech, are nevertheless able (albeit not consistently) to differentiate these lexemes when adherence to traditional norms is demanded (Weinreich, Labov & Herzog 1968:134-5, cit. Andersen 1973:782). Whenever an adaptation of this kind takes place, it is possible to speak of *adaptive rules,* by which speakers adjust their speech to conform to community norms in accordance with their status and roles. The synchronic goal of such rules appears to be that of 'ensuring relative uniformity of usage, regardless of differences in phonological structure among the grammars of the speakers' (Andersen, loc. cit.). In the long run such rules tend to be curtailed and eliminated, but at any given point in the history of a language, every phonology has a number of adaptive rules.

Adaptive rules produce conventional signs: they refer to the extra-linguistic reality of social norms broadly conceived (including style), and are therefore symbols rather than diagrams. Implementation rules differ from adaptive rules, therefore, in semeiotic function. Although adaptive rules are formulated in terms of the phonological structure *sensu stricto* and are subordinate to the latter, they form an additive system which is subject to elaboration and revision throughout speakers' lives (Andersen 1973:781).

To recapitulate, the expression system of language consists of two basic subdivisions, the structured core and the adstructure. The latter has just been described. The former is comprised of a set of diacritic signs which form binary paradigms and a set of interpretants (rules) by which the signs are combined into hypotactic syntagms, on the one hand, and are manifested linearly in speech, on the other. In simultaneous combination, markedness values—the interpretants of phonological signs—partly deter-mine the extent of syntagms and are themselves partly determined by general principles of organization. In sequential combination, markedness determines both the distributional particularities of (the variants of) diacritic signs and their coherence with the contexts in which they occur.

3. The System of Content Signs

The other basic subsystem of language structure is the content signs. These are signs whose signata consist of single content elements (semantic features) or of syntagms of content elements. Depending on whether content signs have simple or complex signata (i.e., one or more content elements), they can be divided into asynthetic and synthetic signs, respectively (cf. Andersen MS:19). The typical content sign has no signans of its own: it relies instead on the signantia of the diacritic (expression) system. Its signata utilize (apart from cases already mentioned above) the signantia of the expression system, and it is the resultant inherent disjunction between content and expression that is overcome in language structure by the presence of an overarching interpretant system—i.e., by the rules that relate content to expression.

At the heart of the content system is the content sign, or morpheme, as it is traditionally called. Like all signs in language, morphemes consist of a signans, a signatum, and an interpretant. The interpretant, here as elsewhere, is the semeiotic relation between signans and signatum, which can be said to be established by a rule of the sort discussed earlier. The great variation observed in morphological systems is due to the manifold ways in which morphemes can differ—'according to the kinds of signantia, the kinds of signata, and the kinds of signatum-signans relations they comprise' (Andersen 1980:3).

Essential to any understanding of the systematic character of content signs is the notion of hierarchy, by which basic linguistic signs (whether the focus is on signata or signantia) are distinguished from sign variants (of signantia). The latter, traditionally called allomorphs, make up what is subsumed under morphophonemics. Morpheme alternants, when they are co-variants of absolute (basic) signantia, are semeiotically subordinate to these latter signs, to which they stand in the relation of 'derived' or secondary entities. Thus, in the typical Indo-European inflectional paradigm, the hierarchy of its constituents accords pride of place to the form of the stem in the maximally unmarked category, e.g. the nominative singular masculine in substantives and the infinitive in verbs (both of which not unexpectedly function as citation forms in dictionaries). In typical examples of morphophonemic alternation (Andersen 1980:4) which produce patterns of relative signantia, consisting in the modification of a real (non-zero) signans—consonant gradation, apophony, accentual alternations, reduplication, and element inversion—there is always a hierarchy among the alternants reflecting the hierarchy of signata of which these co-variants are the means of expression. In some cases, it is not clear (to the learners of a language, no less than to its analysts) whether an alternation is properly morphophonemic or morphological, whether the modification of the sign vehicle is not itself a signans rather than a co-variant of one.

What is important for the theory of grammar generally, and the content system particularly, is the fact that relations between (sets of) signata and signantia that constitute morphological and morphophonemic patterns have a raison d'être that goes beyond mere regularity of cooccurrence. While it is true that all linguistic signs are fundamentally symbolic legisigns, the conventional aspect (their symbolicity) may be modified in the direction of iconicity and indexicality. The indexical nature of the so-called shifters (categories of deixis in one form or another) is one example of the attentuation of the arbitrariness of the linguistic sign (cf. Jakobson 1971:130-47). A much more significant matter is iconicity, embodied in the 'extensive patterns of similarity and difference among the shapes of grammatical morphemes which correspond to the relations of similarity and difference among their meanings' (Andersen MS:21). A typical example (cf. Jakobson 1971: 167 f.) is the correspondence between the opposition plural vs. singular and the relative number of segments in the case desinences of these two numbers in many Russian substantives: regardless of the specific shape of the desinences, each plural desinence is longer by one segment than the corresponding singular desinence. This distribution is of a piece with the most common of such patterns, the specialization of consonants (the larger phoneme class) as expressions of lexical meaning and vowels (the smaller phoneme class) as expressions of grammatical meaning, in such languages as the Semitic group (Trubetzkoy 1958:270, cit. Andersen MS:23). Correspondences like these between content and expression can be understood as diagrams (relations reflected by relations). *The fact that signantia may diagram signata is tantamount to the principle by which a system of content signs is established as a structure.* If not for these pervasive mapping relations between signata and signantia, the content system would amount to no more than an inventory of arbitrary signs, a purely additive system (like the alphabet or the Morse code).

The particular example of the longer desinences (case by case) of the Russian singular vis-à-vis the plural is, however, simultaneously character-istic of linguistic iconicity and somewhat misleading as to its true nature. In this easily generalized example the conceptual correspondence is between extent and number: the grammatical category of plurality is understood to be an iconic analogue of the (greater) length of the case desinence, a relation of quantity. This analogy is in alignment with such phenomena as the so-called 'small vs. large symbolism' (Jakobson 1971:199) imputed to certain phonological relations (cf. Jakobson & Waugh 1979:177 f.).

There is an inherent difficulty, however, in the ontological validity of comparisons of this kind. Given the asymmetry of the content and expression system (discussed in detail earlier in this chapter), there is no direct way of comparing form and meaning in language, and the only access to their congruence is via the interpretants—the units of mediation relating signantia and signata. There may be a kind of naive or intuitive truth to the notion that greater extent naturally reflects greater number, but the existence of counterexamples tends to undermine its validity. For instance, in Russian (to make the comparison homogeneous) the opposi-tion within verbs of determinate vs. nondeterminate subaspect (in the small class of so-called verbs of motion) is expressed inter alia by shorter vs. longer stems. Now, the determinate is the marked member of this opposition, and the nondeterminate is correspondingly unmarked. The longer stem, therefore, appears consistently as the expression of the unmarked form, the corresponding marked form being expressed by the shorter verb stem. This relation between stem length and grammatical meaning is, however, directly counter to that of desinence length and plural number in the example cited earlier: the marked plural form is longer, the unmarked singular correspondingly shorter.

In the face of this discrepancy, a more scrupulous attention to the varieties of semeiosis encompassed by the class of icons becomes important. It is to be recalled that Peirce divided icons into three subspecies—images, diagrams, and metaphors. More precisely, recognizing that a pure icon can only be a possibility, with an object that is a Firstness, Peirce speaks of a sign that may be *iconic,* 'that is, may represent its object mainly by its similarity, no matter what its mode of being' (2.276). This sort of impure icon he then terms a *hypoicon.*

> Hypoicons may be roughly divided according to the mode of Firstness of which they partake. Those which partake of simple qualities, of First Firstnesses, are *images;* those which represent the relations, mainly dyadic, or so regarded, of the parts of one thing by analogous relations in their own parts, are *diagrams;* those which represent the representative character of a representamen by representing a parallelism in something else, are *metaphors.* (2.277)

What appears with greater clarity in the light of these distinctions is the status of imaginal iconic correspondences in the content system of language vis-à-vis the diagrammatic ones. Here, as everywhere in semeiosis, it is a matter of emphasis or relative prominence of one or another aspect of the sign, rather than a matter of all-or-none. Relations of quantity, such as those embodied in the correspondence between desinence length and the grammatical opposition singular vs. plural, have a pronounced imaginal quotient—amounting to the representation of 'simple qualities' and 'First Firstnesses.' The same aspect predominates in the linguistic representation of the order of events in real time: Caesar's acts as reported in the sequence *Veni, vidi, vici* is a straightforward example of the way in which 'the temporal order of speech events tends to mirror the order of narrated events in time or in rank' (Jakobson 1971:350). (This is an instance of a mirror image without the attendant reversal.)

Analogic semeiosis of the sort exemplified by linguistic diagrams proper is much less straightforward and cannot be reduced to the mere representation of simple qualities. Indeed, what appears to be typical of diagrammatization in language is a semeiotic mapping involving the *interpretants* rather than the signans-signatum relation proper. Practically, what this amounts to is the necessary involvement of markedness, of which the most important concomitant is reference to a specific context. To return to the example of the opposition of determinate and nondeterminate subaspect in Russian verbs of motion, the marked stem cooccurs with the marked category, the unmarked stem with the unmarked category. Inasmuch as the marked category is expressed by a stem which is consistently shorter than the stem of the corresponding unmarked category, the length of the stem can be understood as being abridged to mirror the definition, relative restrictedness or narrowed scope, of the marked value. This would place the relations between marked and unmarked values of the stem in perfect alignment with the earlier phonological example, in which abridged (shorter) syllable peaks in English occur before marked tenues (tense obstruents) and unabridged peaks elsewhere (before lax obstruents, before sonorants, and finally). In both examples of congruence between markedness values, units and contexts match: in the phonological case the context is comprised by yet another unit, in the morphological case the context is comprised by a grammatical category.

4. Units, Contexts, and Markedness

Although there is nothing 'compulsory' about the iconic congruence between signs and the contexts in which they occur (*pace* Jakobson 1971:357), it is nonetheless true that language frequently resorts to these patterns of diagrammatization, and the teleology of linguistic change clearly has the establishment of form/meaning diagrams as a goal.

Taking semeiotic congruence to be the raison d'être of both the synchronic status of language facts and the diachronic process characterizing them while they are in *statu nascendi*, it is necessary to detail the ways in which this congruence is achieved. The principle force of iconicity in language is channeled through markedness assimilation and (as we shall see) its corollary, markedness reversal. The cohesion between linguistic facts is rooted in the interpretant system imparting structure to expression and content signs in their cooccurrence.

While it might be misleading to say that 'markedness inheres in the relationships between signs and contexts' (Haiman 1980:529, fn. 12), it is nevertheless important to emphasize the interpretant value of context. The context-sensitive nature of markedness also implies the possible subordination of narrower to broader contexts, in a hierarchical structure. This notion would tally well with the common presupposition concerning the all-encompassing nature of part-whole relationships in language.

Markedness as a species of interpretant is subject to the same qualifications as all interpretants, and none is more pertinent to language structure than its indissoluble link with abduction. As was clear from the extended discussion of Peirce's notion of interpretant in the preceding chapter, the ramified system of Thirds that bind Sign and Object into significational complexes articulates a graded gamut involving a variety of differential factors. One of these is the degree of fixity or codedness of an interpretant vis-à-vis its antecedent sign(s). The determination of degree of codedness of the interpretant-sign-object relation is an abductive process; as such, it is fundamentally fallible (unlike deduction and induction, given the truth of the premises).

The fallibility of abduction means, as far as the theory of grammar is concerned, that there is nothing obligatory, necessary, or inevitable about the coherence of language data *in the short run*. Whereas the overarching teleological thrust of language development tends to direct the cooccurrence of linguistic phenomena into patterns which are iconic, at any given point in the history of a language the process may not yet have run its full course, thereby presenting learner and analyst alike with a mottled picture characterized by variation, discontinuities between grammars of different speakers, and numerous anomalies—in short, with the flux that language always presents side by side with what has become stabilized in it.

With respect to markedness, the non-deterministic character of coherence is nowhere more prominent than in what has been called markedness reversal or markedness dominance (Andersen 1972:45-6). This is the phenomenon whereby a marked context reverses the normal markedness values of the terms of an opposition, including reversal of the relation between the elements of a syntagm ('rank reversal,' Andersen 1972:46, fn. 23).

A straightforward example of markedness reversal in phonology is provided by the neutralization in Standard German of the protensity category in obstruents functioning as syllable codas (Andersen 1972:44-5). All obstruents in this marked function (syllable onsets being unmarked) are realized as [+ tense], the marked value. (This illustrates the potentially wide scope of markedness assimilation: here its reference goes beyond simultaneous or contiguous diacritic signs to embrace a more abstract element of the context, the position of a segment within the syllable.) Since protensity is phonemic in German (Trubetzkoy 1958:75), one would expect the unmarked term of the opposition (the lax obstruent) to appear in position of neutralization, but the dominance exercised by the marked value of the supervening context of syllable coda effects a reversal such that 'the normally unmarked value is evaluated as marked' (Andersen 1972:45). It is, parenthetically, the failure to perceive the role of the syllable as a context that accounts for the common misstatement of this pronunciation rule of German in American linguistic literature (Anderson, loc. cit., fn. 22): it is almost universally referred to as 'devoicing' (in 'word-final position') because the expectation that the unmarked member of an opposition appears in position of neutralization is fulfilled only if voicing is assumed to be phonemic, tenues in the European languages being nonphonemically voiceless (the unmarked value of the *diacritic* category of voice).

There is nothing aprioristically compulsory in this dominance of syllable coda in German, although the accomplished fact of coherence between elements and context may appear to render it so retrospectively (the usual point of view of the analyst). It is possible after all to cite a language—English—where no such neutralization rule obtains, despite the identical status of the category involved (protensity in obstruents).

The generality of the semeiotic principle, together with its optional though teleologically favored nature, can be seen in the following further examples, which affect the content system rather than the expression system. The implementation of grammatical categories is commonly determined by the presence of the marked member of an opposition defining contexts of neutralization; the normally marked member of another opposition is selected.

> In English, for instance, in sentences in a marked status, the assertive vs. non-assertive opposition (*they do know* vs. *they know*) is neutralized, and the normally marked assertive is used to the exclusion of the non-assertive (*Do they know? They do not know.*) Similarly, in the marked subjunctive mood, the past vs. present opposition (*they knew* vs. *they know*) is neutralized, and the normally marked past tense is used to the exclusion of the present (*I wish they knew*). Here, too, the number opposition (*they were* vs. *he was*) is neutralized, the normally marked number being used to the exclusion of the unmarked number (*I wish he were*). (Andersen 1972:45, fn. 23)

It is inherently not possible, despite the widespread insistence on the part of linguists that the justification for the effects contexts have on elements be 'independently motivated' (thus, for instance, in Haiman 1980:529, fn. 12), to discriminate between contexts that do and those that do not condition markedness reversal. That is to say, the determination of a particular rank order in a given hierarchy of contexts may be largely language-specific and subject *as a systematic principle of structure* to the very 'ad-hoc and circular' identifications that linguists fear as analytically illegitimate (Haiman, loc. cit.).

Regardless of the optional force in language of markedness reversal in marked contexts, it is 'an essential characteristic of all human semeiotic systems. For a simple example, consider the distinction between formal and casual dress. In the unmarked context of an everyday occasion, formal wear is marked and casual clothes unmarked; but in the marked context of a festive occasion, the markedness values of normal and casual clothes are reversed' (Andersen, loc. cit.). Furthermore, neither the sign nor the context in which it occurs need have an immutable markedness value, for it is possible that they be mutually defining, as in the example (Haiman, loc. cit.) of 'a bilingual who speaks French at home and English at the office. Marked linguistic behavior for such a person is the use of English at home or of French at the office.' Neither language is either marked or unmarked except when used in a particular social context.

5. Markedness and Derivational Relations

Differences in phonic expression which accompany discrete constituents through a derivational network or family tree are typically compared amongst themselves. Alternatively, differences in expression are juxtaposed directly to corresponding differences in content. Both gambits fail to address the real question: just *why* are certain specific expressions associated with certain specific contents?

The semeiotic values that at once inform sound and meaning are markedness values. Just as the phonological structure is determined ultimately by the markedness relations obtaining between its sets of oppositions, so grammatical and lexical categories organize themselves into a coherent system through oppositions of grammatical and lexical meaning informed by the evaluative dimension that is markedness. The apparent chasm between expression and content is thus bridged.

Taking the position that patterns of meaning are determined by semeiotic value makes it possible to meet head on the problem of the coherence of derivational relations (as, indeed, of all linguistic relations). In many languages there is a set of relationships between words that is sometimes referred to (in the typical process-oriented or mutational mode) as a 'truncation.' Elements present in what is taken to be the deriving base of a derivative are absent in the latter, and the resultant morphophonemic alternation is characterized as including the deletion of certain elements (segments, suffixes). Truncation can be seen as one of five constituents of an exhaustive typology of formal processes accompanying derivation: (1) augmentation (affixation); (2) reduction (truncation); (3) a combination of augmentation and reduction; (4) morphophonemic alternation (including prosodic features)—with or without augmentation or reduction; (5) change of form class only, i.e., without any overt morphophonemic change. Typically, a relationship such as Russian *krépkij* 'strong' // *krepít'* 'make strong' is seen (correctly) in directional (i.e., hierarchical) or (incorrectly) in mutational terms and represented as a truncation of the stem-final *k* of *krépkij* in *krepít'*. This kind of analysis centers exclusively on the morphophonemics of the relationship, utterly oblivious to the fact that there is a difference in meaning associated with the difference in form. Nor does it embrace the knowledge that the verb is factitive and transitive and thereby implements the grammatical opposition defined by the conjoined categories factitive/stative and transitive/intransitive. The consistent inclusion of the grammatical categories at stake is important generally; in this particular example all the more so, as there exists a stative form *krepčát'* 'become strong' in which the *k* of *krépkij* alternates (as regularly elsewhere) with *č*.

An analysis which aspires to explanatory status must come to grips with the formal alternation in the triplet *krépkij* // *krepít'* // *krepčát'* associated with the different categories that implement it. This translates into the demand that the earlier question be reiterated here: why a particular expression for a particular content? Historical exegesis alone, while not wholly irrelevant, will not suffice, since what we need to uncover is the precise semeiotic motivation which permits the forms to subsist synchronically as differentiated expressions of coordinated contents. It is just at this point that we have recourse to markedness and its semeiotic implications.

Truncation, understood as shorthand for the relation between forms which differ in part by the presence vs. absence of a given element of expression, involves an unmarking. A term of a derivational correlation which is taken to be primary (the so-called deriving base) vis-à-vis a specific secondary counterpart (its derivative) is marked, and the latter is unmarked. This assignment of markedness values accords well with the notion that the absence of something (*signe zéro*) is normally unmarked, whereas the presence of that same something is normally marked.

In our example, however, truncation only occurs in the factitive/transitive form, so we must ask: why there and not in the stative? The answer resides in the markedness values of the opposed categories. Since factitive is unmarked, the presence of a truncated form is congruent semeiotically with the value of the category in which the form is implemented. Stative/intransitive is, conversely, marked; and this marked context dictates a marked means of expression—the *č* that is phonologically marked for stridency as opposed to the unmarked *k*. We have here, consequently, an instance of markedness assimilation.

Truncation (and for that matter, all reduction) is normally an unmarking, as has already been asserted. It follows, to be sure, that all augmentation is normally a marking. In an opposition dominated by a marked context, however, the reverse may obtain, in conformity with our second semeiotic universal, markedness reversal. Thus in affective formations (diminutives, hypocoristics, etc.) reduction applies with reversed sign values, so that a Russian or English diminutive like the proper name *Miša* 'Mike' is marked vis-à-vis its neutral counterpart *Mixaíl* 'Michael.' An analysis of reduction in terms of markedness not only reveals the semeiotic coherence of the derivational relations involved but also accounts for the widespread incidence of truncation as a preferred means in forming hypocoristics and diminutives. This observation is tangent with the knowledge that ellipsis, abbreviation, and univerbation are particularly favored processes in the formation of marked (i.e., non-neutral) vocabulary and the marked (social/professional) use of language.

Composition is a particularly revealing testing ground for both the overarching conception of linguistic structure being advanced here and the specific illustrative analysis, in that it subsumes both major types of derivation, lexical and syntactic (cf. chapter 3, section 1). In the face of a [+ sharp] stem-final consonant *v'* in Russian *krov'* 'blood,' it has proven troublesome to interpret the presence of its [– sharp] counterpart *v* in compounds such as *krovopodtëk* 'bruise,' *krovosmešénie* 'incest,' *krovožádnyj* 'bloodthirsty,' etc. However, given the semeiotic analysis of truncation proffered above, it is apparent that what we have here is yet again an unmarking, i.e., the substitution of an [U sharp] sign for a [M sharp] sign as part of the elaboration of a set of relationships (composition) that is structurally homologous with truncation.

The Russian data can profitably be compared to similar phenomena in Japanese. In Japanese compounding is often accompanied by the substitution of a lenis consonant for a fortis in the second constituent of a binomial, so that, for example, *fúufu* 'husband and wife' + *kenka* 'quarrel' fuses in *fuufugénka* 'family quarrel.' Again, assuming that *k* is distinctively [M tense] and *g* is [U tense], the compound shows an unmarked sign over and against the marked sign of the identical constituent when uncompounded. The concomitant alternation in the locus of high pitch is likewise in need of explanation, and the repository of explanantes is, unsurprisingly, the same. Each constituent is liable to a loss of its prosodic characteristics when compounded. Thus *fúufu,* with high pitch on the first mora of the first syllable, becomes totally low(er)-pitched, while *kenka,* with high pitch occurring on any following intraphrasal constituent, acquires high pitch on the first syllable. The prosodic features of both constituents have been superseded by the characteristic prosody of the (Sino-Japanese) compound—high pitch on the first mora of the second constituent. The loss of independent prosodic characteristics by both constituents through composition is an unmarking.

The Japanese 'retraction' of pitch in the second constituent is structurally akin to the alternation of stress position accompanying univerbation and nominalization in English. Phrases like *rènt a cár* or *lòng beách* when substantivized into *rént-a-car* and *Lóng Beach* not only display a loss of individual constituent stress but also a simultaneous retraction of primary stress from all syllables other than absolute initial onto the latter. This phenomenon is to be explained, just as retraction in verbal/nominal pairs like *permít/pérmit, frequént/fréquent, rejéct/réject, envélop/énvelope,* as a markedness assimilation. Initial stress in English is unmarked, non-initial marked. Correspondingly, the category of nominals (substantives, adjectives) is unmarked relative to verbals, which are marked (cf. Jakobson 1980:105). Note that what could be seen here as the iconicity (more precisely, diagrammaticity) of nominal stress when juxtaposed to the unmarked order (Subject Verb Object) of English sentence units is at bottom a markedness assimilation.

6. Further Exemplification and Summary

A theory of grammar informed by Peirce's semeiotic casts the notion of rule in a fundamentally different light from that of its understanding in contemporary linguistics. Specifically, besides their status as interpretants, in a semeiotic theory of grammar rules cease to be viewed as divorced from the sign relations they implement. Rules are perceived necessarily as representing the relations constituting units and contexts and their hierarchies. (We can then claim to have begun the long trek back to the sane methodological postulates of interwar European structuralism.) This view is tantamount to the establishment of a neostructuralist perspective which redefines 'rule of grammar' in a radically different manner.

From at least the time of Saussure, language has been considered akin to (if not a species of) a *game,* whence the conception of rules of grammar as identical in essence to the rules of a game (like chess). Playing a game involves performance along prescribed, standardized patterns which, in chess for example, are called moves. The rules of chess determine the repertoire of permissible moves; also, they determine the domain of correct moves, violation of which is tantamount to not playing the game. The notion of correctness implies an obligatoriness: in certain game situations a certain move is the only mandated one (cf. Wright 1963:6).

All of the conditions attending games render playing them a type of rule-governed behavior. Rules are prototypical of norms, and the jump to the conception of language as rule-governed behavior seems natural:

> The *rules of grammar* (morphology and syntax) of a natural language are another example of the same main type of norm as the rules of a game. To the moves of a game as patterns correspond the set forms of correct speech. To play or the activity of playing a game corresponds speech or the activity of speaking (and writing) a language. Of a person who does not speak according to the rules of grammar, we say either that he speaks incorrectly or that he does not speak *that language.* (Wright 1963:6)

On closer scrutiny, however, the conception of language as rule-governed does not appear as monolithic as made out to be. Linguistic rules are typically represented in the form of operations on entities, in which respect they can be termed mutational. The implicational or conditional meaning in the formula $X \rightarrow Y / \_\_\_ Z$ (read: X goes to Y in the environment Z), appropriate as a notational device for diachronic changes, is also promiscuously transposed into the study of synchrony, where its distortive impact is scarcely perceived. It is distortive primarily because language, which is a system of relations, comes to be represented instead as a system of processes.

When considering pluralization in English, to take a familiar example, a contemporary linguist (like Halle 1964) will formulate as part of his analysis a 'rule' s $\rightarrow$ iz / [+ strident] _____. This notation states that the English plural desinence *-s* assumes the shape [iz] following sub-stantival stems which end in a strident obstruent, i.e., one of the group / s z š ž č ǯ /, as in *asses, phases, ashes, garages, watches, judges,* respectively. The arrow ($\rightarrow$) belies the fact that what is really at stake is not a process but a relation between the alternations of form associated with an invariant grammatical meaning, the plural. The alternant [iz] is actually one of a set of variants which also includes [s] and [z], as in *locks, fops, chiefs, pins, whims, boys,* etc. Given the (well-nigh universal) methodology which 'sets up' basic forms such as the English plural morpheme and proceeds to 'derive' the actually occurring phonetic variants from it by the application of 'rules,' no attention is paid to the question of coherence among the data of the English plural.

Every person learning English must incorporate into his or her knowledge the forms *oxen* and *children*. These forms are purely rule-governed in that the addition of the suffix *-en* to the corresponding singular stems must be learned as a fact of pluralization unconnected with the vast bulk of English words both extant and potential. Indeed, these two exceptions to the 'rules' of English pluralization are unusual precisely because they must be learned by rote, just as many rules of behavior or of games must be learned. The functional coherence assumed to exist between the forms of the English plural and the associated grammatical meaning is, in other words, almost totally absent from the two cited exceptions.

Once this dichotomy is clearly perceived the structural core ceases to be characterized by rules in the conventional sense, since these are characteristic . . . of exceptions! This means that the structural core consists rather of linguistic data that cohere in virtue of certain principles of organization which assure the solidarity of the data.

Perhaps it can now be better understood just how crucial markedness is to an explanatory theory of the structural core of language—that part of language where data cohere—aspiring to make sense of grammar. For it is markedness alone which allows a unitary explanation of linguistic facts at all levels of structure.

English (like French and Russian) evinces a case of concomitant neutralization in its compact obstruents: strident compact obstruents are predictably [+ acute], mellow compact obstruents predictably [- acute]. This means that the markedness values for the feature [± acute] will be reversed in the compact obstruents of English, as in Russian (Shapiro 1972b:355). Hence /š ž č ǯ/ are designated [M str], whereas /k g/ are [U str]. As for /s z/, they are marked with respect to themselves; consequently, when stems ending in /s z/ precede the plural desinence which is identical in specification, the stem-final segment and desinential consonant are marked with respect to each other—which is to say that the condition of multiple markedness obtains (cf. Shapiro 1972a). This is also true, however, of /š ž č ǯ/, which are [M comp] and [M str].

The question as to which of the alternants [s], [z], or [ɨz]—or, perhaps, some other entity—is to be taken as the 'base form' of the desinence can also legitimately be asked. Before attempting an answer, one must understand that this is a question of morphology ('relations between linguistic signs') and not one of morphophonemics ('relations between the contextual variants of the same linguistic sign(s)'; cf. Andersen 1969a:807). The congruence of phonological form (segments, diacritic signs) and the grammatical meaning of plurality is a morphological one which hinges on the markedness value of the category involved. Since plural is assigned the value [M number], the basic sign (morpheme) will mirror this value by implementing the marked term(s) of a phonological distinctive feature. The relevant feature is tense/lax. Consequently, the English plural desinence, like that of the possessive, is *s* (*pace* Andersen 1980:4), /s/ being [+ tense] and thereby [M tense].

With regard to the phonetic realization of the basic plural desinence *s*, the following congruence obtains: stems terminating in lax segments cooccur with the alternant [z] (*pins, whims, bears, drives, bibs,* etc.); those terminating in tense segments cooccur with [s] (*docks, lots, pips,* etc.). Vocalic stems, however, present a problem. In word-final position stressed vowels are always diphthongal, that is to say, only underlying tense vowels, which are [U tense], are permitted. As for unstressed vowels in word-final position, there can be no contrast based solely on the protensity feature; this means that whatever the phonetic realization here, the sign value is [U tense]. It is the unmarked value of word-final vowels that explains not only the [z] of *boys, spas, Annas, bellows,* etc., but the [z] of [ɨz] as well.

The unitary nature of a linguistic theory grounded in markedness has been illustrated above largely by examples from phonology, morphophonemics, and morphology. This should not obscure the fundamental fact that the structure of syntax and lexis is also systematically informed by markedness (cf. Andersen 1972:45, 1975). All levels of linguistic structure are *isomorphous* as to the principles of their organization. A thoroughgoing semeiotic approach to language must ultimately fill in the lacunae that persist in our theoretical understanding of these principles and the different means by which they are implemented in widely divergent languages. An adequate program of theoretical inquiry into language as a system of signs, which the present chapter has sought to prefigure, must set the hermeneutic understanding of immanent structure as its primary goal.

In achieving this end, it will need to address the real problems of linguistic structure subtended by real data, and to attempt to solve them in a uniform fashion which does justice to the principles of isomorphism and iconicity underlying language as semeiotic. It is to this task that the following chapters are devoted.

PART TWO

Language as Semeiotic

III

Phonology

1. Consonantism

A. Japanese Tenues and Mediae

The terms 'tenues' and 'mediae' have traditionally been used to denote the series of obstruents associated with the letters *p, t, k, s,* etc. and *b, d, g, z,* etc., respectively. From the phonological point of view, tenues and mediae subsume two diacritic categories in terms of which they can be opposed: voiced vs. voiceless and tense vs. lax. The diacritic category voiced vs. voiceless presents, from a logical viewpoint, two *contradictory* opposites whose physical counterparts are the presence vs. absence of glottal vibrations. A distinctively voiced media is thus normally constituted by the corresponding tenuis with superimposed glottal vibrations. Since voicing and tenseness are syncategorematic features (in the sense of Shapiro 1972b:352), normally there is a complementary distribution of their physical correlates such that, in languages with distinctive voicing (like Russian), voiced obstruents are phonetically lax and voiceless ones phonetically tense. At the same time, in comparison to languages (like English) which have distinctive tenseness, languages with distinctive voicing manifest tenues which are normally relatively lax and tenuis stops which are as a rule unaspirate.

The diacritic category tense vs. lax, on the other hand, is composed of two *contrary* opposites—greater vs. lesser protensity—typically implemented as a difference between tenues and mediae in the relative duration of the release portion and the tenure portion (Jakobson 1962:550 ff., esp. 555).

With regard to the phonological analysis of contemporary standard Japanese (*hyōjungo*), to the best of my knowledge no one has discussed the tenues/mediae opposition except in terms of the diacritic category of voice. This applies equally to native phoneticians and foreign, traditionalists and generativists; cf. e.g., Jimbo 1927, Shirota 1971, Polivanov 1959, Bloch 1950, Wenck 1966, McCawley 1968. Moreover, despite the eloquent testimony afforded by the diachronic phonology and dialectology of Japanese,[1] historical treatises have likewise never veered from the position that voicing was and is distinctive. In most cases, of course, this situation is simply a reflection of the neglect of the phonological distinctions comprehended by the tenues/mediae series in the history of Japanese.

In reconsidering the problem of tenues and mediae in Japanese from a semeiotic viewpoint, we need to perceive the relevance and importance of phonological rules in facilitating a decision as to which of the two features at stake is distinctive, which redundant. More precisely, we need to exploit the heuristic potential of markedness assimilation by examining pertinent Japanese variation and neutralization rules in its light.

Unlike a language such as Russian, Japanese does not abound in rules of the kind needed. Among the small set available for inspection, one can focus provisionally on two: (1) the voiceless realization of vowels between tenuis consonants and in word-final position before pause (if there is a pitch lowering within the word); cf. Martin 1952:14; and (2) the morphophonemic[2] variation displayed by the preterit desinence ta,[3] viz. /ta/ ~ /da/. Examples of vowel unvoicing are seen below.

čišIki	'knowledge'	cUkúsU	'exhaust'
ókUsañ	'lady of the house'	kOkóro	'heart'
kákI	'oyster'	kEsú	'extinguish'

If one wishes to account for vowel unvoicing in terms of markedness assimilation and to utilize the traditional markedness values for the traditional categories putatively involved, there are major obstacles. First, voiceless vowels are usually considered to be marked for voicing, while voiceless obstruents are considered to be unmarked for this feature. The juxtaposition of marked vowels and unmarked obstruents is incompatible with the principle of markedness assimilation. This impasse leaves us to surmise one of two resolutions: either the traditional markedness assignments err, or the features involved are incorrect. Perhaps this dilemma can be overcome by assuming that the voicing feature is not pertinent to the assessment of the vowel values, and that the correct redundant feature to be invoked is tenseness. However, for reasons that will become clear, this assumption only clouds the picture. Hence, short of challenging the correctness of the traditional markedness values assigned to voiceless vowels and voiceless consonants, the only recourse is to recognize tense vs. lax as the distinctive feature in the Japanese obstruent system (cf. Andersen

1968:175, 1969c:569-70). But this is precisely the prerequisite needed in order to understand the unvoicing of vowels as a markedness assimilation, since tense obstruents are [M tense].

The second case of neutralization which I wish to examine is less straight-forward than that of vowel unvoicing but is still susceptible of the same mode of argumentation and analysis. The relevant morphophonemic rule is exemplified by forms such as those below.

šinu	'die'	*šinda*	'died'
yobu	'call'	*yonda*	'called'
yómu	'read'	*yónda*	'read'
oyóŋu	'swim'	*oyóyda*	'swam'

BUT

arúku	'walk'	*arúyta*	'walked'

ETC.

The alternation /ta/ ~ /da/ of the morpheme *ta* cannot be *explained* (not simply described) as a case of markedness assimilation without assuming that the relevant diacritic category is tense vs. lax. As in the first example considered, the [U voice] value of the redundantly voiced acute nasal *n* does not match the [M voice] value of the desinential obstruent *d*. After yod there is a twofold result, depending on the stem-final segment of the nonpreterit: if that segment is [U tense], so is the desinence-initial segment, hence *oyógu/oyóyda;* if it is [M tense], so is the desinence-initial segment, hence *arúku/arúyta*.

The markedness-theoretic principle of assigning phonological shape to basic forms of morphemes (specifically, desinences) delineated in Shapiro 1972b in connection with the English plural, can be exploited with similar success here, too. Since the preterit is the marked category (cf. Jakobson 1971:136-7) vis-à-vis the nonpreterit in Japanese as generally,[4] we would expect it to be expressed by the marked term of the relevant phonological feature (cf. Jakobson 1971:350-6). Tenseness fulfills this expectation, voicing does not.

Perhaps it would not prove totally amiss to interject here a brief digression on problems of markedness assignment, as adumbrated by Shapiro 1972b and 1974b. In these studies I have attempted to sketch a deductively formulated theory of phonological structure in terms of certain formal and substantive universals of a semeiotic nature. Among the formal universals, the most salient ones pivot on the elaboration of feature hierarchies and the assignment of markedness values. In the event that a feature is physically present in a segment but phonologically redundant, I have hypothesized a reversal of otherwise operant markedness values. Figures 5 and 6 will serve to illustrate the plausibility of these theoretical

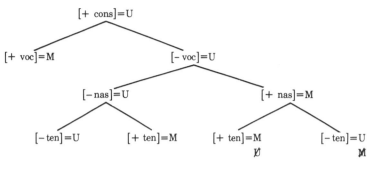

FIGURE 5.

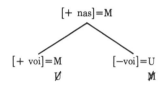

FIGURE 6.

postulates, both generally and specifically as regards the Japanese phenomena which constitute our topic herein. Consider the assignment of values for the tenseness feature in *n*.[5]

Note, crucially, that the inappropriateness of voicing as a distinctive feature in the Japanese consonant system is indicated by the value [M voice] which eventuates for *n*.

I turn now, continuing the line of argumentation, to the set of morphophonemic alternations variously termed *nigori, dakuon,* and (most appositely) *rendaku* by native phoneticians: the change of a 'voiceless' consonant to a 'voiced' counterpart in the formation of certain compounds (cf. Latin *negāre, negōtium, negligō,* etc. and W. Slavic sandhi). The data are summarized (inter alia) by Martin (1952:48-57, 65-6), of which an illustrative sampling is seen below.

kuni	'country'	*šimáguni*	'island country'
sóra	'sky'	*samuzóra*	'cold weather'
tácu	'stand'	*medácu*	'stand out'
yónhyaku	'400'	*sámbyaku*	'300'

ETC.

I would like to suggest an interpretation of this set of correspondences which will corroborate the proposed phonological reinterpretation of

Japanese tenues and mediae. I will do this on the basis of admittedly limited but nonetheless highly suggestive evidence, namely comparative phenomena of word-composition from Russian.

Russian is endowed with a rich morphophonemic and derivational component. In the formation of bahuvrihi and tatpurusha composita, it evinces a somewhat curious and altogether productive alternation of sharp (palatalized) and plain (nonpalatalized) consonant, for example see below.

krov'	'blood'	*krovopodtëk*	'bruise'
grud'	'chest'	*grudobrjúšnyj*	'thoraco-abdominal'
kúdri	'locks'	*černokúdryj*	'black-haired'
brov'	'eyebrow'	*černobróvyj*	'black-browed'

In each pair cited there is a correlation between [M sharp], i.e. [+ sharp], and [U sharp], i.e. [– sharp] base-final segments, such that the unmarked segment of the compositum replaces its marked counterpart but not vice versa.

If we now compare this process to that of Japanese *rendaku,* it would seem plausible to claim that the semeiotic purport is identical, in the face of disparate language-specific particulars. Pursuing this claim, one can then argue that the media which appears in *rendaku* must be valorized as the unmarked term of the phonological opposition, and this evaluation is possible only if the tense vs. lax feature is considered distinctive.

The validity of such a semeiotic analysis is also borne out by a confrontation of prosodic phenomena attendant upon composition. Given examples from English, Russian, and Japanese, respectively, we can discern a typologically homologous process at work.

ENGLISH
> *gráy béard* → *gráybèard*
> *trée* + *tóad* → *trée tòad*
> *bláck héad* → *bláckhèad*

RUSSIAN
> *pár* + *voz'i* → *parovóz*
> (steam + carry → locomotive)
> *ikóna* + *p'isa* → *íkonopis'*
> (icon + write → iconography)
> *búr'a* + *lomáj* → *burelóm*
> (storm + break → fallen wood)

JAPANESE
> *fúufu* + *kenka* → *fuufugénka*
> (husband and wife + quarrel → family quarrel)
> *ánpo* + *jooyaku* → *anpojóoyaku*

(security + treaty → security treaty)
yámato + *kotobá* → *yamatokótoba*
(Yamato + word → native Japanese word)

In each case adduced, the process of compounding entails the obliteration of the prosodic properties of the constituents taken singly and assigns primary stress or pitch, respectively, to a certain syllable or mora. This erasure of suprasegmental properties can easily be interpreted as an *unmárking,* i.e. as a neutralization of distinctiveness or prominence. This interpretation comports very well with our notion of markedness in general and is an important component of a systematic understanding and explanation of the linguistic process at hand as structurally motivated.[6]

The argument for positing the feature tense vs. lax as distinctive in Japanese can be buttressed by adducing perceptual evidence. Polivanov (1959:22), in discussing the development of Japanese consonantism, cites the different ways in which the North Chinese 'semivoiced' series is perceived, respectively, by native speakers of French, English, Russian, and Japanese:

> North Chinese ^{P}b, ^{t}d, ^{k}g, etc. (nonaspirate) are evaluated by the French as voiceless (ditto for the English, whence their customary European transcription *p, t, k*). On the other hand, the Russian speaker perceives them to be voiced, whence their transcription as *b, d, g* by Russian Sinologists (*p, t, k* being reserved for the Chinese aspirates *p, t, k*). Japanese perception of these sounds aligns itself with that of French and English: North Chinese ^{P}b (*p* in European transcription, *b* in the Russian) in the word *bai-lun* 'white dragon' is rendered in a late dialectal Japanese borrowing by *p* (not by *b*!): Nagasaki *pa:ron* (or *pe:ron* in other dialects) 'rowing race during the holiday of the White Dragon.' This kind of interpretation of Chinese 'semivoiced' obstruents in indicated also by the transcriptional practice of Japanese Sinologists.

The convergence of perceptual data between French, English, and Japanese, on one side, and Russian, on the other, gives an additional fillip to the argument elaborated above, since French and English both have distinctive tenseness, while Russian has an opposition of voiced vs. voiceless. Cf., finally, the fact that Japanese shares with English and French (Ladefoged 1971:20) a delay in voice onset, whereas the voicing of Russian mediae commences instantaneously.

This last bit of testimony leads conveniently to some concluding remarks on the relationship between phonetics and phonology, as reflected in the recent literature. I consider Ladefoged 1971, Vennemann 1972, and Shibatani 1973 to be representative—in varying degrees—of what can be called the *naturalness fallacy* in linguistics. Ladefoged advocates the inclusion of scalar phonetic parameters in phonology (seemingly oblivious of the crucial distinction between logically contradictory and contrary oppositions), by which he intends, notably, the concomitant rejection of the binaristic principles championed for several decades by Jakobson. Vennemann analyzes the subphonemic changes wrought by assimilation and concludes (echoing Ladefoged) that phonology must embrace non-binary rules along numerical scales which reflect redundancies such as those pertinent to certain assimilations. Shibatani argues, largely on the basis of phonetic adaptation observable in interlinguistic borrowing, that the phonetic surface structure often supersedes that of underlying morphemic structure. He concludes that 'identifying a natural phonetic representation is a prerequisite to identifying a natural phonological process' (1973:105).

The attention lavished by these authors on phonetic detail and accuracy is praiseworthy and highly emulable. Nevertheless, their alternately implicit (Ladefoged) and explicit (Vennemann, Shibatani) advocacy of phonetic 'naturalness' can only be lamented as a retrogression into the morass of prestructuralism. This step backward, apparently provoked by Chomsky and Halle 1968, illustrates the widespread conflation of form and substance which has hampered recent discussions of the evaluative component in phonology. Here the trenchant caveat of Andersen 1974a deserves to be quoted in full yet again:

> It should be noted that markedness relations pertain to the form of language. They should be consistently distinguished from such notions as relative articulatory complexity, relative optimalness, or relative text frequency, which are facts about the substance of language. For even though it is often the case that, for instance, the unmarked term of an opposition involves less articulatory complexity and occurs more frequently than the corresponding marked term, this is not necessarily so. Markedness is a matter of conceptual complexity and as such is to a considerable extent independent of the substance of language. One of the principal goals of phonology is to determine the precise extent of this relative independence.

Form is the imposition of mind on the physical continuum (substance); phonological feature terms are *oppositive, relative,* and *negative* (Jakobson 1962:294, 626 ff.). This new skirmish with binarism (cf. Martinet's older one), mounted by Ladefoged et al., is based on a fundamental misapprehension of the logical quiddity (as it were) of oppositions in language. They are binary by definition (cf. Jakobson 1962:301, 637), since they constitute minimal paradigms, in which the presence of one member implies the absence of the other (one term is in praesentia while the other is in absentia, and vice versa).

The pursuit of phonological theory in the phantasmagoria of phonetics (universal or otherwise) is redolent of the late 19th and early 20th century search for an explanatory theory of sound change in collocations of phonetic correspondences. The futility of this quest is a predictable consequence of a methodology which equated phonological causes with phonetic effects.[7] The same, unfortunately, must be predicted for all such 'naturalness' theories, as even the fleetingest glance at the history of linguistics would confirm. From the Sanskrit grammarians to the Prague Schoolmen, it has been abundantly clear that linguistic structure is a product of culture not nature.[8] As for the grounding of phonological theory in universal phonetics, suffice it to say—pace Ladefoged, Chomsky, and Halle—that the universality of phonetics is coterminous, no more no less, with the law of excluded middle. As the simultaneous occurrence of polar opposites is banished from logic, so the sole universal constraint on speech sounds (diphthongs excepted) is surely the impossibility of uttering both a given segment and its antithesis simultaneously.

The problem of Japanese tenues and mediae may serve to illustrate the efficacy and, in some measure, the possible ineluctability of the approach to linguistic explanation concomitant with a semeiotic theory of marked-ness. It would perhaps not be an exaggeration to say that explanations, if they are to be found at all, must be sought in the forms with which the conceptualization of linguistic structure is invested; and of which the evaluative component provides the richest, if not the sole repository of explanantes.

B. Russian Consonant Syncope

Phonology is fundamentally a bipartite structure consisting of a set of phonemes and a set of implementation rules. The phoneme set is defined by a hierarchy of diacritic categories. The implementation rules are a set of interpretants by means of which the correct phonetic implementation of an utterance is directly related to a phonological representation of that utterance consisting of phonemes and phonological boundaries.

A semeiotic theory of grammar entails inter alia the assumption that the phonology, like all parts of language structure, constitutes a functional system. This assumption is indispensable to the study of sound systems specifically since it (1) imposes the formal requirement of mutual internal consistency on the statements which constitute a phonological description; and (2) forces the theory underlying the description to explicate the functional coherence among the constituent parts and to provide a method for evaluating the internal consistency of phonological descriptions.

Phonological rules have two functions. First, they translate a phonological representation couched in purely relational terms (diacritic category specifications) into a detailed three-parameter (frequency, volume, time) score which corresponds, in turn, to an acoustic signal. This is the phonetic function of the phonological rules. Second, with regard to the specific nature of these correspondences, the rules produce in the actual utterances a distributional representation of the paradigmatic relations that define the phoneme set (Andersen 1966:9). The nature of this distributional representation is that of a diagram. This is the iconic function of the rule component.

The emphasis on the functional relation between the implementation rules and the hierarchy of diacritic categories underlying the phoneme set entails envisaging this relation as one of strong cohesion—the cohesion characteristic of a functional system. Further, the requirement of internal consistency facilitates and preserves this cohesion by demanding that the phonological rules be so formulated as to refer demonstrably to relations in the hierarchy of diacritic categories.

The phonetic function of phonological rules can be fulfilled by implementation rules which simply assign the proper redundant features to a phonological representation, thus rendering the representation suffi- ciently explicit as to be realizable phonetically. Implementation rules which have the effect of altering distinctive feature specifications, or of deleting, adding, or metathesizing whole segments clearly cannot be interpreted as being uniquely motivated by the rule component's phonetic function.

Neutralization rules, i.e., rules effecting the suspension of a phono- logical feature in phonologically defined environments, provide one of the means by which the relations obtaining within the hierarchy of diacritic categories are manifested. There are two basic types of neutralization: sequential and concomitant. Sequential neutralization can be defined as the suspension of a phonological opposition in an environment char- acterized by reference to its concurrent and sequential context, one and the same realization being assigned to both terms of the opposition (Andersen 1966:25). Both the particular category neutralized and the specific environment in which the neutralization takes place must ultimately be a function of the relations obtaining between the category neutralized and other categories in the hierarchy. Concomitant neutralization can be defined as the suspension of a diacritic category in part of a class of phonemes, specifically the unpaired members of the phoneme class. The unpaired phoneme is unspecified with respect to the diacritic category in question, and it is the function of an implementation rule to specify the proper implementation of the unpaired phoneme in those environments where the category is diacritic for the paired phonemes of the class.

The two basic types of neutralization sketched above are limited in scope to discrete segments of neutralization or specific categories taken singly. It seems profitable, however, to extend the notion of neutralization to blocs of segments, and perhaps even to blocs of diacritic categories. With regard to the former, it seems appropriate to consider, for example, the consistent absence of a segment from a consonant cluster to be an instance of neutralization, since the distinction based on the presence vs. the absence of the segment in question is suspended. This variety of neutralization, which can be termed *bloc neutralization,* as it pertains to the simplification of consonant clusters in Russian, is the chief subject of this section.

The diacritic categories of Russian, together with the phonemes they underlie, are shown in Table 1. In the discussion to be presented below, all statements concerning the distinctive feature definitions of Russian phonemes make specific reference to Table 1.

TABLE 1

Diacritic Categories and Phonemes of Russian

VOCALIC	*a, i, u, e, o, l, l', r, r'*
NONVOCALIC	*m, m', n, n', v, v', j, p, p',*
	b, b', t, t', d, d', k, k', g,
	g', x, x', f, f', s, s', z, z',
	c, č, š, š', ž
CONSONANTAL	*l, l', r, r', m, m', n, n',*
	p, p', b, b', t, t', d, d', k,
	k', g, g', x, x', f, f', s, s',
	z, z', c, č, š, s', ž
NONCONSONANTAL	*a, i, u, e, o, v, v', j*
DIFFUSE	*i, u*
NONDIFFUSE	*a, e, o*
FLAT	*u, o*
NONFLAT	*i, e*
VOICELESS	*p, p', t, t', s, s', š, k, k'*
VOICED	*b, b', d, d', z, z', z, g, g'*
COMPACT	*č, š, š', ž, k, k', g, g', x, x', a*
NONCOMPACT	*t, t', d, d', s, s', z, z', c,*
	p, p', b, b', e, o
GRAVE	*v, v', m, m', p, p', b, b', f, f'*
ACUTE	*t, t', d, d', s, s', z, z', j,*
	n, n', c
STRIDENT	*c, s, s', z, z', f, f', š, š', ž, č*
MELLOW	*t, t', d, d', p, p', b, b', k, k',*
	g, g', x, x', n, n', m, m'
CONTINUANT	*s, s', z, z', š, š', ž, x, x', l, l'*
ABRUPT	*c, č, k, k', g, g', r, r', t, t', d, d'*
NASAL	*n, n', m, m'*
NONNASAL	*t, t', d, d', p, p', b, b'*
SHARP	*t', d', s', z', p', b', f', v'*
	k', g', x', r', l', m', n', š
PLAIN	*t, d, s, z, p, b, f, v, k, g,*
	x, r, l, m, n, š

The phonology of Russian seems to have a rule whereby sequences of two or more identical segments (geminates) are simplified (degeminated) before or after consonant, and before word boundary (Panov 1967:87-8).[9] Let us call this the 'degemination rule.' It accounts for the pronunciation of *trupp* 'troupes' (gen pl) [trúp], *tonn* 'tons' (gen pl) [tón], *atóll* 'atoll' [ʌtól], *kass* 'cashboxes' (gen pl) [kás], *trëxtónka* '3-ton vehicle' [tr'òxtónkə]—cf. *tónna* 'ton' [tón:ə]—etc. Except in the hyperexplicit code (with a potential pause), it holds across preposition/prefix and word boundary, e.g., *rov vválivaetsja* 'the ditch is collapsing' [rófvál'ivəic:ə], *v ssóre* 'in a quarrel' [fsór'ъ] as in *v sóre* 'in the trash.' Actually, the portion of the rule which applies to sequences of identical consonants in the immediate environment of yet other consonants apparently needs to be divorced from the portion which degeminates identical consonants before word boundary. This seems indicated because acute obstruents which undergo assibilation before compact obstruents result in sequences which are not obligatorily simplified (cf. n. 1) before word boundary: *matč* 'match' [máč':], *pritč* 'parables' [pr'íč':] (Panov 1967:88).

Russian also contains a 'bloc neutralization rule' which deletes (syncopates) segments from consonant clusters, e.g. *sčastlívyj* 'happy' [š':is'l'ivɨj], *čéstnyj* 'honest' [č'esnɨj], *poezdka* 'trip' [pʌjéskə], etc. The most general form of this syncope rule embodies the claim (later shown to be only partly correct) that in a given sequence of consonants, be they obstruent or sonorant, the medial member may drop out. However, since clusters of three consonants do occur (*bódrstvovat'* 'be awake,' *vzdërnut'* 'yank up,' *otstranít'* 'banish,' etc.), there is need for restrictions which reveal the regularity of syncope in certain cases. Such restrictions may appear to be derivable from either universal rules of clustering (cf. Cairns (1969) or language-specific rules (Terexova 1966); this is only partly true. In any event, it can be seen that the 'degemination rule' is nothing but a special instance of the 'bloc neutralization rule'—specifically its first portion (two identical consonants in the neighborhood of any third).

The relevant portions of sentences like *oléni už sšíblis' rogámi* 'the stags had already locked horns' or *ètot xlyšč sčástliv* 'this fop is happy' (Panov 1967:87) are subject to this latter rule, hence the pronunciation [uš:ɨbl'is'] and [xl̄š':ás'l'if], respectively.

The syncope rule which applies as expected in *komplimentščik* 'complimenter' [kəmpl'im'én'š'ik] is partially suspended in *osmótrščik* [osmótrš'ik] 'inspector' (cf. *konsérvščik* 'canner,' *kórmščik* 'feeder,' *litávrščik* 'tympanist,' etc.), which is due to the presence of a sonorant immediately preceding -*š*'. The systematicity of this phenomenon will be discussed below.

The syncope rule is applied obligatorily to obstruents before the compact continuant *s, š, š'*. It is also applied—with what appears to be a gradually attenuated obligatoriness—to consonant clusters which do not end in š and ž'. Further echoing the 'degemination rule,' two identical consonants apparently need not be in sequence; as long as they are strident continuants they may be distributed on either side of the medial obstruent of a triplet, as in marksístskij 'Marxist' [mʌrks'isk'ii̯]. This holds across word boundary as well: most séryj 'grey bridge' [móss' erii̯], mozg zébry 'zebra brain' [mózz'ebri̯], matč ténnisnyj 'tennis match' [máč' tén'isnii̯], etc. Identical stops on either side of a fricative are not syncopated: čikágskij 'Chicago' [č'ikákskii̯], rak skatílsja 'the crab slid off' [rákskʌt'íls,ə], Gleb spal 'Gleb slept' [gl'épspál], etc.

Syncope is also obligatory for t or d before n when preceded by s or z: čéstnyj [č'ésnii̯], pózdnij 'late' [póz'n'ii̯], pérstnja 'ring' (gen sg) [p'érsn'ə], bezdna 'abyss' [b'eznə], etc. (Terexova 1966).

Finally, syncope takes place when identical consonants precede a word boundary, regardless of the nature of the segment preceding these identical consonants (specifically, even if it is a vowel).

The question is: how are these distributional facts to be accounted for? The degemination and bloc neutralization rules as distributional statements are partially true, but are they motivated functionally in terms of the relationship between phonological rules and the hierarchy of diacritic categories underlying the phoneme set?

Perhaps the most important aspect of neutralization rules is that the opposition neutralized is normally represented by the unmarked member in positions of neutralization. In the case of bloc neutralization, consequently, one can speak of the syncopated cluster as the unmarked counterpart of the unsyncopated one. Since bloc neutralization is patently a kind of simplification, the assignment of unmarkedness to its result fits well with the notion that only marked units contribute to linguistic complexity (elimination of marked units = simplification; cf. Cairns 1969: 867).

Markedness can also be determined by a consideration of the 'universals of phonological inventory' (Cairns 1969:870-1) or of 'implicational laws' (Jakobson [1941] 1968). Cairns has suggested the following heuristic principle governing the relation between implicational universals and the assignment of markedness:

> If the presence in any language of a set of segments, S, is implied by the presence of another set of segments, T, in the same language, and the converse is not true, then the segments in S are unmarked for at least one feature for which the segments in T are marked.

For instance, since the existence of glides implies the existence of obstruents, glides are marked with respect to obstruents: for the feature of consonantality, obstruents are unmarked and glides marked. Note that this corresponds to the optimality criterion: optimal consonants are [+ cons], hence unmarked for consonantality; glides are [— cons], hence marked for consonantality.

With respect to syncope it does not seem inappropriate to hypothesize that something like degree of markedness must be at work in order that the simplification, in Russian, of all *sks* clusters be reconciled with the preservation of all *ksk* clusters, since the particular segments involved are the same, albeit in different order. The following reasoning seems plausible.

First, of the two types of syllable slopes, codas—which are generally subject to more restrictions than onsets—are marked and onsets unmarked (Andersen 1969b:124). Hence the last member of a prevocalic cluster is never syncopated since, qua onset, it is always unmarked with respect to the rest of the cluster. Second, since the 'archetypal program for vocal tract control' is the sequence *tata* . . . (Cairns 1969:877), obstruent syllable slopes are unmarked in relation to sonorant syllable slopes. Hence the obstruent first member of a post-vocalic cluster is never syncopated, since, qua slope, it is always unmarked with respect to the rest of the cluster. To continue with *sks* and *ksk* as examples, the *k* of *sks* is multiply marked with respect to the segments surrounding it: it is marked twice for compactness (*s* is unmarked), once each with respect to each *s*. In the case of *ksk,* however, neither *k* can syncopate because both are in unmarked syllable slope position, neutralizations taking place in marked positions only; furthermore, *s,* which does occur in a marked position, is not multiply marked (i.e., at least doubly marked) with respect to *k*.

The sequences *stn* and *zdn* are subject to obligatory simplification in Russian (Terexova 1966:83). If one inquires why the medial segment invariably drops, the answer appears to be the same (cf. Shapiro 1972b:349-50): *t* and *d* are marked for abruptness while *n* is unmarked; *t* and *d* are marked for stridency (being mellow stops) while *s* and *z* are unmarked for stridency (cf. Cairns 1969:871). This double markedness of *t* and *d* between *s* or *z* and *n* is a degree of complexity both necessary and sufficient for syncope to take place in marked positions in Russian.

In order to facilitate further explanation it must also be mentioned that any segment is marked when contiguous to itself. Since the optimal or archetypal sequence of segments is *tata* . . . (i.e., the recurrent concatenation of the optimal consonant, the diffuse obstruent *t,* and the optimal vowel, the compact *a*), in which the vowel and the consonant represent polar opposites, then markedness with respect to this unmarked structure would be gradually introduced and heightened by having the segments go from least alike to most alike. Two segments are most alike when they are identical. Hence the most marked sequences are either *aa* or *tt*.

Returning to examples of identical compact continuants in sequence, it is the doubly marked segment which is syncopated. Thus in the sequence *ššš* of *už sšibl'is'* the medial segment is marked with respect to its righthand neighbor; it is also marked with respect to its lefthand neighbor. Both neighbors, being either preceded or followed by vowels, are unmarked.

In the cluster *trš'* of *osmotrščik* the sonorant does not drop, not simply because it is a sonorant but because it is not multiply marked in relation to its immediate environment.

In the cluster *ntš'* of *kompl'iméntščik, t* is marked for abruptness with respect to *n,* which is unmarked for abruptness. It is also marked for acuteness with respect to *n,* which is unmarked for this category.

Consonant clusters consisting of one or two sonorants and one or two obstruents (e.g., *trš', jtš', rgš', rmš', rvš'*) undergo the syncope rule optionally, meaning that there is a degree of free variation.[10] The reason is that the non-nasal sonorants (liquids, glides) are always marked for consonantality with respect to obstruents since they are either [+ voc] or [— cons]. Nasals, being the optimal sonorants (they are the only consonants having formant structure), are always marked for consonantality with respect to obstruents.[11] The presence of this immutable markedness of sonorants with respect to obstruents can always potentially prevent the syncope rule from applying obligatorily.[12]

One of the most important implications of the iconic function is its role in determining whether a category is diacritic for a given segment. Since the rules are interpretants which translate paradigmatic relations defining the hierarchy of diacritic categories into their syntagmatic counterparts, it is the rules—and only the rules—that will indicate to learner and analyst alike whether a phonetic characteristic in a segment is relevant phonologically. Phonological rules can also indicate that the category vacillates between distinctiveness and redundancy; such a situation would constitute the functional manifestation of variability as an inherent property of language as a sign system.

We have seen that, for instance, *mozg zebry* 'zebra's brain' pronounced without pause will yield [mózz'ébři] since the [+ comp] /g/ is doubly marked, once with respect to each of its neighboring /z/'s. On the other hand, in a phrase like *v zágs xotéli* '(they) wanted (to go) to the registry office' pronounced without pause, there is no consonant syncope since no preconsonantal segment is multiply marked with respect to its neighbors. In the case of certain clusters (*stk, zdk, ste, ntk, ndk, ntk, ndk*) there is variation among speakers. Thus *pianístka* 'pianist (f.)' or *zagvózdka* 'hitch' are pronounced [p'ιʌn'ískə], [zʌgvóskə] or [p'ιʌn'ístkə], [zʌgvóstkə]; and *kostljávyj* 'bony' is pronounced [kʌs'l'ávii̭] or [kʌstl'ávii̭] while *ščastlivyj* 'happy' is invariably [š':is'l'ívii̭]. Experiments with native speakers (Ganiev 1966) show that *t* tends to be syncopated in common words of the elliptic code and preserved otherwise.[13]

The /t/ or /d/ of these clusters can be variously interpreted (by speakers!) as redundantly or distinctively [+ abrupt], since in the Russian sound pattern their designation with respect to other features is sufficient to distinguish /t/ and /d/ from mellow continuants. In case they are interpreted as distinctively abrupt, their markedness value is [U abr], and syncope does not occur. However, if they are interpreted as redundantly abrupt, then their markedness value will be reversed to [M abr], and syncope will occur in virtue of their multiple markedness with respect to contiguous consonants. Thus the ambiguity of the distinctive feature relations is mirrored by the ambiguity (here: optionality) of the implementation rule, thereby instantiating one of the chief consequences of the iconic function.

This species of variation is commonly circumscribed in a functional manner. The same syncope rule which is optional is *stl* and *stk* clusters is (as we saw) obligatory in *stn* and *zdn* clusters, hence *čéstnyj* 'honest' [č'ésnɨj], *pózdno* 'late' [póznə], etc. The obligatoriness of the rule in these latter clusters has the functional effect of indicating that in a certain environment *t* and *d* are *never* interpreted as being distinctively [+ abr], just as in a second environment they are *sometimes* interpreted as being distinctively [+ abr]; and, finally, when prevocalic they are *always* interpreted as distinctively [+ abr]. This logical threefold result is characteristic of functional variation when reference is made in its definition to the sequential (rather than the purely concomitant) environment. It is the iconic counterpart in the rules of the variability inherent in the hierarchy of diacritic categories and the markedness relations defining the hierarchy.

The degemination rule, in its application to geminates before word boundary, can also be motivated in terms of markedness. To take *mássa* 'mass' as an example, the second *s* is marked for syllabicity while the first is unmarked. As long as a vowel follows the second *s*, the geminate character of the stem final can be preserved ([más:ə], [məs:ʌv'ík] *massovík* 'mass propagandist,' etc.).[14] However, when the second *s* appears directly before word boundary, as in the gen pl *mass*, it is no longer in onset position as regards the syllable slope; it is in coda position, which is the marked one. Hence, the second *s* in coda position is doubly marked and must syncopate, giving [más].

Geminates which are not divided by morpheme boundary occur only in non-native words. Indeed, Russian stems do not end in identical segments, the exceptions being participles and adjectives with geminate *n* arising from a single *n* on either side of a morpheme boundary, e.g. *imennój* 'nominal,' *podënnyj* 'quotidian,' *perevedënnyj* 'translated,' *pročítannyj* 'read,' etc. The appearance of geminates before stressed vowels is similarly possible in native Russian words when a morpheme boundary intervenes: *ssóra* 'quarrel,' *vvóz* 'importation,' etc. Hence any occurrence of underlying geminates not split up by a morpheme boundary can be considered marked. It is also the case that even those Russian (native) stems which end in geminate *n* simplify when followed by word boundary: *edínstvennyj* 'lone'~ *edínstven* (cf. *edínstvenna* et al.), *oživlënnyj* 'excited' ~ *oživlën* (cf. *oživlënna* et al.), etc. Even these geminate *n*'s not before word boundary are subject to simplification, in a hierarchical order. Geminate *n* does not simplify if it occurs at any point before the stress. This is the wholly unmarked position for geminates. Geminates which occur immediately after the stressed vowel are usually unsimplified but may be simplified in the elliptic subcode.[15] Geminates which occur in any other position with relation to the stress are most susceptible of simplification, hence in the most marked position. If non-native words—the category which includes occurrences of geminates unbroken by morpheme boundary—are examined in the light of the scale of markedness established for native geminates, then the picture becomes somewhat clearer. For native words the preservation of geminates is most unmarked before stressed vowels; for non-native words the occurrence of geminates is most marked in this position, foreign words being marked for nativeness. To put it in a different way: since gemination is most common in the presence of post-geminate stress and inter-geminate morpheme boundary, the absence of inter-geminate boundary accompanied by post-geminate stress is the most marked state for geminates in non-native words. This high degree of markedness is what accounts for the simplification of geminates in foreign words with post-geminate stress and their more common maintenance in position immediately following the stressed syllable (cf. Avanesov 1968).

The wide applicability of the markedness based approach to bloc neutralization (specifically, consonant syncope) may be more readily apparent when data from other languages are considered. Even a fleeting glance at the history of English, for instance, reveals that the consonant clusters of *dumb, knee, knife, wright, tight, walk, lord (<hláford), balm, palm, bomb, two, sword, glisten, whistle,* etc. were all simplified because one of the consonants was multiply marked with respect to the other. Similarly, a solution to the problem of vowel/zero alternations in the history of East Slavic (see chapter 4; cf. Isačenko 1970), lends itself to such treatment: cf. the dialectal changes, artificially banished from literary Russian, of *žurávl'* 'crane' → *žuráf'/žuravél',* *rubl'* 'ruble' → *rup'/rúbel',* etc.

C. *The Problem of Russian š'*

The sign function of phonological rules consists in the distributional mirroring of the constitutive relations of the phonological system. And it is this iconicity that distinguishes phonology from morphophonemics (Andersen 1969a:826-7). Phonological implementation rules, in contradistinction to morphophonemic rules, 'produce overt signs (allophonic variation, neutralization) of the distinctive feature relations that define the phonemes.' The relations are conceptualized by language learners and users in terms of an evaluative system—markedness.

The old problem of phonological analysis I wish to address here, using a Russian case, is that of the monophonemic status of a sound vs. its divisibility into several phonemes and resultant polyphonemic (usually biphonemic) status. Trubetzkoy (1958:51-9) dealt with this problem, as have (among others) Chao ([1934] 1963), Martinet (1939), and more recently Schane (1968). Specifically, I will be concerned with the re-examination of the status of the sounds [š':] and [ž':] in contemporary standard Russian, about which numerous scholars have had their special say, including Avanesov (1948), Bulygina (1971), Isačenko (1969, 1971), Reformatskij (1967), Veyrenc (1966), Zinder (1963), Flier (1980, 1982), and Thelin (1974, 1981). Earlier in the century Baudouin ([1912] 1963:230) opted for the biphonemic solution, while his illustrious pupil Ščerba (1957: 171) leaned towards a monophonemic one. Isačenko (1971) utilizes the approach of Halle (1959:51-2) and arrives at an apodictically enunciated conclusion (supporting Zinder) that the sounds in question must be viewed as biphonemic, namely /s/ + /č/ and /z/ + /ž/ or /ž/ + /ž/. Had he taken note of the comprehensive study of Veyrenc, Isačenko's conclusion may have been less sure: Veyrenc adduces cogent arguments that must be taken into account. Flier and Thelin argue at cross purposes, and both fall short of a solution.

I will confine myself here to an *aperçu* of phenomena relating to [š':], about which see also Barinova (1966), Borunova (1966), Panov (1968:81-102). Mutatus mutandis, the argumentation sketched hereinafter applies with equal force to [ž':].

According to the latest Soviet sources, there are essentially two varieties of contemporary standard Russian pronunciation as regards [š':]. The first variety has a long soft (palatalized) š wherever the orthography uses the letters щ, сч, шч, зч, жч. The second variety has this sound only where no clear cut prefix/preposition boundary intervenes; otherwise it has a sequence [š'č'] or [s'č'] and occasionally [š':]. The length of [š':] is neutralized in syllable coda position and phonetically present in syllable onset position (i.e., the 'basic' one).

Taking the second variety of pronunciation as a diagnostic case, it becomes clear that there has to be some coherent explanation for the occurrence of the biphonemic sequence at preposition boundaries (i.e., beyond simply describing that it occurs at this boundary). An explanation of this kind, I submit, is most successfully framed in terms of markedness. Let us call the position of occurrence of [š':] (rather than [š'č'] or [s'č']) the stem-internal position. This position is unmarked as against stem-external position, i.e., at preposition or word boundary, since the latter position is marked (neutralizations and cases of contextual variation which occur stem-internally are frequently excluded stem-externally). Further, the phonetic sequence [š'č']/[s'č'] can also be assumed to be marked vis-à-vis the unmarked [š':], since the degree of heterogeneity of the former exceeds that of the latter. We can see, now, that there is a correlation, via markedness, between the position and the sound(s). In the unmarked stem-internal position, the unmarked [š':] appears to the exclusion of [š'č']/[s'č']. In the marked stem-external position, the marked [š'č']/[s'č'] appears—but not to the exclusion of [š':]. This last datum is understandable in the light of Brøndal's 'principle of compensation': the marked position does not combine with the marked sound(s) unless it also combines with the unmarked sound.

The degree of markedness of a stem-external position increases proportionately with the bookishness or foreignness of the item (cf. Borunova 1966:63 ff.) This in turn enhances the frequency of [š'č']/ [s'č'] at the expense of [š':]. The effect of book learning and universal literacy is then to reduce positions of neutralization and to accentuate differentiation—in the present case at boundaries, but also generally (cf. Shapiro 1968:44-5).

In the preceding section I attempted to demonstrate that consonant deletion rules in Russian are governed by markedness considerations. Specifically, I suggested that in a consonant cluster of more than two segments it was the multiply marked one (relative to its neighbors) that was syncopated. This finding is in direct conflict with the assertions of Isačenko (1971). If [š':] is to be regarded as the phonetic realization of *sč*, then we cannot account for the pronunciation of such items as *kámenščik* 'mason' [kám'ьn'š'ik], since the sequence *n'sč* should drop *s* which is [M acute] and [M abrupt]. Moreover, the biphonemic treatment of [š':] and the resultant derivation of the allomorphs *ščik/čik* from an underlying *sčik* or even *skik*—as is done in Worth (1968), as well as Isačenko (1971) and Shapiro (1972a)—must be adjudged fundamentally sterile, since this 'derivation' explains nothing about the particular distribution of allomorphs, viz. dental and palatal obstruents plus *čik*, but *ščik* elsewhere. On the other hand, if we invoke markedness and consider [š':] to be both monophonemic and the basic (underlying) initial obstruent of the suffix, then things begin to fall into place. The variant *čik* has an initial segment which is marked for stridency; hence its concatenation with stems whose final obstruents are marked for acuteness, e.g. *perevódčik perevód* + *čik* 'translator,' *kabátčik kabáč* + *čik* 'taverner,' *okútčik okúč* + *čik* 'heaper,' *izvózčik izvóz* + *čik* 'cab driver,' *perepísčik perep'ís* + *čik* 'amanuensis,' *perebéžčik perebéž* + *čik* 'renegade.' The basic variant *ščik* begins with a segment which is [U strident]; hence its combination with stems which end in [U acute] obstruents, e.g. *garderóbščik garderób* + *š'ik* 'cloakroom attendant,' *zabastóvščik zabastóv* + *š'ik* 'striker.' Note that this explains why items like *anšlagščik anšlág* + *š'ik* 'headline setter' are now tolerated by the language.

Proponents of the biphonemic solution, who appeal to morphophonemic alternations to press their case, fail to distinguish between (1) the obvious necessity of considering 'morphological factors' (cf. Reformatskij 1970) in arriving at answers to phonological problems; and (2) the quite separate matter of the *sign function* of phonological rules as distinguished from that of morphophonemic rules. The assignment of phonemic status to [š':] is fully compatible with and corroborative of the markedness relations which characterize the hierarchy of diacritic categories underlying the Russian phonemes. At the same time, the biphonemic hypothesis is based on the workings of the morphophonemic component, i.e., on rules which have a different sign function and which typically reveal little or nothing about the constitutive relations of the contemporary phonological system.

In conclusion, however, one might point out the feasibility of effecting a reconciliation of the opposing views—attributable to the respective tenets of the Moscow and Leningrad Schools of phonological doctrine—by adapting the remarks of Andersen (1972:18, fn. 11) and considering the sequence [š'č']/[s'č'] to represent the phonetic realization of a phonemic segmental diphthong. We note that the order of elements as regards markedness values accords with the principle of intra-segmental variation (*š* and *s* are [U strident], *č* is [M strident]). This rapprochement is facilitated by the knowledge that sequences such as *bez ščuki* 'without the pike' and *vešč' ščekotlivaja* 'delicate matter' are pronounced with a [š':] of normal duration.

2. Vocalism

A. Russian Unstressed Vowels

The most striking characteristic of the phonological system of Russian is the alternation of phonetic values as between stressed and unstressed syllables, a phenomenon known as vowel reduction.[16] The five-vowel system under stress is qualitatively reduced to a three-vowel system in unstressed syllables; in its grossest form these alternations can be represented as in Figure 7 (letters stand for phonemes). Actually, to make this scheme a bit more accurate, one ought to note that the stressed diffuse (high) vowels /i u/ do not change qualitatively when not under stress—not in the traditional norm, anyway.[17] Like all the other vowels they are reduced quantitatively (are of shorter duration), but unlike the others they undergo no further change.

That Russian vowels undergo reduction in unstressed syllables is typologically to be associated with the presence of strong dynamic stress in

FIGURE 7.

this language: it is a well known tendency for languages with this kind of stress to exhibit concomitant reduction in unstressed syllables. But in contrast to the conventional view that sees vowel reduction simply as the physical consequence of strong dynamic stress (uneven distribution of articulatory energy over the utterance span), I take the view that the observed variations are signs and are, therefore, motivated semeiotically. This view implies that phonetic variation—like all variation—has a function, one which includes but also ultimately transcends phonetic substance.

Function in the semeiotic sense has, first of all, to do with the iconic, the indexical, and the symbolic aspects of linguistic signs. The first of these aspects—the iconic—has special relevance to phonological structure, since it is the iconic function that makes manifest, or diagrams, the relational values by which the system of diacritic categories is defined.[18] The functional relationship between category values and the way they are realized in speech is, on the semeiotic view, an expression of the strong cohesion obtaining between form and substance in phonology (as elsewhere, in grammar and lexis).

In the light of this conception of phonological structure, therefore, when confronted by systematic variation of the sort presented by Russian unstressed vocalism, one ought to probe beyond the physical parameters of speech to inquire into semeiotic raison d'être. That strong dynamic stress is often associated with vowel reduction cannot explain the behavior of unstressed vowels in Russian. There are, after all, other languages—Slavic ones at that—where strong dynamic stress does not imply vowel reduction (e.g. Ukrainian); or produces a different kind of reduction as to phonetic outcome (e.g. Bulgarian).

The motivation of vowel reduction (where it occurs, with or without concomitant strong dynamic stress) must reside in the fulfillment of the iconic function. Since the iconic function implicit in variation is said to realize or diagram the relations which define the underlying system of diacritic signs, the question really has to do with the precise nature of the relations that obtain between terms of phonological oppositions.

Besides the phonetic specifications, expressed as polar values (plus and minus) of phonological diacritic categories, each of the two terms of the minimal phonological paradigm has a semeiotic value, which is constituted by markedness. That is to say, each term embodies one of two possible semeiotic evaluations of the polarity (asymmetry) characterizing the phonological paradigm. In this respect, phonological paradigms are in perfect conformity with the content system of language, since 'every single constituent of any linguistic system is built on an opposition of two logical contradictories: the presence of an attribute ("markedness") in contraposition to its absence ("unmarkedness")'.[19]

Assuming that Russian unstressed vocalism is a semeiotic diagram (icon) of the markedness relations defining the vowel system of Russian, what needs to be investigated are the particular ways in which the diagrammatization is accomplished. The first place to start is the status of stressedness itself, a point which can easily be overlooked in any treatment of the topic. It makes sense to speak of the unstressed vocalism *en gros* only in opposition to the stressed vocalism. Since it is the relation between stressed and unstressed syllables that is at stake, and relations, as has already been made clear, are expressed in terms of markedness values, what needs to be emphasized first is the markedness of unstressed syllables vis-à-vis the unmarkedness of stressed syllables (cf. Trubetzkoy 1975:182). Unstressed syllables in Russian are positions of neutralization vis-à-vis the vowel system of the stressed syllables: the five-vowel system under stress is reduced (as we saw) to a three-vowel system when not under stress. Since the marked term of an opposition is that which is more narrowly defined, it can be seen that vowel reduction in Russian is a sign of the marked status of unstressed syllables; and, conversely, the absence of reduction in stressed syllables is a sign of their unmarked status. There is, in other words, an over-arching semeiotic cohesion between the markedness values of the *contexts* (stressed/unstressed syllables), on one hand, and the markedness values of the *vocalic sub-systems* which manifest themselves in those contexts, on the other. As will become clear below, this fundamental type of cohesion—between contexts and units (here: vowels)—is also at the basis of the explanation of Russian unstressed vocalism.[20]

The basic (i.e., stressed) system of Russian vowels is constituted by five vowels and three distinctive features as in Table 2. With the exception of

TABLE 2

	compact	diffuse	flat
/a/	(+) U	(—) M	(+) U
/i/	(—) M	(+) U	(—) M
/u/	(—) M	(+) U	(+) U
/e/	(—) M	(—) M	(—) M
/o/	(—) M	(—) M	(+) U

the flatness of /a/, all of the feature specifications (plusses and minuses) are distinctive; the markedness values (M's and U's assigned in accordance with the principles of Shapiro 1976:36-45) take this into account. For the problem of unstressed vocalism, flatness is not relevant, only compactness and diffuseness. Indeed, the central feature involved in vowel reduction is diffuseness. The two vowels /i/ and /u/ that are unmarked for diffuseness do not undergo qualitative reduction precisely because of their markedness value: in conformity with the status of unstressedness, only those vowels that are [M dif], i.e., / a e o/, change their quality as well as their duration.

The actual phonetic variants which appear as the unstressed counterparts of /a e o/ are:

$$/a/ - (\alpha >) \Lambda > \partial \qquad /i/ - i (>i^e) > \text{ь}$$

The greater-than sign (>) indicates the greater duration of the variant preceding it, corresponding to the number and the position (excluding absolute initial) of unstressed syllables in the phonological word, first pretonic being segregated (together with absolute initial) from post-tonic and all other pretonic syllables. The parenthesized alpha (α) represents a possible (and quite common) more open pronunciation of neutralized /a o/ in absolute initial and, for some speakers, in phrase-final position (Verbickaja 1976:59). This variant has been characterized as a feature of Muscovite speech (Panov 1979:160) corresponding to the Leningrad caret (ʌ), a less open vowel (Matusevič 1976:100), although the standard, Muscovite-oriented handbooks of R. I. Avanesov (1956, 1972) make exclusive use of the caret without further commentary.[21] The schwa (ə) occurs normally in positions other than first pretonic, after hard consonants. The sign [ь] denotes a shorter, laxer, slightly lower, and less fronted version of [i]—a kind of 'front schwa,' as it is occasionally transcribed.

The realizations in unstressed syllables deriving from /a o e/ could just as well be designated by the one phonetic symbol [i]. This would correctly render the negligible qualitative differences between vowel variants of increasingly lesser duration. It is, nevertheless, a phonetic fact that speakers differ in the degree to which these differences are negligible, and the standard practice is to reflect these subtleties (perhaps because of a normativist bias). Hence the common use of [i^e] to designate the vowel variant occurring after soft consonants in first pretonic position (corresponding to [ʌ]); and [ь] to designate the vowel occurring after soft consonants in other unstressed syllables (corresponding to schwa).

The main unstressed vowel variants can be ranged according to the acoustic parameters of duration and formant structure (the first two formants being the only linguistically relevant ones); the data are taken from Matusevič (1976:100-20) (Table 3).[22]

TABLE 3

	duration (msec)	F_1 (Herz)	F_2
[ʌ]	90	700	1000
[ə]	80	700	900
[i]	70	350	2000
[ь]	67	600	1950
[e]	69	500	2200

TABLE 4

[a]	196	700	1000
[i]	140	350	2000
[ɨ]	120	200-300	1600-1800
[u]	155	200-300	550-600
[e]	155	500	1300-1700
[o]	165	500	800-900

A comparison with the figures for stressed vowels is instructive (Table 4). It can readily be seen that, given the imprecision of formant structure as a criterion, duration appears to be the main physical differentiator of unstressed vowels vis-à-vis their stressed counterparts (cf. Verbickaja 1970), although length is not phonemic in Russian. We know from auditory and perceptual studies, however, that qualitative differences not readily discriminable by instrumental means are still phonologically relevant differentiators (Verbickaja 1976:47-59, 86-100), and this is borne out by proprioceptive awareness of articulatory differences. These differences can be expressed in terms of the diacritic categories which differentiate stressed vowels. The phoneme /a/ which subsumes the phonetic variants [ɑ ʌ ə], occurring chiefly after hard consonants, is specified basically as [+cmp], hence [U cmp]. The unstressed variants subsumed by /a/, which represent an articulatory and acoustic deflection away from the maximal openness of /a/, can thus be construed as discrete points on a continuum going from maximal compactness towards diffuseness (noncompactness). In relation to the [U cmp] value of /a/, these variants represent a graded increase in markedness for the category of compactness. Conversely, the phoneme /i/ which subsumes the phonetic variants [i iᵉ ь], occurring after soft consonants, and [ɨ ɨᵉ], occurring after hard consonants, is specified basically as [+dif], hence [U dif]. The unstressed variants subsumed by /i/, representing an articulatory and acoustic deflection away from the maximal closeness of /i/, can similarly be construed as discrete points on a continuum which begins at maximal diffuseness and goes towards compactness (nondiffuseness). Relative to the [U dif] value of /i/, these variants articulate a graded increase in markedness for the category of diffuseness.

The two features engaged in Russian unstressed vocalism, compactness and diffuseness, are syncategorematic (in the sense of Shapiro 1976:44) and, subsequently, complementary. An icon of this fundamental complementarity is provided by the complementarity of the contexts in which the unstressed variants subsumed by /a/ and /i/ occur. Specifically, [ɑ ʌ ə] are found chiefly after hard consonants, whereas [i iᵉ ь] are found after soft.[23]

The coherence between contexts and units with respect to Russian unstressed vocalism also manifests itself in the fact of /a/ and /i/ being the phonemic cover for the reduced vowels. Since /a/ occurs mainly after hard consonants and /i/ after soft, this distribution is clearly an instance of markedness assimilation,[24] whereby the vowel evaluated as [U cmp] coheres with the consonant evaluated as being unmarked for sharpness (palatalization); and the vowel evaluated as [M cmp] coheres with the consonant evaluated as being marked for sharpness. In the latter case, the vowel is /i/ rather than /u/ because of a secondary tonality assimilation: since the consonant is [M shp], the vowel is [M fla] in addition to being [M cmp].

The main arena of cohesion between contexts and units, to which we now turn, is that involving the variants of /a/ and /i/, i.e., Russian unstressed vocalism proper. The overarching formal correlate of the systematic nature of the variation at hand is hierarchy or ranking, expressed in the first instance by the bifurcation of vowels into stressed and unstressed (Figure 8).

The interesting thing at this point is the existence of a few words in which the stressed vowel is not one of the normal five vowels but rather one of the two characteristically unstressed variants [ə ь]. Panov (1967:44, 1979:33) cites the expletive čtób t'eb'é! [štə́pt'ib'é] as the only example with stressed [ə], but this is not so: the reportative particle *mol,* when it begins an utterance is also pronounced with stressed [ə]. Similarly, [ь] appears under stress in the reportative *d'éskat'* [d'ьskət'].[25] To be sure, in all three cases the vowel can also be pronounced fully, i.e., as [o] and [e], respectively. For those speakers who do not habitually pronounce a full vowel in these

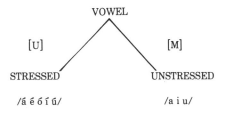

FIGURE 8

words, the reduced vowel is lexicalized, and all lexicalizations are necessarily marked vis-à-vis the regularities of the rest of the phonological system (Figure 9).

The category of unstressed syllables and the vowels implementing it is further bifurcated by the first major subsidiary opposition, that of (absolute) initial vs. noninitial. Initial is defined here as the very first segment in a word, preceded by another word ending in a vowel; or by a pause. In this position the unstressed vowel undergoes the least qualitative and quantitative change vis-à-vis its stressed counterpart (Bondarko 1977:112). In conformity with our earlier understanding of deflection away from the unmarked value as a relative increase in markedness, initial position is evaluated as unmarked, noninitial position as marked (Figure 10).

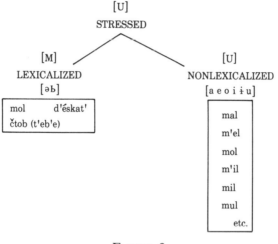

FIGURE 9

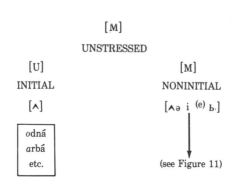

FIGURE 10

What is important to notice here, as in the preceding case, is the cohesion between contexts and units. Words in which the stressed vowel is a lexicalized (otherwise unstressed) variant (*mol, čtob, d'éskat'*) display not just any reduced vowel but precisely the one evaluated as marked in the series of variants—here [ə] and [ь], respectively. Thus, we have the situation of a marked context—a lexicalized pronunciation—being fulfilled by a marked vowel. This semeiotic coherence is replicated mutatis mutandis in the pronunciation of the unmarked [ʌ] in initial position—the context evaluated as unmarked relative to noninitial syllables, e.g. [ʌdná], [ʌrbá]. In fact, we will see this pattern of semeiotic coherence between the markedness values of contexts and that of vowel variants being sustained throughout the hierarchy as it bifurcates further down through the ranks of categories.

The second major subsidiary opposition, following immediately upon the opposition initial vs. noninitial, is that between position after soft consonants vs. not after soft consonants (Figure 11).[26]

The normal vowel variant after soft consonants is a realization of /i/, hence [i^(e)] in first pretonic position and [ь] in all other unstressed syllables, e.g. *l'esá* [l'i^e sá], *m'asá* [m'i^e sá], *m'ol'i* [m'i^e l'í]; but *časovój* [č'ьsʌvój],

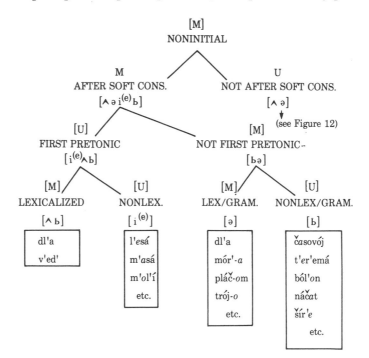

FIGURE 11

t'eremá [t'ʙr'i^emá], *ból'on* [ból'ʙn], *náčat* [náč'ʙt], *šir'e* [šír'ʙ], etc. Caret and schwa do not appear after soft consonanfs except in lexicalized or grammaticalized forms. The preposition *dl'a* is the only case of lexicalization; it is also the sole example of a preposition whose final prevocalic consonant is soft. In any event, the standard pronunciation is [ʌ] and [ə], depending on whether the vowel is one or more syllables (resp.) away from the stress, e.g. *dl'a vás* [dl'ʌvás], but *dl'a m'en'a* [dl'əm'i^en'á], etc. The relative fronting perceived in the second example is, of course, due to the doubly palatalized environment; contrast *dl'a mojovó* [dl'əməi̯i^evó], etc.

The grammaticalized pronunciation of the nonfront [ə] for the expected [ʙ] is confined to certain (mainly substantival) desinences and the 3pl of the indicative verb (2nd conjugation), e.g. *mór'a* [mór'ə], *pláčom* [pláč'əm], *trójo* [trói̯ə], *v'íd'at* [v'íd'ət], etc.[27] In general, the number of instances of this pronunciation is being curtailed over time, and it would be safe to predict its ultimate disappearance, even in standard speech.

There exists one instance of the lexicalized pronunciation of [ʙ], in the clitic *v'ed'*, which is invariably pronounced with the so-called second degree of reduction—or simply with [i]—no matter how close or far from the stressed syllable, e.g. *v'ed'já* [v'ʙt'já], like *v'ed' on'í* [v'ʙt'ʌn'i], etc.

So much for reduced vowels after soft consonants. The other branch of the hierarchy is dominated by the opposite node, i.e., not after soft consonants, which likewise splits further into first pretonic vs. non-first pretonic; and lexicalized vs. non-lexicalized (Figure 12).

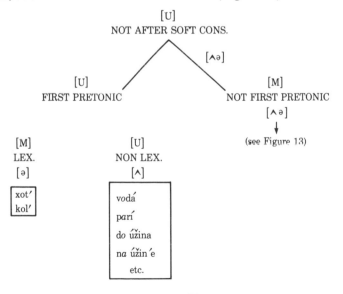

FIGURE 12

The normal reduced vowel in noninitial position and not in first pretonic after other than a soft consonant is schwa; here caret will occur only in certain vowel chains. In first pretonic, however, caret is normal, with schwa occurring only in the lexicalized abbreviations of the relative clause head words *xotjá* and *koli,* viz. *xot'* and *kol',* both of which may have a schwa in standard speech, although lesser grades of reduction are heard as well. Hence the expected fulfillment of an unmarked context by the unmarked vowel variant in *vodá* [vʌdá], *parí* [pʌrɨ́], *do úžina* [dʌúžinə], *na úžin'e* [nʌúzɨn'ь], etc.

It is at this point that the question of the pronunciation of vowel chains looms, chains one or none of whose vowels is stressed. Sequences of vowels in Russian have generally failed to receive fully adequate treatment in the handbooks; the account here is based on Avanesov (1972), Panov (1967), Shapiro (1970), and Ward (1975), the last-cited item being the most complete factual summary available. (Figure 13).

An unstressed vowel which finds itself in a syllable other than the first pretonic after a hard consonant will be pronounced invariably with the

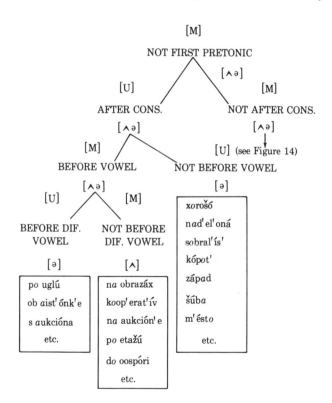

FIGURE 13

second degree of reduction, i.e., with a schwa, unless it is followed by a vowel, in which case the outcome will hinge on the kind of vowel that follows. Hence the expected pronunciations in items like *xorošó* [xərʌšó], *nad'el'oná* [nəd'ьl'iᵉná], *sobral'ís'* [səbrʌl'ís'], *kópot'* [kópət'], *zapad* [zápət], *šúba* [šúbə], *m'ésto* [m'éstə], etc. As soon as vowel chains are involved, however, there is a split, depending on whether or not the vowel in question is preceded by a vowel, in which case other factors will come into play (see below); or whether it is preceded by a consonant, on one hand, and followed by what sort of vowel, on the other. In a vowel chain consisting of more than two vowels, each pair of vowels is taken separately, without there being any dependency relation between such pairs. In pairs preceded by a consonant and having a diffuse vowel as the second member, the first member will undergo the second degree of reduction expected of vowels in position other than first pretonic, e.g. *po uglú* [pəuglú], *ob aist'ónk'e* [ʌbəis't'ónk'ь], *s aukcióna* [səukciɔnə], etc. But the presence of a nondiffuse vowel renders the position of the unstressed syllable irrelevant, and the variant which appears here is caret rather than schwa, e.g. *na obrazǎx* [nʌʌbrʌzáx], *koop'erat'ív* [kʌʌp'ьrʌt'íf], *na aukción'e* [nʌʌukción'ь], *po etažú* [pʌetʌžú], *do oospóri* [dʌʌʌspórɨ], etc.[28]

This situation must be compared directly to the behavior of vowel chains in other contexts (Figure 14). As soon as the vowel at stake is both preceded and followed by another vowel, the presence of a diffuse vowel to its immediate right becomes irrelevant, and the variant is a caret, e.g. *na aukción'e* [nʌʌukción'ь], *do oospóri* [dʌʌʌspórɨ], etc.

In all of the vowel chains examined so far, the stressed syllable has been to the right of (followed) the vowel in question. At the lowest rank of the entire hierarchy, however, the position of the stress—either to the right (following) or to the left of (preceding) the vowel—becomes a contextual factor. As long as the stressed syllable is to the right of the vowel, and the vowel is before a consonant, the first grade of reduction (caret) will obtain, e.g. *n'ï odnovó* [n'iʌdnʌvó], *u adr'esóv* [uʌdr'iᵉsóf], *koop'erat'ív* [kʌʌp'ьrʌt'íf], etc. But as soon as the vowel at stake appears after the stressed syllable, the character of the stressed vowel again becomes a discriminating factor, precisely in the same way as before; a stressed diffuse vowel occasions the pronunciation of schwa, e.g. *víorat'* [vɨɔrət']—this being the only such example cited in the literature;[29] and the presence of a stressed nondiffuse vowel occasions a caret, e.g. *pràot'ec* [práʌt'ьc], *n'é o kom* [n'éʌkəm], *n'é ot kovo* [n'éʌtkəvə], etc.

It is worth pondering why a diffuse vowel should have the effect of conditioning the second degree of reduction in vowel chains. One can speculate that it has something to do, first of all, with the special status of vowel chains in Russian, where the unmarked syllabic structure is CVCV..., i.e., regular alternation of consonants and vowels. Assuming,

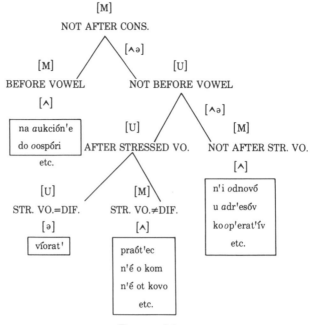

FIGURE 14

then, the marked status of vowel chains, one can go a step further and surmise that the degree of markedness of a vowel chain varies directly with the number of vowels enchained. Practically speaking, this makes 3-vowel chains the most highly marked, 2-vowel chains the second most highly marked.

Now, while all unstressed syllables are marked as a class vis-à-vis stressed syllables, the existence of vowel chains in unstressed position can be evaluated as a case of hypermarking (cf. chapter 4, section 2), the usual outcome of which is the reversal of the values that would otherwise obtain (markedness reversal). For the problem at hand, this reversal means that in hypermarked contexts the kind of semeiosis that is otherwise sustained— called replicative semeiosis—is supplanted by a kind normally reserved for morphophonemics, i.e., chiastic semeiosis (cf. chapter 2, section 2). In other words, instead of the marked variant schwa appearing in marked contexts and the unmarked variant caret in unmarked contexts (marked- ness assimilation), the signs apply with reversed values, articulating a com- plementarity, or chiasmus, between units and contexts.

This (chiastic) form of semeiosis is itself subject to gradience. Thus 3- vowel chains, being the most highly marked sequences, are constituted throughout by caret, e.g. *do oospóri* [dʌʌʌsporɨ], *na aukción'e* [nʌʌukción'ь], *do aórti* [dʌʌórtɨ], etc. But 2-vowel chains can be fulfilled by either caret or schwa, depending on two further factors in the case of prestressed chains (stress on the leftmost member); and three factors in the case of post-stressed chains (stress following the chain). In both pre-and post-stressed chains, the character of the leftmost, resp. rightmost vowel is criterial (Figure 15).

The complementarity between vowel value and the value of the context is complete, which returns us to the question posed earlier regarding the role of diffuse vowels in vowel chains. We can see that the value of the vowel varies inversely with the value of the context. Diffuse vowels are unmarked for diffuseness; as a context in which chiastic semeiosis occurs, they condition a value of the cooccurring unit that is their opposite, viz. marked, here schwa (*víorat'*). Nondiffuse vowels are marked for diffuseness; when they comprise the context, the resultant variant is the unmarked caret (*práot'ec*).

But the gradience extends beyond the diffuseness or nondiffuseness of the appropriate vowel; whether the vowel is to the left (precedes) or to the right of (follows) the vowel whose value is being determined is also criterial. In Russian, sequential neutralization habitually takes the rightmost member of the series as determinative of the whole series (as in voicing neutralization, for instance), a phenomenon otherwise known as regressive assimilation. The opposite-directed assimilation—progressive assimilation—is a rarity in Russian. Hence the markedness value of each of these assimilations is unmarked and marked, respectively. Consequently, when the diffuse vowel precedes in the vowel chain, the result is a caret (*n'i odnovó*); when it follows, it is schwa (*po uglú*). Chiastic semeiosis thus informs the entire distribution of vowel variants in Russian vowel chains.

The picture of Russian unstressed vocalism presented so far is characteristic of normative speech. Within the standard, however, col-

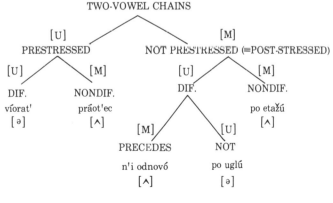

FIGURE 15

loquial pronunciations in informal settings have been given increasing legitimacy by Soviet writers on the subject, and a full account would have to take at least some departures from the traditional norm into consideration. I now turn, therefore, to two such classes of phenomena.

It has been observed for some time that unstressed vowels in absolute final position (i.e., in open syllables) may be of greater duration than word-internally, approaching the duration of absolute initial position in their most prolonged realization; conversely, they can also go in the opposite direction in allegro tempo, to the point of obliteration by syncope (cf. Matusevič 1976:97). In her fine instrumental study, Verbickaja (1976:59) treats the phenomenon in a way which lends itself to easy translation and incorporation within the framework of the present analysis. Her findings are arranged in Table 5 (abbreviated and adapted). Verbickaja's general emphasis is on relative duration, but for the purposes of a semeiotic analysis what is significant is the greater degree of openness of the reduced vowel that is possible in final position. This qualitative nuance can be reflected in the analysis simply by the recognition of a distinction between auslaut and nonauslaut within the category of noninitial unstressed syllables. Three further categories are, of course, also relevant as in any analysis: the soft vs. nonsoft character of the preceding consonant; first pretonic syllable vs. non-first pretonic; and lexicalized/ grammaticalized vs. non-lex/gram. Ignoring the problem of vowel chains, the hierarchy would look like Figure 16. Vowels of identical quality but of lesser duration are marked, in accordance with the general principle enunciated at the outset of this section; hence their uniform appearance in marked contexts in the above hierarchy.

TABLE 5

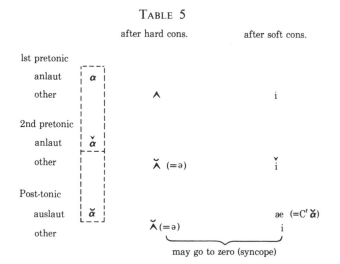

may go to zero (syncope)

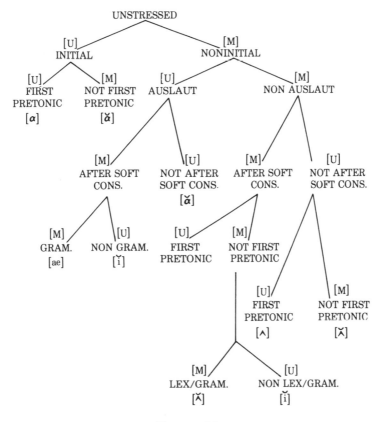

FIGURE 16

The second class of phenomena which depart from the norm (described in detail by Paufošima 1980) is much more clearly dialectal in origin and can in no way be called normative.[30] It involves (inter alia) two major contraventions of the established norm: (1) qualitative reduction of unstressed /i u/ to schwa, e.g. *v ispolnénii* [vəspaln'én'ii], *iz Budapésta* [izbədap'ésta], *vipolnjáli* [vəpaln'ál'i], *s istoričeskim* [səstar'íč'ʊsk'im], *buxgaltérija* [bəvalt'ér'iịa], etc.; (2) reduction of /a o/ (also /e/) in unstressed position to [u] instead of the normative schwa, e.g. *popul'árnyx* [pupul'árnɨx], *na Ukraíne* [nuukraín'iᵉ], *dopuskájut* [dupuskáịut], etc. In some of the cases cited by Paufošima (1980:63), the phonetic notation indicates a labialized schwa rather than a straightforward [u]. Furthermore, there seems to be an assimilative process at work (reminiscent of Russian dialects) whereby the implementation of one or the other of these two nonnormative reductions is dependent on the quality of the vowel in the following syllable, thus *Ljapunóva* [l'upunóva], *zakutók* [zukutók], *Debjussí* [d'ub'us':í], etc.; but *gruzovickí* [grəzəv'ič'k'í], *v Uzbekistáne* [vəⁱ zb'ik'istan'ъ], *rybolóvnogo* [rəbalóvnəvə], etc. Generally, Paufošima's examples reveal a distribution which hinges on the presence of /u/ in the following syllable for the appearance of [u] as the unstressed variant of /a o e/; and schwa elsewhere (with or without fronting or labialization, depending on the softness or hardness of the following consonant).

These intrusions of vowel harmony (for that is what we have) in the pronunciation of standard Russian can be understood, like all cases of vowel harmony, as instantiations of markedness assimilation. This is not the place for a full-blown analysis of Paufošima's data; but the reader is referred to Shapiro (1974b) for the markedness-based framework (and very brief discussion of Russian dialect examples) permitting a uniform semeiotic interpretation of the data.

Returning, in conclusion, to the system of Russian unstressed vocalism in the traditional standard which has been the main subject of the present section, the clear advantages of a semeiotic analysis must be emphasized anew. Jakobson's pronouncement that 'all linguistic phenomena—from the smallest components to entire utterances and their interchange—act always and solely as signs' (1971:703), if taken seriously, makes it incumbent on the linguist to seek out patterns of semeiosis even in such seemingly random phenomena as the minute phonetic variations of Russian unstressed vowels. From a programmatic and methodological standpoint, this search for sensible organization in phonetic data is a highly preferable alternative to ad hoc reliance on purely physical considerations such as target-value of vowels or the distribution of acoustic energy. Aside from the fact that the phonetic facts are outward manifestations (icons, more precisely diagrams) of an inherent order—and not vice versa—the accumulation of instrumental studies has led, not to explanations of linguistic phenomena, but to an increasing awareness of the severe limitations of the entire approach. It is widely acknowledged by phoneticians themselves that the phonetic continuum is just that, whereas phonological units are discrete entities, the search for whose discrete physical correlates has time and again proven to be vain. Even the phonetic properties used to define the distinctive features or diacritic categories of phonological analysis are already one order of abstraction above the actual phonetic surface, with which they maintain, of course, a regular interrelationship allowing speech to be realized (cf. Andersen 1979).

Nor can the manipulative strategies of transformational-generative phonology (or any of the alternative phonologies spawned by it) aspire to explanatory hegemony. For along with those who recur without hesitation to the purely physical bases of speech, the practitioners of all such approaches are doomed to the failure that comes from disregarding the crucial lessons of inter-war European structuralism (exemplified most aptly for phonology by Jakobson 1962:280-310 and 1978).[31]

The lessons in theory and method that this study of Russian unstressed vocalism has to offer center on four points. First, where there exist patterns of variation, it is these surface phenomena that must be addressed directly as explananda; an attempt must be made to understand, for instance, why phonetic facts can at all subsist alongside each other. Even so-called automatic alternations are in need of an explanation which reveals the systematic nature of the relations between the alternants. Second, it must be grasped that there is a coherence of facts at the core of structure; and that the coherence resides in the patterned cooccurrence of contexts and units. The circularity inherent, furthermore, in all manifestations of coherence must not be viewed as a defect: it is of the very nature of language as a hermeneutic object and cannot be stressed enough, particularly in the face of the received understanding of 'independent motivation' as criterial for linguistic theory (cf. n. 20 above). Third, contexts must be recognized as possessing semeiotic values of the exact same kind as units, namely markedness values. Fourth and last, coherence must be understood as a coordination of the markedness values, of contexts and units in their cooccurrence . This fact, a formal universal, imparts to language structure the encompassing cohesion that, as we have witnessed, embraces even the apparent vagaries of phonetic variation.

B. Changes in the Russian Vowel System

To recapitulate some of the main points of chapter 2 and earlier sections of this chapter, the conception of phonological structure as fundamentally semeiotic makes the following assumptions:

(1) terms of phonological oppositions (distinctive features) are signa (signs) each consisting of a signans (signifier) and a signatum (signified);

(2) terms of phonological oppositions constitute a binary paradigm in which the presence of one term necessarily implies the absence of the other, and vice versa;

(3) the several signantia (sign vehicles) are expressed as polar specifications of features, i.e., plus (+) vs. minus (—) a given opposition;

(4) being purely diacritic, all phonological signantia are conjugate with one and the same signatum (their meaning), namely 'otherness';

(5) phonological paradigms cannot occur singly or in isolation and must inhere in synthetic domains or syntagms traditionally called phonemes;

(6) phonemes are rank ordered, hypotactic structures in which one or a set of features is subordinate to one or a set of other features;

(7) the relation obtaining between terms of phonological oppositions is fundamentally asymmetric in virtue of the terms' polarity (plus vs.

minus); and secondarily symmetric in virtue of their binariness;

(8) the semeiotic manifestation of the asymmetry of phonological relations is expressed by an evaluative component—markedness—which endows each term of an opposition with a semeiotic value, so that each phonological paradigm consists of a marked and an unmarked term. 'Marked' is the more narrowly defined or conceptually complex term; 'unmarked' the less narrowly defined, conceptually less complex term;

(9) the markedness relations which characterize each phonological paradigm and thereby underlie the syntagms of feature terms (phonemes) are rendered manifest and palpable by implementation rules;

(10) in addition to a purely phonetic function, implementation rules have a diagrammatic (iconic) function, which is to say that they manifest the relation of equivalence between disparate phonological signantia. Equivalence obtains between two terms identically valorized as marked or unmarked;

(11) the cohesion characteristic of any functional system such as phonological structure consists in the congruity between the (productive) implementation rules and the (extant) relations underlying the hierarchy of diacritic signs, hence the set of phonemes or syntagms which the hierarchy defines;

(12) since the corpus of utterances from which each new generation of learners must abduce (infer) a phonological system is necessarily ambiguous (i.e., permits of alternative interpretations), the phonology of the learner may differ in a number of significant ways from that of the teaching generation. This is the chief source of phonological change;

(13) a change in phonetic output normally corresponds to a change in the phonological implementation rules, since rules are normally coherent with the category relations and hierarchies underlying the phoneme set.

Given these cardinal assumptions of phonology as semeiotic, I wish now to examine a hypothesis which flows from the last of these assumptions; more precisely, from an extension thereof.

In the typologically oriented studies of Andersen (1974a, 1975) one can discover the first coherent conceptualization of alternative rankings of phonological categories as motivations for the positing of structurally different phonological systems. The emphasis in these valuable programmatic essays, however, is exclusively on resolving the question, which of two categories is diacritic, which redundant in two or more languages; and on accomplishing this resolution by invoking a different rank order of related categories. Thus, for instance, in focusing on the vocalic tonality classes constituted by the features grave/acute and flat/nonflat in Japanese and Russian, Andersen asserts that 'it is essentially a difference in rank that separates the Russian and the Japanese vowel systems . . . in Russian, flatting is phonemic, and different values for the phonetic feature of gravity occur in complementary distribution. In Japanese, on the other hand, gravity is phonemic, and the phonetic feature of flatting is assigned by an implementation rule' (1975:70).

Despite the firmness of this assertion, different rank order must still be adjudged only a possible mode of explanation. One can also assume that the rank order of two syncategorematic (i.e., closely related, conjugate) features such as compact/noncompact and diffuse/nondiffuse or grave/ acute and flat/nonflat remains unchanged so long as only one of the two is distinctive. In order to explain the different implementation rules and resulting differences in distribution of features between, say, Japanese and Russian, one can invoke an entirely different formal universal, namely markedness reversal (designated by a slash, e.g. U̸ M) in redundant features. According to this principle of phonological structure, the markedness values that would normally obtain for features, were the latter distinctive in a given segment, are reversed in case they are redundant. Thus the Japanese system of two tonality classes can be represented as in Figure 17, where the assignment of markedness values is made in accordance with the formal universals enunciated in Shapiro 1972b. The Russian system (here the so-called Old Muscovite [= OM]) employs the same order of features; however, the markedness values for the gravity feature are the exact reverse of those in the Japanese system (Figure 18).

The reversals of values for the flatting feature in Japanese occur in virtue of this feature's redundancy. In Russian, on the other hand, the reversal of flatting values is due to the reversal in the superordinate gravity feature. Be that as it may, what eventuates is identical markedness values for the flatting feature in both Japanese and Russian—despite its redundancy in the former.

The utilization of ordering considerations as an explanans of typological differences in the redundancy of tonality features needs to be tested further before its general validity can be determined. At the same time, phonological theory can perhaps be advanced by investigating alternative rankings of distinctive features with a view towards establishing this kind of reordering as a source of phonological change. It is to this task that I now turn; the data to be examined pertain to the development of unstressed

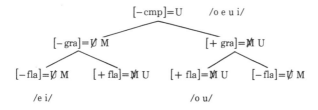

FIGURE 17

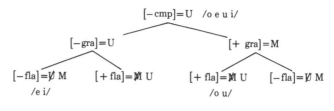

FIGURE 18

vowels in Russian, roughly from the latter quarter of the eighteenth century to the present.

The problem of Russian vocalism chiefly concerns the 'reduction' of vowels in the syllable immediately preceding the stress, i.e., the so-called 'first pretonic' syllable. In this position, vowels have had a special development which is in need of an explanation. Specifically, up until the beginning of this century, the standard Russian of Moscow and St. Petersburg (based chiefly on the Moscow dialect) contained a set of neutralization rules which effected the following realizations of first pretonic vowels. After phonemically plain (= nonpalatalized or 'hard') consonants, the distinction between /a/ and /o/ was suspended and represented by a reduced vowel [ɑ]. Hence the pronunciations *vodá* 'water' [vɑdá], *travá* 'grass' [trɑvá], etc. The identical vowel was pronounced in absolute initial position: *oknó* 'window' [ɑknó], *arbá* 'wagon' [ɑrbá], etc. After phonetically (i.e., nondiacritically) plain consonants— the so-called 'unpaired' hard consonants—the neutralization rule embraced /e/ in addition to /a/ and /o/; but the realizations differed depending on which of the unpaired hard consonants preceded which vowel. After /š/ and /ž/ the realization was identical for all three vowels, viz. [eⁱ], hence *žará* 'heat' [žeⁱrá], *žená* 'wife' [žeⁱná] (cf. pl. *žёny*), *žerló* 'muzzle' [zeⁱrló] (cf. pl. *žérla*), *šagí* 'steps' [šeⁱg'i], *šelká* 'silks' [šcⁱlká] (cf. sg. *šёlk*), *v šerstí* 'in wool' [fšeⁱrs't'í] (cf. sg. *šerst'*). After /c/, however, the realizations diverged such that /e/ was rendered as the expected [eⁱ] but /a/ and /o/ were reduced to [ɑ]: *cená* 'price' [ceⁱná] (cf. pl. *cény*), *cedít'* 'strain' [ceⁱd'it'] (cf. 2nd sg. *cédiš'*); but *carít'* 'reign' [cɑr'ít'], *capkóvka* 'hoeing' [cɑpkófkə] (cf. *cápka* 'hoe'), *cokóčut* 'they clang' [cɑkóč'ut] (cf. *cókot* 'clanging'), etc.[32]

After (phonemically and phonetically) sharp (= palatalized or 'soft') consonants, the distinction between /a/, /e/, and /o/ was uniformly suspended and realized in the single reduced vowel [eⁱ]: *tjanút'* 'pull' [t'eⁱnút'], *javljátsja* 'appear' [i̯eⁱvl'ác:ə], *časý* 'watch' [č'eⁱsɨ], *lesá* 'forests' [l'eⁱsá], *edá* 'food' [i̯eⁱdá], *v čestí* 'in honor' [fč'eⁱs't'í], *ni čertá* 'nothing' [n'ič'eɪ rtá] (cf. sg. *čërt* 'devil'), *eži* 'hedgehogs' [i̯eⁱ ẕ̌ɨ] (cf. sg. *ëž*), etc. (Panov 1967:301).

Although the diffuse (high) vowels /i/ and /u/ normally were exempt from the kind of qualitative reduction ascribed to the other three vowels, the non-discrimination of underlying /i/, on the one hand, and /e/, /o/, or /a/, on the other, was not unknown in the standard Russian of the time (Panov 1967:303). Thus *milá* 'nice' and *melá* 'swept' (both feminine forms) could be pronounced identically as [m'eⁱlá].[33]

The situation in 19th century Russian can be recapitulated by means of Table 6.

TABLE 6. 19th century Standard Russian

First Pretonic	After Hard Cons./Anlaut	After Soft Cons.	After /c/	After /š ž/
/a/	ɑ	eⁱ	ɑ	eⁱ
/o/	ɑ	eⁱ	eⁱ	eⁱ
/e/	eɪ	eⁱ	eⁱ	eⁱ
/i/	ɨ/i	i/eⁱ	ɨ/eⁱ	ɨ/eⁱ
/u/	u	u	u	u

In the beginning of the twentieth century, however, this older norm began to be supplanted by a standard pronunciation in which no distinction obtained between first pretonic /a/, /e/, and /o/, on the one hand; and /i/, on the other, after soft consonants and the phonetically hard /c/, /š/, and /ž/. This pronunciation was called *ikan'e* 'pronouncing [i]', since the phonetic realization of /a e o/ came to be close to and practically identical with /i/, e.g. *tjanút'* [t'eⁱ nút'] → [t'inút'] ~ [t'iᵉ nút'], *časý* [č'cⁱ sɨ́] → [č'isɨ́] ~ [č'iᵉ sɨ́], *edá* [i̯eⁱ dá] → [i̯idá] ~ [i̯iᵉ dá], *žará* [že̱ⁱ rá] → [ži̱rá] ~ [ži̱ᵉ rá], *šagi* [šeⁱ g'í] → [ši̱g'í] ~ [ši̱ᵉ g'i], *cena* [ceⁱ ná] → [cɨná] ~ (ci̱ᵉ ná), etc. The new situation for all practical purposes is summarized diagrammatically in Figure 19.

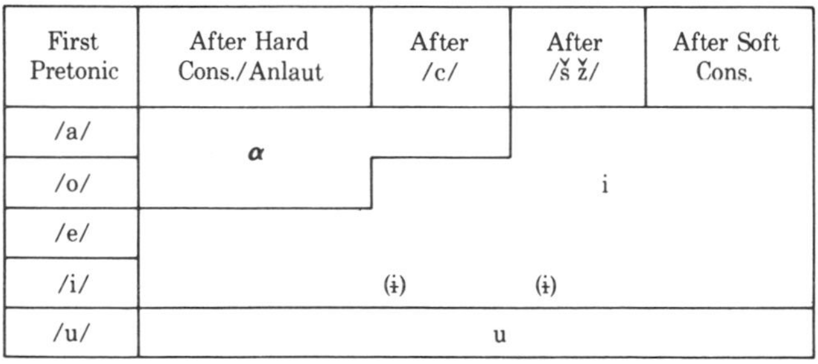

First Pretonic	After Hard Cons./Anlaut	After /c/	After /š̱ ẕ̌/	After Soft Cons.
/a/	*α*		i	
/o/			i	
/e/			i	
/i/		(i̱)	(i̱)	
/u/	u			

FIGURE 19. Standard at the beginning of the 20th century (= 'Old Muscovite')

This is, essentially, the state of affairs in present-day standard Russian, with the following exceptions. Instead of [ɑ], which is a rather open variety of reduced /a/, the all but universal pronunciation now exhibits /ʌ/, which is a higher, less open, shorter version of [ɑ]; and, although [i] is exceedingly prevalent, most orthoepists (e.g. Avanesov 1972) continue to recommend [iᵉ] as an equal and preferred variant. The most radical departure from the Old Muscovite norm in first pretonic vocalism, however, has to do with /a/ after /š ž/. Except for certain archaisms such as žalét "pity' [žiľet'], lošadéj 'horses, gen.' [ləšid'éi̯] (and all other oblique cases of the pl.), etc., first pretonic /a/ after /š ž/ now universally reduces to the vowel expected after phonetically hard consonants, namely [ʌ], hence standard žará [žʌrá], šagí [šʌg'i], etc. Thus the contemporary situation can be summarized as in Figure 20.

The essential difference, then, between the OM and CSR unstressed vowel systems resides in the treatment of /a e o/ after /š ž/. OM merges the three qualitatively reducible vowels after all consonants but /c/. At this stage, all nondiffuse vowels are neutralized in unstressed position, and the neutralized sound is specified as [ɑ] after hard paired consonants and /c/; and as [iᵉ] or [ɨᵉ] after others. CSR, on the other hand, dissociates the realizations of /a/ from /e/ and /o/ after /š ž/; and /a o/ from /e/ after /c/. The fact that in OM diffuse and nondiffuse vowels are consistently kept apart in unstressed position suggests that the hierarchy of features ranks diffuse/nondiffuse above compact/noncompact (Figure 21).

First Pretonic	After Hard Cons./Anlaut	After /c/	After /š ž/	After Soft Cons.
/a/	ʌ			
/o/			(ɨ)	i
/e/		(ɨ)	(ɨ)	
/i/				
/u/	u			

FIGURE 20. Contemporary Standard Russian (CSR) Vocalism

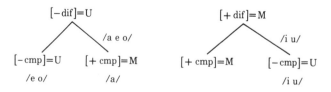

FIGURE 21. Old Muscovite Vowel System (partial)

With reference to this hierarchy and its relative rank order of diffuse/nondiffuse vis-à-vis compact/noncompact, we can formulate the following rules to account for vowel reduction in OM. First, /a o/ are implemented as /e/ ([eⁱ] automatically after sharp consonants and [eⁱ] after hard) when the immediately preceding consonant is one of /č š ž/; and as /a/ (phonetically [ɑ]) after /c/. Second, all three qualitatively reducible vowels /a e o/ are rendered as /e/ (phonetically [eⁱ]) after sharp consonants unmarked for stridency (the latter set including all soft consonants but /c/); and as /a/ (phonetically [ɑ]) after plain consonants similarly unmarked for the stridency feature.[34] Note that the environment specifications contained in the two rules are mutually exclusive.

The first innovation in the OM rule component is the introduction of *ikan'e*, well documented at the turn of the century among young Muscovites by Košutič (1919). In terms of the relations which characterize the feature hierarchy of OM (Fig. 22), this innovation can be easily understood as the confirmation of an equivalence between the markedness values of /e/ and /i/: though opposed by diffuseness, their unmarked status for compactness facilitated the change of reduced vowels as necessarily nondiffuse to that of facultatively diffuse. Existent prior to and concomitant with the inception of *ikan'e*, however, was the inherent ambiguity of /i u/ with respect to their markedness value for the compactness feature. Since these two phonemes were unopposed to a [+ dif + cmp] counterpart, their markedness value could be reversed from U to M in accordance with the principle of markedness reversal in redundant features. But the exploitation of this ambiguity entailed an eventual reinterpretation of the feature hierarchy, failing which the rules of vowel reduction would have ceased to be phonologically motivated in the sense of the eleventh assumption of a semeiotic theory of phonological structure enunciated earlier, that productive rules necessarily mirror the hierarchy of diacritic category signs by being congruous or coherent with the relations which underlie it. The equation of /i u/ with /a/ as both [M cmp]—i.e., the consistent assignment of a marked value to /i u/ in virtue of their interpretation as redundantly [— cmp]—was the key triggering factor in the reordering of the diffuseness and compactness features relative to each other (Figure 23).

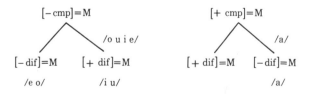

FIGURE 22. CSR Vowel System (partial)

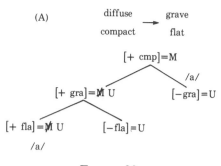

FIGURE 23

Before proceeding to the rules corresponding to this hierarchy it should be noted that the relationship between the two tonality features, gravity and flatness, is directly contingent on the internal rank order of the superordinate features, compactness and diffuseness. Indeed, as in OM (Fig. 18), when diffuseness ranks above compactness, then gravity is superordinate to flatness and the resultant markedness assignments are, illustratively, as follows for /a/ (Figure 23). However, when compactness ranks higher than diffuseness, as in Fig. 22, reflecting the situation in CSR, the flatness feature is superordinate to the gravity feature, with the additional difference that the pertinent feature term is acuteness rather than gravity, but the markedness assignments are identical; cf. Figures 18 and 24.

Now, in conformity with the hierarchy of CSR (Figure 22), the two rules which accounted for vowel reduction in OM were recast to reflect the severance of /a/ from /e o/ after /š ž/, occasioned originally by the introduction of *ikan'e*. First /e o/ came to be implemented as /i/ after /š ž c č/. Second, there came about uniform implementation of /a e o/ after sharp, resp. plain consonants: after the former, the phonetic value is [iᵉ];

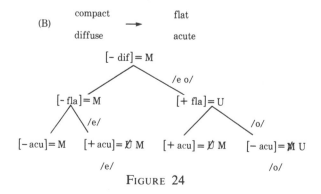

FIGURE 24

after the latter, the phonetic value is [ʌ]. Thus /a/ now behaves after all [M str] segments exactly as it does after [U str] segments, e.g. šagí [šʌg'í], žará [žʌrá], carít' [cʌr'it'], časý [č'iᵉsɨ́], tjanút' [t'iᵉnut'], etc.

It is clear, moreover, that the elimination of the pronunciation of /a/ as /i/ after /š ž/ was an altogether natural consequence of the introduction of *ikan'e* and the concomitant reordering of the hierarchy of diacritic signs, since this OM pronunciation was inconsistent with the new hierarchy which ranked compactness above diffuseness. The maintenance, therefore, of *ikan'e* after /š ž/ as part of OM must be viewed as the outcome of adaptive rules, which slowly but inexorably gave way to the new norms, leaving only the residue of archaisms such as *žalet'* [žɨl'ét'], *lošadej* [ləšɨd'éj], *pod bešamel'ju* [pədb‚ьšɨm'él'ju], etc.

The several phonological changes examined in connection with the recent historical development of Russian unstressed vocalism are, of course, not uniformly similar in kind. The first change—the innovation known as *ikan'e*—was 'caused' (if one can speak of causation) by the exploitation, by a new generation of speakers, of a phonological ambiguity in the hierarchy of diacritic signs which corresponded to the implementation rules of the older generation. As soon as this reinterpretation had been introduced, a reversal in the rank order of the two diacritic categories in question became at least a strong possibility. This second structural ambiguity was duly exploited by succeeding generations of Russian speakers. And it was this second change, the restructuring of the hierarchy, which led to or 'caused' the pronunciation of first pretonic /a/ to be dissociated from that of /e o/ after /š ž/.

IV

Morphophonemics and Morphology

1. Anaptyxis and Russian Word Structure

A. Substantival Derivation

The cornerstone of a general understanding of word structure, specifically of morphophonemics, is what I have called the *principle of markedness complementarity* (Shapiro 1974c:34; cf. Shapiro 1972:359). Grossly considered, this principle states that oppositely marked stems and desinences attract, identically marked stems and desinences repel. For instance, to illustrate using data genetically unconnected with Russian, in Japanese one may assume that vocalic stems (i.e., those ending in a vowel) are unmarked, while consonantal stems (i.e., those ending in a consonant or glide) are marked.[1] Similarly, we may assume that vocalic desinences (those beginning in a vowel) are unmarked, whereas consonantal desinences (those beginning in a consonant or glide) are marked. One may (and, ultimately, must) assume this when confronted, first of all, by the alternations of the nonpreterite desinence *u* ∼ *ru: tabe-ru* 'eat,' *iki-ru* 'live,' *nusum-u* 'steal,' *kos-u* 'cross,' etc.

The nonpreterite unmarked tense is realized by a marked desinence alternant *ru* and an unmarked desinence alternant *u*. With unmarked stems such as *tabe,* the principle of markedness complementarity dictates the juxtaposition of *ru,* the marked nonpreterite desinence. Conversely, with marked stems like *yom* 'read,' the same principle dictates the juxtaposition of *u,* the unmarked nonpreterite desinence.

The preterite desinence *ta* is marked, being consonantal, hence the concatenation with it of unmarked (vocalic) stems, as in *tabeta* 'ate' and *ikita* 'lived.' When it comes to consonantal stems, which are marked, the

preterite desinence remains *ta*. However, in accordance with the principle
of markedness complementarity, the stem final [M str] segment of the
nonpreterite alternates with an [U str] segment in the preterite stem (Table
7).

TABLE 7

Japanese Verbs

	nonpreterite			preterite
ŋ ~ y	oyog-u	'swim'		oyoy-da
m ~ n	yom-u	'read'		yon-da
k ~ y	aruk-u	'walk'		aruy-ta
b ~ n	yob-u	'call'		yon-da
w ~ t	kaw-u	'buy'		kat-ta
r ~ t	kar-u	'cut'		kat-ta
s ~ s	sas-u	'pierce'		sas-ita[2]
n ~ n	sin-u	'die'		sin-da

Note that stems ending in *s* and *n* (*sas* and *sin*) do not alternate the stem
final segment (cf. n. 2), since these segments are both unmarked for
stridency.

The above analysis of Japanese conjugation is by way of introduction
to a detailed examination of vowel/zero alternations in the Russian
substantive. My aim once again is to capture the essentially semeiotic
nature of the morphophonemic alternations in terms of a theory of
markedness which includes (inter alia) the principle of markedness
complementarity.

Russian, along with the other Slavic languages, evinces alternations of
vowel with zero throughout its morphophonemic component. Historically,
these alternations correspond to the so-called jers, which were reduced
vowels in Common Slavic. In all the Slavic languages these reduced vowels
were either lost or developed into 'full' (unreduced) vowels, depending on a
host of factors. In Old Russian their syncope in certain positions and their
maintenance in others, within one and the same stem, gave rise to the
alternations that now abound in Russian. Isačenko (1970) marshalled
much of the pertinent data and formulated an impressive array of plausible
rules to describe both the diachronic and the synchronic situations.[3]
However, neither he nor any other student of the problem produced a
coherent explanation of the phenomenon itself. What follows is an attempt
to explain vowel/zero alternations in terms which are of sufficient
generality as to be applicable as explanantes of typologically congruent
morphophonemic phenomena in other languages as well. These terms will
facilitate an answer to the question regarding the nature of the relationship
between derivation and inflection raised by Stankiewicz (1962) and Worth
(1967a, 1967b, 1968b) among others. The patent concreteness of the sign

system represented by Russian morphophonemics will also suggest important inferences about the deep vs. surface structure dichotomy, buttressing those of the preceding section.

In order to understand the process of vowel alternating with zero in stems, we must start with the markedness values of certain oppositions within pertinent grammatical categories. Russian substantives which have a $\emptyset$ desinence in the nom sg can be one of two genders, fem or masc. The value of this $\emptyset$ is contextually dependent on the value of the category which it expresses formally (cf. Shapiro 1972b). Specifically, in a marked grammatical context zero has the opposite sign value, viz. unmarked; and vice versa.

Since Russian substantival desinences simultaneously express membership in several grammatical categories (gender, number, case), the markedness value of a desinence must be *synthetic,* i.e., representative of all pertinent categories.[4] The synthetic markedness value is assigned on the basis of presence vs. absence of a marked category among the categorial correlates of a given desinence.[5] Thus, in accordance with this criterion, nom sg desinences are designated [U des] while gen pl are designated [M des]. The synthetic markedness value of $\emptyset$ assigned in terms of these relations is M in the context of nom sg and U elsewhere in the paradigm.

As a working hypothesis one can go a step further and posit the condition of complementarity obtaining between stem and desinence as regards their respective markedness value (again, the principle of markedness complementarity). More specifically, if one assumes the syntagmatic manifestation of grammatical units to proceed by concatenation of opposite valued entities (U + M or M + U, rather than U + U or M + M), then the markedness value of a stem preceding a $\emptyset$ desinence must differ from the value of that desinence. However, these relationships between stem and desinence obtain only if there is no change in the stem shape as regards vowels. If there is such a change—i.e., an alternation of vowel and zero—the markedness value of the stem before a zero desinence is reversed, and it is this new, reversed value that is utilized in derivation (but not in inflection).[6]

This line of argumentation can be exploited to comprehend peculiarities of the Russian declensional system insofar as vowel/zero alternations are concerned. Six substantives of the 3rd (chiefly fem) declension display a vowel/zero alternation: *ljubóv'* 'love,' *neljubóv'* 'dislike,' *cérkov'* 'church,' *rož'* 'rye,' *lož'* 'falsehood,' *voš'* 'louse.'[7] The vowel *o* is present in the nom sg and instrumental sg while being absent elsewhere in the paradigm. In other words, the vowel appears just in case the stem is attached to either a zero desinence or one that begins with a nonvocalic segment (the *j* of *ju*).[8] As in Japanese, Russian desinences are unmarked when vocalic, marked when consonantal. This means that, in conformity with the principle of markedness complementarity vis-à-vis stem and desinence values, one should expect the unmarked form of the stem to occur before *ju,* a marked desinence. This is, indeed, what takes place (Figure 25).

Note that for derivational purposes the sign value of the stem is reversed so that *voš'* = Ʋ M and *ljubóv'* = Ʋ M. It is this reversed value which manifests itself in *ljubóvnyj* [adj], *vóška* [dim], etc.

A similar pattern can be detected in the 1st (masc) declension, with important consequences for derivation. Consider the following schema for *bagor/bagra* 'gaff' and *lob/lba* 'forehead' (Figure 26).

The value of the Ø desinence of the nom sg is M, since the category is evaluated synthetically as U. This makes the stem U. In derivation, however, due to the discrepancy in stem shape between the maximally unmarked form and the other forms in the paradigm, the markedness values are reversed *in the pre-zero shape only,* rendering the latter M.[9] This reversal occurs in *bagór/bagrá* and all other syllabic stems. However, in dealing with nonsyllabic stems like *lob/lba* syllabicity may become relevant. More precisely, the fact that nonsyllabic stems are marked for syllabicity, syllabic stems being unmarked, effects yet another reversal in markedness values. Thus *lob,* the pre-zero stem shape, ends up—after two

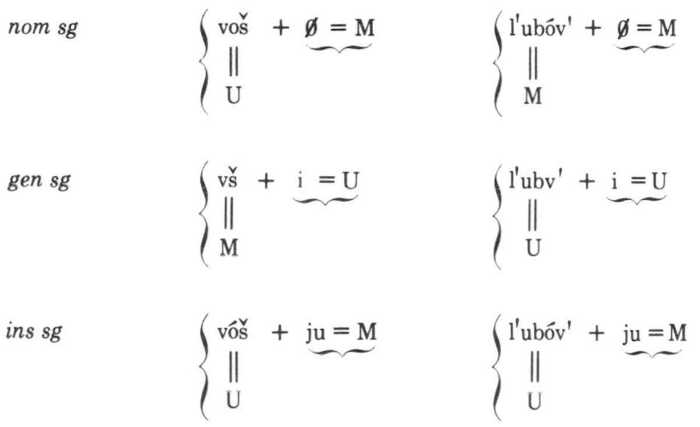

$$
\begin{aligned}
nom\ sg \qquad & \left\{ \begin{array}{l} \text{voš} \ + \ \emptyset = M \\ \quad \| \\ \quad U \end{array} \right.
& \left\{ \begin{array}{l} \text{l'ubóv'} + \ \emptyset = M \\ \quad \| \\ \quad M \end{array} \right. \\[2em]
gen\ sg \qquad & \left\{ \begin{array}{l} \text{vš} \ + \ i = U \\ \quad \| \\ \quad M \end{array} \right.
& \left\{ \begin{array}{l} \text{l'ubv'} + \ i = U \\ \quad \| \\ \quad U \end{array} \right. \\[2em]
ins\ sg \qquad & \left\{ \begin{array}{l} \text{vóš} \ + \ ju = M \\ \quad \| \\ \quad U \end{array} \right.
& \left\{ \begin{array}{l} \text{l'ubóv'} + \ ju = M \\ \quad \| \\ \quad U \end{array} \right.
\end{aligned}
$$

FIGURE 25.

$$
\begin{aligned}
nom\ sg \qquad & \left\{ \begin{array}{l} \text{bagór} \ + \ \emptyset = M \\ \quad \| \\ \quad Ʋ\ M \end{array} \right.
& \left\{ \begin{array}{l} \text{lob} + \ \emptyset = M \\ \quad \| \\ \quad Ʋ\ M\ U \end{array} \right. \\[2em]
gen\ sg \qquad & \left\{ \begin{array}{l} \text{bagr} \ + \ á = U \\ \quad \| \\ \quad M \end{array} \right.
& \left\{ \begin{array}{l} \text{lb} + \ a = U \\ \quad \| \\ \quad M \end{array} \right.
\end{aligned}
$$

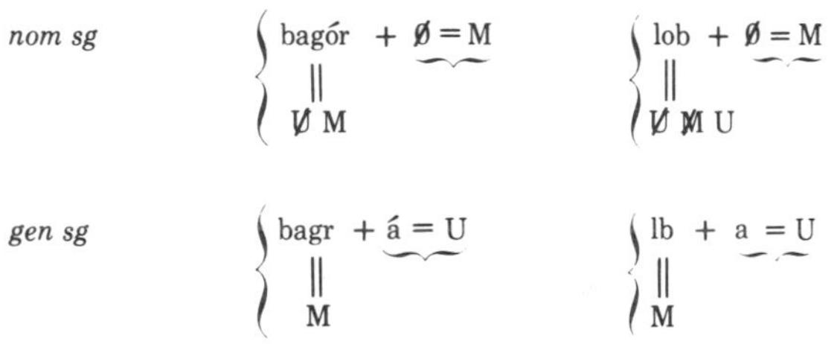

FIGURE 26

markedness reversals—being an unmarked stem (see below for counter-examples).

Before going any further, I would like to clarify the meaning of markedness reversal as it applies to hierarchies of contexts (among the latter are grammatical as well as phonological categories). If syllabicity, for instance, is said to effect a reversal of a markedness value that would otherwise obtain, this simply means that syllabicity has taken rank precedence over any other pertinent contexts in the hierarchy of contexts in which the relevant units are embedded. As importantly, these reversals must not be taken to mean some sort of process in time, such as a mutation or transformation. The meaning, consequently, of the assertion that there are two reversals in the above example—one attributable to the fact of a stem occurring before a zero desinence, the other attributable to the stem's syllabicity—is that syllabicity takes precedence in the hierarchy of contexts over two other contexts, that of (1) stem shape before desinences other than zero, and (2) stem shape before zero desinences. It is in this specific way that all of the grammatical categories and environment conditions that are part of structure can be seen to have a semeiotic relevance matching that of particular units. There is thus no contextless unit, nor unitless context in language, despite the evident possibility of isolating one from the other for purposes of analysis or inventorization.

Reversal occurs when elements of structure are dominated by a marked context, and it is this markedness dominance that is the semeiotic principle at work here. A change in rank associated with markedness dominance is to be understood as a diagrammatization of the semeiotic values of the units and contexts involved.

The process of complementary concatenation in derivation fuses unmarked stems with marked suffixes and marked stems with unmarked suffixes. In the case of derivational suffixes, as opposed to inflectional suffixes (desinences), it is the vocalic suffixes that are marked and the consonantal ones that are unmarked (cf. the Japanese situation). Hence, derivatives such as *bagórščik* 'gaffer' and *lobovój* 'forehead' [adj] can be analyzed in the following manner:

$$[M] \quad + \quad [U]$$
$$\text{bagór} \quad + \quad \text{šč} \quad + \quad \text{ik} \quad + \quad \emptyset$$

$$[U] \quad + \quad [M]$$
$$\text{lob} \quad + \quad \text{ov} \quad + \quad \text{ój}$$

It is instructive to examine the way in which the process of concatenation affects certain Russian diminutives, viz. masc substantives in #*k* and *ik*. If one assumes (contrary to the usual practice) that suffixes containing a vowel/zero alternation instead of a stable (full) vowel are consonantal, the #*k* is assigned to the category of unmarked suffixes, while *ik* is assigned to the category of marked suffixes. In such masc diminutives as *čéxlik* 'cover,' *kóvrik* 'rug,' *órlik* 'eagle' whose correlate nondiminutive stems display a vowel/zero alternation (e.g. *čexól/čexlá*), it is the unmarked form of the stem that appears with the marked form of the suffix. Conversely, the concatenation of the unmarked suffix #*k* occasions the utilization of the marked stem form, hence *kogotók* (*kógot'/kógtja* 'talon'), *nogotók* (*nógot'/nógtja* 'nail'), etc. Note, importantly, the difference in stem shape between *čéxlik,* on the one hand, and *čexolók* (Dal' 1934:1292) or *čexól'čik,* on the other, wherein the sole conditioning factor is the markedness value of the suffix. In this connection, the shape of the presuffixal element in *čexól'čik, kovĕrčik* 'rug' [dim], *vixórčik* 'cowlick' [dim] can be seen to be #*c,* that is the diminutive suffix functioning here as a concatenator (cf. Shapiro 1967).[10]

Feminine and neuter diminutives are no less corroborative of the concatenation principle enunciated above. In order to ascertain this, consider first the relationships expressed by the following chart using *zemljá* 'land' and *sukn6* 'linen' as examples (Figure 27).

Accordingly, the stem shape which contains a vowel is M and will appear in any derivatives utilizing an unmarked suffix. This situation can be exemplified by such formations as *zemél'ka, sukónce, búločka* (*búlka/ búlok* 'roll'), *okóško* (*oknó/ókon* 'window'). In fact, the entire network of graded affectives (cf. Stankiewicz 1968), insofar as their morphophonemics is concerned, conforms to the principle of markedness complementarity, e.g. *golová/golóvka/golóvočka* 'head,' *síto/sítce/sítečko* 'sieve,' *bob/ bobók/bobóček* 'bean.'

The markedness values of stems which undergo no anaptyxis on the inflectional level but do so on the derivational level require special attention. In contradistinction to consonant clusters preceding desinences, those clusters (excepting *st* and *zd*)[11] which precede derivational suffixes are all potentially susceptible of anaptyxis.[12] Most such clusters, as will become evident below, do undergo anaptyxis; however, only those ending in a glide—which is marked for both vocalicity and consonantality—must perforce undergo it. Hence any cluster ending in *j* will intercalate the vowel

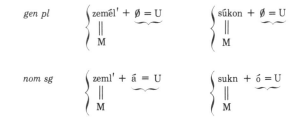

FIGURE 27.

e before it, e.g. *pit'ë* 'drink' → *pitéjnyj* [adj], *stat'já* 'article' → *statéjka* [dim], etc.

With respect to the processes to be analyzed, stems must be distinguished by declension type, reflecting their different treatment before marked and unmarked zeros (cf. Figures 27 and 28). Masculine stems ending in a consonant cluster before the ∅ desinence of the nom sg maintain the markedness value assigned them by extension of the criterion governing synthetic markedness, viz. U. Thus the stem value of *korábl'* 'ship,' which intercalates no vowel between the stem final consonants of the nom sg, is U. This, in turn, means that the corresponding marked shape of the stem is anaptyctic, i.e., *korabel'*. Indeed, it is the latter form of the stem that appears before unmarked derivational (viz. consonantal) suffixes: *korabél'nyj* [adj], *korabél'ščik* 'mariner'; cf. *koráblik* [dim] and *korablíško* [pej]. Similarly, consider the behavior of *vengr* 'Hungarian.' It is the marked form of the stem, viz. *venger,* which appears before consonantal derivational suffixes: *vengérka* [fem], *vengérskij* [adj]. *vengérec* [obsolete masc].[13] This process is not confined to the older vocabulary; note, for example, *dirižábl'* 'dirigible' but *dirižábel'nyj* [adj]. The analysis proffered here also has the advantage of obviating the necessity for invoking dialect borrowing in cases like *žurávl'* 'crane' but *žuravél'nik* 'geranium.' It should be borne in mind, on comparing e.g. *ugórskij* 'Ugric' [adj] (cf. *úgry* 'Ugrians') with *négrskij* 'negro' [adj] or *gágrskij* 'Gagra' [adj], that anaptyxis—with its semeiotic motivation—can now be circumvented in contemporary standard Russian, especially in non-Russian nomina propria. At the same time it is important to realize that *négrskij* is a rarer version of *negritjánskij,* while *gágrskij* is replaced in colloquial Russian by *gágrinskij* (Superanskaja 1966:259). Clearly, however, in the face of *njujórkskij* 'New York' [adj], *oksfórdskij* 'Oxford' [adj], *sévrskij* 'Sèvre' [adj], *njukásl'skij* 'Newcastle' [adj], etc. there can be no doubt that the rules are easily bent to accommodate foreign items. Nonetheless, it is the foreignness of the exceptions which proves the systematic validity of the rules.[14]

In nonmasculine items, whose stem occurs before the ∅ desinence in the gen pl, it is markedness reversal which figures prominently in the occurrence of anaptyxis. The stem value of *týkva* 'pumpkin,' *búkva* 'letter,' *iglá* 'needle,' *igrá* 'game,' *baraxló* 'junk,' etc. for the purposes of derivation is opposite that expected, since these items fail to undergo anaptyxis in the gen pl *though they ought to* (see section B, below). Hence, before ∅, the assigned value M is reversed to U, entailing the corresponding assignment of M to the anaptyctic stem shapes *tykov, bukov, igol, igor, baraxol,* etc. The latter shapes are extant in derivatives containing consonantal suffixes: *týkovka* [dim], *búkovka* [dim], *igólka* [dim], *igól'nyj* [adj], *igórka* [dim], *igórnyj* [adj], *baraxólka* 'flea market,' *baraxól'nyj* [adj], *baraxól'ščik* 'junkman,' etc. The latter three items are particularly revealing, for no gen pl form of *baraxló* (a collective singulare tantum) exists. This means that markedness reversal is here effected on the extant stem shape *baraxl*, such that its value as M is reversed to U, in turn rendering *baraxol* marked; cf. *kéglja* → *kégel'nyj* [adj] 'tenpin.' Similarly, fluctuation in the form of the gen pl does not alter the derivational result. Thus *usád'ba* 'estate,' whose gen pl is either *usád'b* or *usádeb*, nonetheless gives rise to *usádebnyj* [adj], since the markedness value of the anaptyctic stem shape is M regardless. Given gen pl *usádeb*, whose markedness value is M, *usádebnyj* results from the concatenation of the anaptyctic stem with the unmarked consonantal suffix # *n*. Given *usád'b*, whose markedness value is also M, the presence of a consonant cluster which ought to undergo anaptyxis but does not in stem final position before ∅ entails a markedness reversal, such that the non-anaptyctic stem shape becomes U, rendering, in turn, the anaptyctic shape M. The result in either instance, consequently, is *usádebnyj;* cf. *dýšlo/dýšl* ~ *dýšel* → *dýšel'ce* 'thill' [dim]. This accounts, incidentally, for the total absence of formal doublets in items derived from stems (like *usád'ba*) which vacillate in the gen pl, and more generally, before any ∅ desinence.

In some isolated instances of verb/substantive derivational relations, the substantive displays a stable full vowel while the correlate verb syncopates it. The 3rd declension feminines *lest'* 'flattery,' *čest'* 'honor,' and *mest'* 'revenge' are correlated with the verbs *l'stit'* 'flatter,' *čtit'* 'honor,'[15] and *mstit'* 'avenge' (cf. Isačenko 1970:92-3).

The examples of Figure 28 are to be augmented by, on the one hand, *čéstnyj* 'honest,' *počët* 'esteem,' *čéstvovat'* 'honor,' *čëtkij* 'distinct,' *otméstka* 'spite'; and on the other, by *čtec* 'reader,' *učtívyj* 'polite,' *mstítel'* 'avenger.' Note that *l'stec* is regular despite the fact that the suffix # *c* appears, since the stable full vowel (gen *l'stecá*, dat *l'stecú*, etc.) renders the suffix marked, i.e., tantamount to a vocalic one; cf. *čtec/čtecá*.

A similar relationship can be discerned in *plésen'/pléseni* 'mould' → *plesnevét'* 'to be covered with mould,' *plesnevój* [adj]; and *kópot'/ kópoti* 'soot' → *koptít'* 'smoke.'

By a process of abduction from the above examples, certain foreign loan words in Russian are shaped in conformity with the relations characterizing *lest'* → *l'stit'* (cf. Worth 1968c:121-2). Although *mébel'*

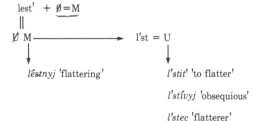

FIGURE 28.

'furniture' displays no alternation of vowel and zero, the related verb is *meblirovát'* 'furnish.' This kind of infrequent alternation is not limited to feminine stems, however. Thus *šáber/šábera* 'scraper' is correlated with *šábrit'*.[16] The only coherent hypothesis which suggests itself by way of explanation is as follows.

The last vowel of the stem, when unstressed and followed by a liquid, can be interpreted as one which *ought to syncopate* before real (i.e., non-zero) desinences. This interpretation is motivated in part by utilizing the converse of the relations dictating anaptyxis—the presence of a stem final consonant cluster, e.g. *cífra* 'figure,' gen pl *cifr,* but *cíferka* [dim] (cf. Čurganova 1971:533). It is further supported by the existence of older autochthonous alternating items such as *lest'* ~ *l'stit'*. Indeed, the latter example and its aforementioned congeners can only be explained in precisely the same manner, by the action of markedness reversal on the value of the pre-zero stem shape. This is reflected in Fig. 28. The reversal changes the value U to M and is conditioned by the situation whereby an alternation ought to exist in the substantival paradigm but does not in fact occur. (Cf. the reversal of *tykv,* motivating *týkovka* above.)

The semeiotic scheme adduced above in explanation of Russian vowel/zero alternations appears to be defective in two respects. First, it does not clarify the discrepancy between items such as *lbíško* 'forehead' [pej] and *rotíško* 'mouth' [pej], i.e., those with non-syllabic bases (cf. *lob/lba, rot/rta*). Second, it does not explain the (stress conditioned) discrepancies between items in *-en'* and adjectival derivatives in *ist,* e.g. *kremén'/kremnjá* 'flint' → *kremnístyj, kóren'/kórnja* 'root' → *kornístyj, grében'/grébnja* 'crest' → *grebnístyj,* on the one hand; and *kámen'/kámnja* 'stone' → *kamenístyj, stúden'/stúdnja* 'galantine' → *studenístyj,* on the other.

With respect to nonsyllabic bases, as was noted earlier, there may or may not be a markedness reversal conditioned by syllabicity. That is to say, the fact that a given base is nonsyllabic may or may not constitute a semeiotically relevant context. Consequently, different derivational stems will or will not evince the nonsyllabic shape of the base, the choice being tied to specific items. Furthermore, this ambivalence gives rise to doublets, e.g. *rtíšče* ~ *rotíšče* 'mouth' [aug], *rotóvyj* ~ *rtóvyj* 'oral,' *l'nóvyj* ~ *lënovyj* 'flaxen.' Schematically, the choice can be represented as in Figure 29.

Given the relations of Figure 29, one might assume that syllabicity is more often pertinent than not. Thus, for tentative illustrative purposes, if one examines the various correlates of *lob,* it appears to be the evaluation of the anaptyctic stem shape as unmarked that motivates *lobán* 'person with a prominent forehead,' *lobástyj* 'with a big forehead' [adj], *lóbik* [dim], *lobotrjás* 'lazybones,' *lobovój* [adj]; also *belolóbyj* 'white foreheaded'

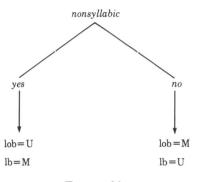

nonsyllabic

yes   no

lob = U   lob = M
lb = M   lb = U

FIGURE 29

[adj] and all other bahuvrihi composita (cf. Isačenko 1972), wherein the zero suffix is evaluated as marked. On the other hand, *lbíško* [pej] and *lbíšče* [aug] are motivated by the relations conditioned in 'part by the irrelevance of syllabicity, as are *lobók* 'pubis' and *lóbnyj* [adj]. The predominance of the latter evaluation becomes transparent when one confronts the *lob* word family with that of *lën* 'flax.' Here it is *l'njanój* [adj], *l'novód* 'flax raiser,' *l'nóvyj* [adj], *lenók* [dim]. But the picture is essentially a variegated one: cf. *lëd* 'ice,' *ledokól* 'icebreaker,' *ledjanój* [adj], *ledóvyj* [adj], *ledók* [dim], *ledenét'* 'grow icy,' *l'dína* 'ice floe,' *ledýška* 'small piece of ice,' *l'dístyj* 'icy,' etc. A look at Dal' (1934) will suffice to confirm this impression of variegatedness.

With respect to the possible stress conditioning of *kremnístyj* vs. *kamenístyj*, it should first be pointed out that the evidence of Dal' is much more mottled than that of the standard lexicographic sources. Russian dialects have both *grebnístyj* and *grebenístyj*, *kamenístyj* and *kamnístyj*, *korenístyj* and *kornístyj*. At the same time, we find only *studenístyj* and *kremnístyj*. This state of affairs can be interpreted as hinging on the stress of the base. If one assumes that stress assignment rules generally mirror the markedness values of stem variants, then fixed stem stress in words in *-en'* is at variance with the divergent stem values of these items due to the vowel/zero alternation. Thus *stúden'/stúdnja* with fixed stem-initial stress manifests a discrepancy between the markedness values of the variable stem shapes—M before ∅ and U before real desinences—and the stress assignment. The marked stem shape should be stressless, the unmarked stressed. This is, indeed, the situation with *kremén'/kremnjá*. Hence in the abstract context of a discrepancy between stem value and stress, the expected derivational value of the pre-zero stem shape is reversed. For *stúden'* this yields the value U (Ʋ M U)—after two reversals. For *kremén'*, where there is no discrepancy, only one reversal takes place— the one

entailed by the differing inflectional stem shapes—and the variant *kremén'*
is evaluated as M (Ṿ M). These considerations, therefore, constitute the
explanantes of *studenístyj* and *kremnístyj,* respectively.

Let us summarize the conditions under which markedness reversal is
said to occur in the inflectional paradigm vis-à-vis the implementation of
inflectional stems in the derivational system.

A. Masc nom sg, where there is an inflectional vowel/zero alternation
in the paradigm, e.g. *bagór/bagrá → bagórščik, kovër/kovrá → kóvrik.*

B. Gen pl, where anaptyxis fails to occur despite the presence of the
appropriate stem final cluster, e.g. *tykv ~ týkovka, igr ~ igórnyj, dyšl ~
dýšel'ce, usád'b ~ usádebnyj.*

C. Stems which do not appear before ∅ e.g. *baraxlo ~ baraxólka,
kéglja ~ kégel'nyj.*

D. Nonsyllabic stems (optional), e.g. *lob ~ lobotrjás ~ lobovój, lëd
~ ledóvyj ~ ledýška.*

The analysis of the Russian data just completed furnishes us with
several theoretical implications which go to the heart of a number of
contemporary methodological issues in linguistics. First, it lends a
significant measure of credence and coherence to the largely intuitive
assertions of scholars like Stankiewicz (1962) and especially Worth (1967a,
1967b, 1968b) who have groped to hypostatize their notion that a
fundamental cleavage exists between the (albeit interdependent) inflectional and derivational systems. Simultaneously, the proclivity to identify a
methodological advance in treating this problem with the establishment of
rigorous formalisms, typified by Worth (1967b, 1968a), can now be
adjudged as a tack unconducive to explanatory insight. For it is only by
considering the constitutive entities of morphophonemics as parts of a
semeiotic—a system of signs—in which grammatical categories and their
sign values are not only pertinent but inexcludable, that the precise relation
between inflectional and derivational stem can be made perspicuous. The
feasibility of kneading the data into one or another formalized descriptive
configuration must not be permitted to obfuscate the fundamentally
semeiotic nature of all grammatical phenomena.

The analysis pursued in the foregoing pages is also relevant to the
question of the sign function of morphophonemic rules (raised by
Andersen 1969a). The sign values which morphophonemic rules make
reference to can now be acknowledged as more complex than those
referred to by phonological rules. Nevertheless, the relatively small
measure of productivity characteristic of morphophonemic rules does not
interfere with their fundamentally semeiotic nature. In short, morphophonemic rules must not be viewed merely as a 'junk pile' of old
phonological rules which have fallen into desuetude. One cannot emphasize
their semeiotically motivated character enough, there being only a

difference in details of implementation from that of phonological rules.

Finally, one aspect of the semeiotic explored above merits careful scrutiny inasmuch as it permits certain telling inferences about the deep vs. surface structure dichotomy which lies at the base of much contemporary linguistic theorizing. The behavior of Russian stems with regard to vowel/zero alternations was explained by making explicit reference to the markedness values with which these stems were endowed in their *surface* manifestations before zero desinences. Indeed, one of the significant and ultimately most fruitful methodological gambits exploited in the analysis was the deliberate avoidance of generalized 'deep structure' stem shapes as points of departure. In examining the difference, for example, between *zemljá* and *zemél'nyj,* the notion of an underlying stem shape (*zem' #l'*) was eschewed as irrelevant, and it was rather the sign values of the stem—in varying but nonetheless concrete grammatical environments—that proved pivotal to the erection of a successful explanatory edifice.

B. Nominal Inflection

The specific problem to be confronted here, continuing the analysis of anaptyxis, is the delineation of the conditions attendant upon the appearance in Russian inflection of a vowel between two consonants of a cluster containing two or more consonants. I have limited myself to an examination of this process—the alternation of vowel and zero—as it bears upon nominal inflection. The conjugate problem of specifying the conditions surrounding the maintenance of a vowel between two consonants of a stem falls outside my purview. As has been true generally, the ultimate aim here is once more the semeiotic motivation of the data.

Of the four possible ways in which consonant clusters can change—syncope (of one or more consonants), metathesis, anaptyxis (vowel insertion), and permutation (segment switching)—Russian morphophonemics evinces an overwhelming preference for anaptyxis (cf. Isačenko 1970 and Worth 1968), leaving syncope to be effected by the phonological implementation rules (cf. chapter 3, section 2) while eschewing the other two altogether.

The fundamental rule of inflectional anaptyxis in Russian consonant clusters is roughly this: two immediately contiguous consonants, both marked for the stridency feature, will intercalate an inserted vowel (*e* or *o*; v. below) before a zero desinence.[17] If there are more than two consonants in a cluster, at least two contiguous ones of which are [M str], the vowel is nevertheless inserted before the final one, e.g. *korčem* 'tavern [gen pl]'. This 'anaptyxis rule' may be viewed as effecting a simplification of the grammar, in that a marked sequence becomes an unmarked one.

The only consonant clusters which never undergo insertion are, understandably, *st* and *zd,* since these are the only sequences which are always unambiguously interpreted as [U str] + [U str]. Although /t d/ are susceptible of interpretation variously as [U str] or [M str] in other contexts, they appear to be invariably [U str] when preceded by *s* or *z* and followed by ∅.

All sequences other than *st*/*zd*, therefore, can undergo anaptyxis, but there is a graded gamut of susceptibility which hinges on markedness values and their assimilation.

Although the usual distinctive feature treatment of Russian (e.g. Halle 1959) has not regarded the liquids /l l' r r'/ as being distinguished by acuteness, there appears to be some evidence (cf. Panov 1967:126) that /l l'/ may be distinctively [—acute], /r r'/ distinctively [+acute].[18] The redundancy or distinctiveness of acuteness in liquids appears to depend on the sequential context. Indeed, if the consonant which flanks a liquid is itself distinguished by the acuteness feature, so is the liquid; and conversely, if the contiguous consonant is redundantly [±acute], acuteness is similarly redundant in liquids. Since it is unmarked for a feature to be distinctive in a particular segment and marked for it to be redundant in that segment, this rule can be viewed as a markedness assimilation rule.

The rules mentioned so far have an obvious and important connection. The sign value of liquids with respect to the stridency feature (which is invariably redundant in them) will depend on the second rule. Practically, this means that acuteness is distinctive in liquids when the latter are preceded or followed by any segment other than velars and palatals (and other liquids). Although the 'liquid rule' does not appear to be firmly established in Russian as yet, we can nonetheless attribute the preponderant majority of distributional facts to its workings. The veracity of this assertion can be checked not only against the preferred (Avanesov and Ožegov 1959) forms of the gen pl *dýšl* 'pole' and *kárg* 'hag,' but also by the diachronic shift from older *ívolog* 'orioles,' *távolog* 'meadow-sweets,' *ígol* 'needles,' *ígor* 'games' to the CSR forms *ívolg, távolg, ígl, ígr*. (Cf. *vólex* 'alder trees,' *íkor* 'calves' in Kirparsky 1967:125-7, CSR *ól'x, íkr*). Also *mókor* 'wet' → *mokr*. Cf. *tjagl* 'taxes' ~ *tjágol* (Zaliznjak 1967: 270), *kúkol* 'dolls' ~ *kukl, svëkol* 'beets' ~ *svëkl* (Toporov 1971:161-2).

Since liquids must be distinguished by either acuteness or abruptness, they are not subject to the rule (unless acuteness is distinctive in them) which varies the distinctiveness of abruptness in segments which are susceptible of such a vacillation, viz. /f f' p p' b b' t t' d d' m m' n n' l l' r r'/, depending on whether the surrounding consonants are or are not diacritically abrupt. This 'abruptness rule' goes together with a rule which specifies the status of the (syncategorematic) features of abruptness and stridency in nasal consonants. Nasals are diacritically nonstrident when redundantly abrupt, and vice versa.

Resulting from the application of these two rules are gen pl *svërl* 'drills,' *vobl* 'voblas,' *utr* 'mornings,' *nedr* 'wombs,' *pros'b* 'requests,' *capf* 'pins,' *limf* 'lymphs,' *rifm* 'rhymes,' *pal'm* 'palm trees,' *travm* 'traumas,' *kosm* 'manes,' *voln* 'waves,' *ved'm* 'witches,' *bel'm* 'wall-eyes,' *obójm* 'chargers,' *vojn* 'soldiers,' *pojm* 'flood-lands,' etc. Cf. also the nom sg masc *ritm* 'rhythm,' *dërn* 'turf,' *tërn* 'sloe,' *čëln* 'dug-out,' *dobr* 'kind,' *mudr* 'wise,' *ostr* 'sharp'; but *pólon* 'full.'

The varying distinctiveness of the abruptness feature in the appropriate segments results in differing shapes of stems which are phonologically identical. Thus, in *sedló* 'saddle'/GP *sëdel,* the /d/ has been definitively interpreted as nondiacritically abrupt. Consequently, /l/ is diacritically abrupt, and both segments are, moreover, thereby assigned the value [M str]. Hence, the appearance of an anaptyctic vowel. But in *pútla*/GP *putl* or *pódlyj* 'mean'/masc short *podl,* /t d/ are interpreted as diacritically abrupt, implying the opposite interpretation for /l/. Ultimately, this means that /t d/ are assigned the value U str, as is /l/. Therefore, anaptyxis does not occur. Cf. *óstr* and *ostër, mudr* but *bëder* 'thighs,' *mëtel* 'brooms' but *titl* 'tittles.'

Essentially the same analysis explains, on the one hand *vóbla*/gen pl *vobl,* and, on the other, *skrebló* 'flint tool'/gen pl *skrëbel.* If the markedness values of the segments involved are compared with respect to the stridency feature, then there will invariably be no two contiguous [M str] segments. This accounts for *vobl.* However, comparison of values with respect to abruptness will yield the two contiguous [M abr] segments conditioning anaptyxis, hence *skrëbel.*

This is precisely the analysis that explains vacillations such as gen pl *rusl* 'channels' ~ *rúsel, remësl* 'trades' ~ *remësel* (Zaliznjak 1967:270); or *čresl* 'loins' ~ *črésel* (Toporov 1971:161). Since /s/ is immutably distinguished by the abruptness feature (being [— abr]), there can be no fluctuation in its markedness value with respect to stridency, which is [U str]. However, /s/ is at the same time invariably [M abr], while /l/ is also [M abr] in the context of /s/. It is, to summarize, the ambiguity inherent in the distinctiveness and the markedness values of the syncategorematic features of abruptness and stridency that is complemented by and in part manifested through the anaptyxis rule of Russian nominal inflection.

The changes in gen pl forms undergone by stems like *arbá* are indicative of the preferred phonological interpretations in CSR. The older gen pl was *árob* (Zaliznjak 1967:270), at least as a possibility alongside *arb.* The former was eliminated, the latter retained. This must mean that contemporary speakers of Russian do not interpret /b/ as distinctively abrupt, at least in stem final position; cf. the elimination of *ízob* (Kiparsky 1967:126) as a possible variant of *izb.*

The relationships reflected in the 'abruptness rule' do not obtain when nasals are preceded by velars or palatals, i.e., by segments which are [M comp]. In that case, neither abruptness *nor* stridency is distinctive in nasals; hence /n/ is [M str], while /m/ is [U str]. This is again to be explained by markedness assimilation: in the context of segments marked for compactness, it is the marked property, redundancy, that characterizes the nasals with respect to abruptness and stridency.

As a direct consequence, one gets, on the one hand, gen pl *paradígm* 'paradigms,' *fižm* 'farthingales,' *sintágm* 'syntagmas'; on the other, *nóžen* 'scabbards'/*nožón, knjažón* 'princesses,' *mošón* 'pouches,' *ókon* 'windows,' *kúxon'* 'kitchens'; cf. masc nom sg *ogón'* 'fire.'

When there are more than two consonants in the stem final cluster, the rules continue to apply in the manner described. Thus, *korčém* (gen pl of *korčmá*) results because /m/ is [M str] and is contiguous to /č/, which is likewise [M str]. But in *astm* 'asthmas' (if the /t/ is unsycopated) /t/ is interpreted as diacritically abrupt.

When the nasals precede rather than follow velars or palatals, the abruptness rule may or may not apply, yielding doublets: gen pl *déneg* 'money'—*den'g* 'old coin,' *šáneg* 'pie'—*šan'g* (Toporov 1971:154). Since the anaptyctic forms are the only ones recognized as normative, the consistent implementation of the rule appears to be stabilizing here. This is supported by masc nom sg forms such as *frenč* 'service jacket,' *reváns* 'revenge'; cf. gen pl *zamš* 'suede,' *velikánš* 'giantesses.'

With the exception of *lask* 'caresses' (cf. *lások* 'weasels') and *vojsk* 'armies' any stem containing a final cluster ending in /k/—regardless of whether this segment is a suffix—will undergo anaptyxis in the gen pl: *bánok* 'cans,' *mások* 'masks,' *júbok* 'skirts,' *kírok* 'picks,' *kišók* 'guts,' *dosók* 'boards,' *kóšek* 'cats,' *šljúpok* 'boats,' *márok* 'stamps,' *pálok* 'sticks,' etc. This is equally true of masc short forms of adjectives: *lóvok* 'agile,' *xrúpok* 'fragile,' *tjážek* 'heavy,' etc. The only phonological factor which can be adduced to account for this property in /k/, as contrasted with clusters ending in /g/ or /x/ (cf. *pasx* 'Easters,' *kirx* 'churches'), is that /k/ receives an extra mark—over and above its doubly marked status as [M str] and [M abr]. In substantives this extra mark can only be attributable to the grammatical context (i.e., the genitive plural), since masc nom sg forms do not insert a vowel before /k/, cf. *park* 'park,' *vosk* 'wax,' *tal'k* 'talc,' *tomagávk* 'tomahawk,' *bank* 'bank,' etc.

A comparable situation can be observed when stems end in /n/ or /c/. In the first instance anaptyxis always occurs in the appropriate adjectival form, unless /n/ is preceded by itself, in which case two solutions are available (see below). Thus, whereas substantives may vacillate in the gen pl—e.g. *exídn* 'malicious' ∼ *exíden*, *dómen* 'furnaces' ∼ *domn*—in adjectives we find *búren* 'stormy,' *dréven* 'ancient,' *stróen* 'slender,' *dostóin* 'deserving,' *pólon* 'full,' *tésen* 'cramped,' *tóčen* 'exact,' *smešón* 'funny,' etc. Anaptyxis occurs, moreover, even when the cluster is /nn/: *stránen* 'strange,' *blagovónen* 'fragrant,' *neprikosnovénen* 'inviolable,' etc. However, in certain adjectival stems, esp. those whose participial or Church Slavonic origins are still patent, the other solution, namely syncope, is implemented: *božéstven* 'divine,' *blažén* 'blessed,' *derznovén* 'daring,' *svjaščén* 'holy,' etc. In colloquial Russian this distinction tends to disappear (Zaliznjak 1967:240): *médlen* 'slow' ~ *médlenen, neožídan* 'unexpected' ~ *neožídanen, voínstven* 'bellicose' ~ *voínstvenen, svjaščén* ~ *svjaščénen, ískren* 'sincere' ~ *ískrenen.* A distinction can be made between adjectival and participial use in such cases as *opredelén* 'appointed' (pcpl) ~ *opredelénen* (adj).

Substantival stems ending in /nn/ never undergo anaptyxis; rather, one of the identical segments is syncopated: *vann* [ván].

In the second case, that of /c/, a vowel is inserted if /c/ is clearly interpretable as a diminutive suffix: *krepostéc* 'fortresses,' *ozérec* 'lakes,' *bérec* 'tibias,' *bljúdec* 'saucers,' *dvérec* 'doors,' *špórec* 'spurs,' etc. Anaptyxis also occurs in old lexicalized diminutives: *koléc* 'rings,' *kryléc* 'porches,' *ovéc* 'sheep.' Otherwise no vowel is interpolated: *šújc* 'left hands,' *ubíjc* 'killers,' *propójc* 'drunkards,' *influénc* 'influenza.' In *myšc* 'muscles,' despite its being a lexicalized diminutive, no anaptyxis occurs. In *jaíc* 'eggs' (cf. *propóic, tróic* 'trios'), the /j/ of *jajcó* is not primary; it is derived from a vowel chain /ai/ by the application of a morpheme structure rule which states that unstressed /i/ not preceded by morpheme boundary is automatically reduced to /j/ in native Russian stems. Thus: *jájca* 'eggs,' *jajcevód* 'oviduct' but *jaíčnica* 'omelette,' *jaíčnik* 'ovary,' etc.

The behavior of /j/ in stem final position is unconnected with the anaptyxis rule. Since the morpheme structure rules of Russian do not permit /j/ to appear after a consonant when not followed by a vowel (yod is the only such segment; this is to be explained by its being marked for both vocalicity and consonantality), the insertion of a vowel is the only way of unmarking the stem while preserving its consonantal structure intact (i.e., without syncopating yod); hence: gen pl *statéj* 'articles,' *svinéj* 'pigs,' *sudéj* 'judges,' *epitimíj* 'punishments,' *skaméj* 'benches,' etc. Therefore the vowel/zero alternation attendant upon the suffix *j* is a predictable concomitant of a Ø desinence after /j/, i.e., *poberéžij* 'coasts,' *pitéj* 'houses,' *žitíj* 'existences,' *vólčij* [adj] 'wolves,' *čéj* 'whose,' *góstij* 'guests,' etc.

To conclude this inquiry into the phonological determinants of one sector of the morphophonemics of contemporary standard Russian, one might perhaps draw the inference from the processes examined that certain facts about the phonological system cannot be discovered without recourse to phenomena outside the phonology sensu stricto. Specifically, the distinctiveness/redundancy of a particular category, and thereby the correct markedness values, may prove to be identifiable only through the functioning of the morphophonemic component. At the same time, it is the markedness values of segments and the limitations inherent in their juxtaposition that govern these very same morphophonemic rules.

2. Russian Conjugation

Russian conjugation has a rather special place in the history of linguistics, quite apart from its intrinsic interest as a topic of inquiry. Thirty years ago, Roman Jakobson published his celebrated article 'Russian Conjugation' in *Word*. which became the seedbed for the overarching conception of language that came to be known as transformational-generative grammar (cf. Birnbaum 1970:31, Halle 1977:141, Worth 1972:80).[19] With respect to the particular historical role played by Jakobson, a confrontation of 'Russian Conjugation' with its important interwar antecedent 'Zur Struktur des russischen Verbums' (1932) appears to lend credence to the idea that the entire post-Prague period represented in many ways a dissipation of the intellectual energy that had earlier resulted in genuine breakthroughs in linguistic theory and augured more. To be sure, 'Zur Struktur' was but one panel of an eventual triptypch. It focused on the grammatical categories of the Russian verb and analyzed them in terms of markedness while reserving treatment of morphophonemic alternations for a future study. The latter was, indeed, executed as Jakobson 1948; and the triptych completed by Jakobson 1957.

Jakobson's application of the concept of markedness to morphology was utilized by Trubetzkoy in his path-breaking *Das morphonologische System der russischen Sprache* (1934), the 'first structural description of the morphophonemic system of a contemporary literary language' (Stankiewicz 1976:109). For all its merits, however, there is no real attempt made in this short book to integrate the fine discussion of grammatical categories with the thorough analysis of morphophonemic alternations.

A good starting point in a semeiotic analysis of Russian conjugation is Trubetzkoy's outline (based on Jakobson 1932) of the grammatical categories of the Russian verb (1934:5-10)[20] Taking inflection in Russian as a whole, Trubetzkoy notes that the hierarchy of categories is dominated first of all by the opposition between verbal and nonverbal inflection, within which the former is further bisected by the opposition infinitive (unmarked) vs. all other verbal forms (marked).[21] The latter, in turn, comprises the opposition of participles (marked) vs. nonparticipial (unmarked) forms, i.e., the finite verbal forms proper. At this point in the hierarchy the 'purely verbal categories' part company with the 'classes transitional to the adverbs and adjectives' (Jakobson [1948] 1971:119). Participles are split by the opposition of passive (marked) vs. nonpassive (unmarked). The passive is further divided into predicative (marked) vs. nonpredicative (unmarked), while the active (= nonpassive) dominates the opposition between adverbals, or gerunds (marked), and attributive (unmarked) forms. In the other branch of the hierarchy, the nonparticipial forms are first bifurcated by the opposition of the imperative (marked) vs. the indicative (unmarked); secondarily, the latter splits up into preterite (marked) vs. nonpreterite (unmarked). In schematic outline the whole network of oppositions defining Russian conjugation is as in Figure 30.

It is particularly important to take note of the markedness values of the major and minor categories, for it is these values that will be seen to cohere with the values of verbal stems and suffixes in both their morphological and phonological aspects.

All Russian inflected forms comprise a stem and a desinence. A stem is defined as the portion of the form that lies to the left of (immediately precedes) the desinence. A desinence may consist of one or more suffixes (including zero). If there is more than one suffix in a desinence, any suffix but the final one is nonterminal, while the final suffix is free. Desinences consisting of at least one nonterminal suffix are complex, as opposed to simple desinences.

Russian verb stems are of two fundamental kinds, vocalic and consonantal, depending (respectively) on whether they terminate in a vowel or in a consonant. Because of its hierarchical status as maximally unmarked, the infinitive acts partly as a diagnostic in determining stem type. Any stem which exhibits a vowel before the infinitive desinence that it lacks in the nonpreterite is a vocalic stem; this final vowel is its theme vowel.[22] Any stem which exhibits a consonant before the nonpreterite desinences that it lacks when immediately preceding the infinitive desinence

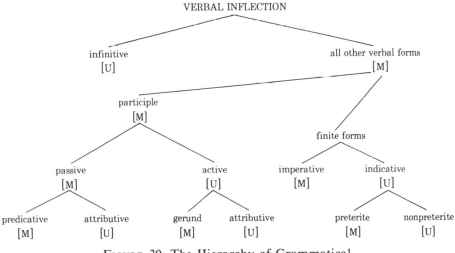

FIGURE 30. The Hierarchy of Grammatical
Categories in Russian Conjugation.

is a consonantal stem. Each stem type, vocalic and consonantal, can manifest one or both of two stem shapes (alternants). If a stem shape terminates in a vowel, it is vocalic; if it terminates in a consonant, it is consonantal.

The correct understanding of the notions stem and stem type is crucial. When the stem is characterized as being vocalic or consonantal, this means that the hierarchical status of a particular stem and the set of morphophonemic alternations with which it is associated in the conjugational paradigm are defined by whether it terminates in a vowel or a consonant. This fundamental division is hence not a classification for the convenience of the analyst but an expression of the immanent patterned relations subsumed hierarchically by the stem. The invariance represented by the stem is thus *in the relations* (cf. Jakobson 1977:1030), not in the form of the stem as we are forced to render it graphically for lack of any other mode of representation. The importance of this understanding of invariance cannot be overemphasized for the theory of grammar. Our recourse to a kind of shorthand for purposes of exposition must not distort the fact that the notion of a stem *inheres in the whole* of the pattern of forms to which it stands as its designated representative, regardless of the concrete shape it assumes in this or that particular member of the paradigm.

Not counting miscellanea, Russian has seven stem types, all but one of which are vocalic. The vocalic stems, designated by their stem-final vowel, are: *-i, -e, Č-a, -u, -a, -o*. The stem *Č-a* differs from *-a* in that the former necessarily has a palatal obstruent (*č, š,* or *ž*) or yod preceding the thematic vowel. Stems in *-u* are necessarily preceded by *n*, stems in *-o* by *r* or *l*. A large and productive class of stems in *-ova* will require special comment later.

The consonant stems, designated by their final consonants, may terminate in any one of the following: *-s, -z, -k, -g, -b, -r, -v, -j, -t, -d, -n, -m*. Additionally, stems which drop the suffix *-nu* in the preterite may have the final consonant *-p* or *-x*.

Russian has two conjugations, the so-called First (IC) and Second (IIC) Conjugations. Using the stems *v'od* 'lead' and *l'et'é* 'fly' as examples of the two conjugations, respectively, the nonpreterite indicative paradigms look like the chart below. Barring the 1sg. desinences, which are identical, the difference between the two patterns in each case resides in the nonterminal desinential vowel. In IC it is the *o* (2sg., 2pl., 3sg., 1pl.) and *u* (3pl.); in IIC it is *i* and *a*.

PERSON	SINGULAR		PLURAL	
1	v'od -ú	l'eč-ú	v'od'-óm	l'et'-ím
2	v'od'óš	l'et'-íš	v'od'-ót'e	l'et'-ít'e
3	v'od'-ót	l'et'-ít	v'od-út	l'et'-át

Thus in addition to the categories represented in Figure 30, Russian has person and number distinctions which find their fullest expression in the nonpreterite indicative. The category of person is implemented by the opposition impersonal vs. personal. The former is realized by the 3rd person, the latter further split into 1st and 2nd person (Figure 31).

The markedness values are assigned in accordance with the discussion in Jakobson [1956] 1971:137. Factoring in the category of number, for which singular is the unmarked value and plural the marked value, we get the following *synthetic desinence values* (where superscripts reflect the number of marked nodes comprising the specific personal form); values for the category person are to the left of the hyphen, values for the category number to the right (Figure 32); 1sg. is the category which has the greatest differentiation between its person/number constituents as to value; and 3pl. is the category with the second greatest degree of differentiation.[23] The emphasis here is on internal difference. Given the value of U for number, the highest degree of deflection for the category person away from that value along the markedness continuum is M^2; that degree is realized in 1sg. Conversely, given the value U for person, the highest degree of deflection for number is M, realized in 3pl. This means that the semeiotic structure of the desinences is different in each case and that, moreover, 1sg. and 3pl. are conceptually the most marked ones owing to their degree of internal differentiation. 1sg. as a synthetic entity implements the maximally marked person and the unmarked number. 3pl. implements the maximally unmarked person and the marked number. They are thus completely complementary in their structure with regard to the semeiotic values which comprise them (which cannot be said of any of the remaining members of the Russian nonpreterite indicative paradigm).

This complementarity is evidently one of the fundamental and ubiquitous series of complementarities that inform the structure of Russian conjugation. Congruent with the principle of markedness complementarity (ch. 4, sec. 1), oppositely valued stems normally combine with oppositely valued desinences; as a corollary, identically valued stems and desinences

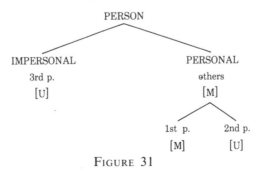

FIGURE 31

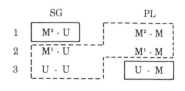

FIGURE 32

normally do not so combine. In Russian inflection, desinences are marked
if they begin with (or are constituted by) a vowel. The reverse is grosso
modo true of stems: they are marked if they end in a consonant, unmarked
if they end in a vowel. The structure of any inflected Russian form thus
normally reflects the fusion of two complementary entities. However, as
will be seen below, the markedness values of stems do not hinge simply on
the identity of their final segments, so that the complementarity can be of
several kinds.

The distribution of the two conjugations according to stem type is as
below.[24] The difference between the vocalic stems centers on the final
consonant, i.e., on the character of the consonant which immediately
precedes the theme vowel. In those stems which are subsumed by IC (cons.,
-*u*, -*a*, and -*o*) the final consonant is necessarily nonsharp, whereas in those
stems subsumed by IIC the consonant is necessarily sharp. Given the fact
that [+ shp] = [M shp] and [— shp] = [U shp], it is reasonable to conclude
from the operation of the principle of markedness complementarity that IC
and the stem types subsumed by it are marked, IIC and the stem types
subsumed by it unmarked. Furthermore, as we shall see later, -*a* (with a
distinct class of exceptions) and -*o* stems have characteristics that
necessitate their being understood as hypermarked, i.e., with a degree of
markedness over and above the other IC stems.

First Conjugation (o/u)	*Second Conjugation (i/a)*
cons. stems	*i* and *e* stems
u stems	
a stems	
o stems	*Č-a* stems

In the paradigm of the nonpreterite indicative there is a fundamental
complementarity between unmarked and marked stem types as regards the
alternation of the final consonant(s) in the stem. Any Russian consonant
other than *j* and *l* which appears in predesinential position can alternate in
respect of the feature sharp/nonsharp, a process called *neperexodnoe
smjagčenie* 'bare softening' by Russian grammarians. This results in the

following possible pairs of sounds in the nonpreterite indicative: $k \sim k'$, $t \sim t'$, $d \sim d'$, $s \sim s'$, $z \sim z'$, $p \sim p'$, $b \sim b'$, $f \sim f'$, $v \sim v'$, $m \sim m'$, $n \sim n'$, $r \sim r'$.[25] But there is also a second type of alternation, called *perexodnoe smjagčenie* 'substitutive softening,' in which rather than have a simple shift from hard (unpalatalized) to soft (palatalized) without any other changes in the character of the consonant, there occurs 'a concomitant change in the basic place of articulation (shift of velar or dental to palatal) or a change of one phoneme into a cluster (epenthesis of a palatalized consonant)' (Jakobson [1948] 1971:126). This second type of softening results in the following other pairs in the nonpreterite indicative: $k \sim č$, $sk \sim šč$, $g \sim ž$, $zg \sim žž$, $t \sim č$, $st \sim šč$, $d \sim ž$, $zd \sim žž$, $s \sim š$, $z \sim ž$, $p \sim pl'$, $b \sim bl'$, $f \sim fl'$, $v \sim vl'$, $m \sim ml'$.

Now, regarding the distribution of the alternants, unmarked stems (*-i*, *-e*) manifest the alternation in only one of the 'outer' desinences (see n. 23), namely the 1sg., e.g. *nos'í* 'wear'/*nošú*, *l'ub'í* 'love'/*l'ubl'-ú*, *v'ert'e* 'twirl'/*v'erč-ú*, etc. The 'inner' forms are unchanged (see below).

noš-ú	nós'-im	l'ubl'-ú	l'úb'-im	v'erč-ú	v'ért'-im
nós'-iš	nós'-it'e	l'úb'-iš	l'úb'-it'e	v'ért'-iš	v'ért'-it'e
nós'-it	nós'-at	l'úb'-it	l'úb'-at	v'ért'-it	v'ért'-at

Marked stem types (cons. and *-u*, but not the hypermarked *-o*, *Č-a*),[26] on the other hand, manifest the alternation in all of the 'inner' forms and in *neither* of the 'outer' (see below).

	p'ok 'bake'	živ 'live'	gnú 'bend'
	p'ok-ú	živ-ú	gn-ú
Sg.	p'oč-óš	živ-óš	gn-óš
	p'oč-ót	živ-ót	gn-ót
	p'oč-óm	živ-óm	gn-óm
Pl.	p'oč-ót'e	živ-ót'e	gn-ót'e
	p'ok-út	ziv-út	gn-út

If we understand the presence of a palatalized consonant in final position to signify a marking of the stem (owing to the [M shp] value of the cons.) and an unpalatalized consonant to signify an unmarking (owing to the [U shp] value of the cons.), then the complementarity is defined as below.

(1) in *unmarked* stem types, only *one* of the 'outer' desinences occasions *marking* of the stem;

(2) in *marked* stem types, *both* of the 'outer' desinences occasion *unmarking* of the stem.

The hypermarked stem types manifest an altered stem shape (vis-à-vis the infinitive) throughout the nonpreterite indicative paradigm (see below).

poro 'rip'		p'isa 'write'	
por'-ú	pór'-om	p'íš-ú	p'íš-om
pór'-oš	pór'-ot'e	p'íš-oš	p'íš-ot'e
pór'-ot	pór'-ut	p'íš-ot	p'íš-ut

In the light of the complementarity of the unmarked and marked stem types, the hypermarked must be evaluated as unmotivated. This assessment is corroborated by historical evidence (Vinogradov and Švedova 1964:155-65, cf. Krysin 1974:199-207) which show that for -a stems there has been a long and decided tendency to convert to -aj stems, i.e., to cons.; thus e.g. *gloda—glodáj*, 'gnaw,' *poloska—poloskáj*, 'rinse,' *maxa—maxáj* 'wave,' *kápa—kápaj*, etc. The -o stems have also tended to change their non-preterite indictive conjugation during the last 50-70 years by joining the class of IIC [sic!] verbs (Panov 1968:142). Since they are all stem-stressed in the 'inner' forms and that of 3pl., the difference between the two conjugations comes down to the 3pl., where the desinence -ut is being replaced by -at. In other words, -o stems are beginning to conjugate like unmarked stems owing to the constant presence of a stem-final soft consonant (unlike any other IC verbs). This is supported by the irregular behavior of three -a stems: *gna* 'drive,' *sípa* 'pour,' *spa* 'sleep.' In each of the three, the nonpreterite indicative is conjugated as a IIC verb, hence: *gon'-ú /gón'-at, sípl'-u/síp'-at*,[27] and *spl'-ú/sp'át*. In fact, potentially any 3pl. which has stem stress and whose stem-final consonant is soft can join IIC, e.g. *stla* 'spread': *st'el'-ú/st'él'-at* (instead of the orthoepic *st'él'-ut*), etc. Given this tendency, it becomes understandable why the Old Muscovite pronunciation of CSR *gón'-at, l'úb'-at, nós'-at*, etc. reflecting the structure *gón'-ut, l'úb'-ut, nós'-ut*, etc. was short-lived in the recent history of Russian and has just about been expunged from the standard language altogether (Avanesov 1972:159, cf. Panov 1968:137-43).

There is a further relation of complementarity informing the structure of the nonpreterite: between the character of the theme vowel and that of the stem-final consonant. In those stems whose final consonant can vary in accordance with the alternations of bare and substitutive softening,[28] the markedness value for the (tonality) feature of flatness varies inversely with the value of the consonant for the (tonality) feature of sharping. Thus in -a and -o stems, there is a marking of the stem throughout the nonpreterite indicative because of its coherence, via complementarity, with the value [U fla] of the theme vowel:[29] *p'isa/p'iš-ú, p'íš-ut, kl'ev'eta/kl'ev'ešč-ú, kl'ev'éšč-ut, poro/por'-ú, pór'-ut, koló* 'prick'/*kol'-ú, kól'-ut, ora* 'plow'/ *or'-ú, ór'-ut, slá/šl'-ú, šl'-út, stla/st'el'-ú, st'él'-ut*, etc. However, there is a clearly-defined set of (IC) exceptions in -a where the stem marking occurs in the 'inner' forms only: *bra* 'take'/*b'er-ú, b'er'-ót, b'er-út, rva* 'tear'/*rv-ú, rv'-ót, rv-út, žda* 'wait'/*žd-ú, žd'-ót, žd-út, žážda* 'crave'/*žážd-u, žážd'-ot*, *žážd-ut, stona* 'moan'/*ston-ú, stón'-ot, stón-ut.* These exceptions are all subsumed under one or more of the following classes, the first two of which are rank-ordered vis-à-vis each other (see A.-D. below).

A. stem-final cons. in *-r*: *bra* 'take,' *žra* 'wolf,' *vra* 'lie,' *orá* 'shout,' *dra* 'flay,' *sra* 'shit,'[30] *po=prá* 'crush'
B. monosyllabic stems: *rva* 'tear,' *žda* 'wait,' *lga* 'lie,' *ržá* 'neigh,' *zva* 'call,' *tka* 'weave,' *ská* 'roll'
C. reduplicative stems:[31] *sosá* 'suck'/*sos-ú, sos'-ót, sos-út; žážda*
D. stem-final cons. in *-n*: *stona*

What binds these four categories of exceptions is their marked value. As opposed to stems like *stla* or *slá* whose final consonant is the [U abr] *-l*, those with the [M abr] sound *-r* manifest a markedness reversal. The presence of the [M abr] *r* as a stem-final consonant renders this a marked context in which the normal (unmarked) situation of stem marking throughout the nonpreterite indicative paradigm is replaced by the marked situation (here, in this group of stems) of marking only the 'inner' forms. Similarly, monosyllabicity is marked vis-à-vis polysyllabicity (cf. Jakobson [1948] 1971:126) in verb stems, so that the second class of exceptions (B) above is likewise to be explained as the result of a markedness reversal. In the case of the two reduplicative stems *sosá* and *žážda,* it is unmarked for Russian verb stems to have a heterogeneous segment structure (i.e., alternation of CV sequences of different and complementary Cs and/or Vs). The two exceptional stems are the only ones in *-a* which are at variance with this structure; hence the absence of marking in the two marked categories, 1sg. and 3pl. Finally, the stem *stona* with its final cons. *-n* exhibits the marked value of the paradigm in virtue of the marked status of *n* with respect to stem-final position: *-a* stem final consonants are normally obstruents, not sonorants, unless the stem is monosyllabic; cf., most directly, the functioning of the other nasal *m* in perfect alignment with other labials, i.e., obstruents: *dr'ema* 'doze'/*dreml'-ú, dr'éml'-ut,* just like *tr'epa* 'pat'/*tr'epl'-ú, tr'épl'-ut,* etc.

In this (latter) connection, it should be noted that *-u* stems, which are invariably preceded by *n* (the so-called *-nu* verbs), behave in exactly the same way as *stona*. This can be explained, just as in *stona,* by the marked status of *n*. However, it should also be noted that unlike *a* and *o, u* while unmarked for flatness is the only one of the three which is differently valued for diffuseness (under any interpretation of the Russian vowel system). Hence, whereas in the case of *a* and *o* there is marking of the stem throughout the nonpreterite indicative, in the case of *-nu* the marking is limited to forms implementing only those categories which are unmarked, i.e., the 'inner' categories.

We now come to the central question of coherence in Russian

conjugation, namely the particular shape the stem takes in a particular form. Jakobson's analysis only went so far as to predict the environments in which the shapes occurred but stopped short of explaining why the shapes occurred where they did. The answer lies in the relations schematized by Figure 31 and the principle of markedness complementarity.

The distribution of stem shapes in Russian conjugation is determined by principles 3 and 4.

(3) in a category further undifferentiated by a verbal category markedness values are replicated: unmarked categories are implemented by unmarked stem shapes, marked categories by marked stem shapes;

(4) in a further differentiated category the subordinate unmarked members are implemented by complementary markedness values: unmarked categories are implemented by marked stem shapes, marked categories by unmarked stem shapes.

The practical consequences of these principles show up, on the one hand, in the infinitive and imperative; and, on the other, in the indicative (preterite and nonpreterite).

The infinitive and the imperative are the only categories which meet the conditions of the first principle above. More precisely, all stem shapes occurring before the infinitive desinences *(t', st', st'i,* and *č*)[32] are vocalic (Flier 1978b: 274ff; cf. Bromlej and Bulatova 1972:178-88) and unmarked in that they implement a category which is further undifferentiated by a subordinate verbal category and is itself unmarked. This means, in turn, that corresponding stem shapes ending in a consonant are marked. The infinitive, as the maximally unmarked category in the hierarchy of Russian conjugation, thus serves as an inherent diagnostic in the assignment of markedness values to stem alternants (see chart below). The finite forms subsume the imperative and the indicative, of which the former is not further differentiated by a strictly verbal category and therefore conforms to the same principle of replication of markedness values as the infinitive (see chart below).

infinitive

[U]	[M]	
p'é-č	p'ok-	'bake'
nos'í-t'	nos-	'carry'
grí-st'	griz-	'gnaw'
n'o-stí	n'os-	'carry'

imperative

[M]	*stem*		*infinitive*
l'eź'-∅	l'éz-	'climb'	l'é-st'

pláč-∅	pláka-	'cry'	pláka-t'
klad'-í	klad-	'place'	klá-st'
žm'-í	ža-/žm-	'press'	žá-t'
p'ok'-í	p'ok-	'bake'	p'é-č
xoxoč-í	xoxota-	'guffaw'	xoxotá-t'
poj-í	pojí-	'give to drink'	pojí-t'
živ'-í	živ-	'live'	ží-t'

The distribution of the imperative desinences ∅ and -i is determined by the type of stress in the nonpreterite indicative and secondarily by the presence of a consonant cluster in stem-final position. Normally, fixed stem stress in the nonpreterite indicative occasions ∅—unless there is a consonant cluster stem-finally, in which case the desinence is -i:[33] pláč-u/pláč-∅, stávl'-u 'place'/stáv'-∅; but prígn-u 'jump'/prígn'-i, číšč-u 'clean'/číst'-i, etc. Otherwise—i.e., if stress is not fixed on the stem—the imperative desinence is normally stressed -i: v'od-ú 'lead'/v'od'-í, živ'ú/živ'-í, etc. In either case, the stem shape is the marked one (cf. the unmarked shape in the infinitive), in conformity with the value of the imperative and its being undifferentiated further by a strictly verbal category.

It should be noted that the marking of the stem in the imperative extends to the stem-final consonant. The specific type of marking is determined by the value of the stem type. Here the opposition is between hypermarked stems, on the one hand, and all remaining stem types, on the other. The former implement the more marked degree of softening—viz. substitutive softening—while the latter implement the less marked degree of softening—viz. bare softening. The fact that the stem-final consonant undergoes marking is coherent with the marked status of the imperative and its subjection to the first (i.e., replicative) principle of coherence above.

Since the form of the imperative desinence is directly contingent on the accentual properties of the stem, an explanation of the distribution of ∅ and -i must take account of the markedness values of stress. In advance of a systematic treatment of stress in Russian conjugation below, we must here acknowledge with Trubetzkoy (1975:182) the unmarked status of the stressed syllable in Russian. In morphology this translates into the relation of a marked value for unstressed stems and an unmarked value for stressed stems. Since Russian stress is permutative (cf. Jakobson 1965a:150), the opposition is between stressed syllables and all other syllables; in syntagmatic terms this is tantamount to the concatenation of one unmarked syllable with one or more marked syllables.

The distribution of the desinence alternants is also tied up with their semeiotic value. In accord with a principle governing the value of grammatical zero enunciated in Shapiro 1972:357, the ∅ of the imperative is unmarked (cf. Jakobson [1965b] 1971:194-5), since it varies inversely with the synthetic markedness value of the grammatical category or categories it expresses (imperative = M). This means, correspondingly, that the value of *-i* is M. If, therefore, this assignment of semeiotic values for desinence alternants comports with the role of stress in the imperative, then the unmarked value for stress (the stressed syllable) ought to be complementary to the marked value for the desinence. We can see that this is indeed the case: the absence of stress on the stem necessarily entails *-i* (except with the obligatorily stressed prefix *ví* = 'out'), and the presence of stress on the stem (in the absence of a supervening consonant cluster in stem-final position) necessarily occasions the stresslessness—hence the prosodically marked value—of the grammatically unmarked ∅.

There is one particularly revealing case of complementarity in the morphophonemics of the Russian imperative that deserves special mention. As Jakobson ([1948] 1971:124) pointed out, the sequence of yod + *i* occurs only if the stem ends in *ji-*; thus *dojí* 'milk'/*doj-í, pojí* 'give to drink'/*poj-í, tají* 'hide'/*taj-í*, etc.; but *stojá* 'stand'/*stój-∅, bojá-*. . . *s'a* 'fear'/ *bój-∅-s'a, sm'ejá-* . . . *s'a* 'laugh'/*sm'éj-∅-s'a, p'í/p'j* 'drink'/*p'éj-∅, p'é/pój* 'sing'/*pój-∅, kl'ová* 'peck'/*kl'új-∅, celova* 'kiss'/*celúj-∅, ví/vój* 'howl'/*vój-∅, d'élaj* 'do'/*d'élaj-∅, vestaváj/vstaj* 'rise'/*vstaváj-∅*, etc. What is pertinent here is the supersedure of stress as a determinant: despite desinential stress in 1sg. of stems like *stojá/stoj-ú, kl'ová/kl'uj-ú, p'é/pój/pjo-ú*, the desinence remains ∅ and the stress in the imperative falls on the last stressable syllable; cf. *govor'í* 'talk'/*govor'-ú, govor'-í* and likewise *dojí/doj-ú, doj-í*, etc.

This superficially peculiar distribution of imperative desinence alternants after stems in *-j* has an explanation. The first, encompassing consideration is that *j* is (1) a glide, hence marked for both vocalicity and consonantality; and (2) marked for acuteness, as opposed to the other two Russian glides (cf. Andersen 1969c), *v* and *v'*, which are [U acu]. No other sound in the Russian system is triply marked for these three features. The multiply marked status of yod accounts for the patterned variance of stems in yod from the general picture of the Russian imperative. Now as to the distribution of ∅ and *i*, stems with the theme vowel *-a* after *j* have in common with consonant stems in *j* that they both have marked values: *-ja* stems are marked vis-à-vis *ji* stems in virtue of the fact that *a* is [M dif] and *i* is [U dif],[34] and consonant stems are marked generally vis-à-vis vocalic stems. Once again, complementarity prevails: the marked stems take unmarked desinences, the unmarked stems marked desinences.

The special subset of stems in *-ava* and *-ova*, despite the peculiarities of stem shape in the indicative, are just like any other *-a* stem, except that the *j* which is stable in non-*ova* stems in *j* manifests itself in them only before the desinences of the nonpreterite indicative and the imperative, e.g. *vstavá/*

vstaj-ú, vstaváj-∅, uznavá 'find out'/*uznaj-ú, uznáj-∅, davá* 'give'/ *daj-ú, dáj-∅, kl'ová/kl'uj-ú, kl'új-∅, celova/celúj-u, celúj-∅.*

Two final peripheral sets of data from the formation of the imperative require comment. In stems (prefixed or unprefixed) where the stress falls on a syllable other than the stem-final one, *-i* can appear instead of ∅ (cf. Zaliznjak 1977:97 and passim): *stáv'i* 'place'/*stáv'-∅* but *ví-stav'i* alongside *ví-stav',* *súnu* 'stick out'/*sún'-∅* but *ví-sun'i* alongside *vi-sun'-∅, káśl'anu* 'cough'/*káśl'an'-i* (no **káśl'an'-∅* but pl. *kásl'an'-∅-t'e* according to Zaliznjak, 97), *za-kúpor'i* 'plug'/*za-kúpor'-i* alongside *za-kúpor'-∅* (but only pl. *za-kúpor-∅-t'e*), *u-v'édom'i* 'inform'/*u-v'édom'-i* alongside *u-v'édom'-∅,* etc. At the same time, the reverse is not true: given an unprefixed stem which is never stem-stressed in the indicative, the addition of *ví-* will never give rise to *-∅,* so that like *v'od* 'lead'/*v'od'-í* only *ví-v'od* 'lead out'/*ví-v'od'-i,* pl. *ví-v'od'-i-t'e* is possible.

This situation has a natural explanation in alignment with all the others proffered earlier. The Russian morphophonemic pattern as regards stress position articulates a basic dichotomy between stem-final stress and all others. Moreover, stress on the final syllable of the stem (where the stem is polysyllabic) is evaluated as marked, stress on any other syllable as unmarked. This relationship transpires, for instance, from the fact that in observing the accentual properties of substantival inflection we see that stem-final stress in the singular is incompatible with a mobile stress paradigm, whereas any other position of the stress in the singular can be altered in the plural, e.g. *provizór* 'pharmacist'/pl. *provizóry, podrúga* 'girlfriend'/pl. *podrúgi, selénie* 'settlement'/pl. *selénija;* but *proféssor*/ pl. *professorá, krasotá* 'beauty'/pl. *krasóty, men'šinstvó* 'minority'/pl. *men'šin-stva, óblako* 'cloud'/pl. *oblaká,* etc. Thus in the imperative, stress on any but the stem-final syllable is unmarked; and by the principle of complementarity this stress is more closely compatible semeiotically with the marked desinence *-i* than with the unmarked ∅.

The second set of peripheral data has to do with the role of consonant clusters in stem-final position. Ordinarily, the presence of a cluster occasions *-i* regardless of stem stress. However, the existence of doublets like *čist'-∅/číst'-i* 'clean,' *pórt'-∅/pórt'-i* 'spoil,' *móršč-∅/móršč-i* 'wrinkle,' *kórč-∅/kórč-i* 'distort,' etc. (cf. Zaliznjak 1977:102 and passim) shows that *-∅* is possible if the cluster's last segment is [M str].[35] Again, the marked stem-final is congruent with the unmarked desinence.

It is instructive to examine just how complementarity affects the structure of Russian verb desinences. In the nonpreterite indicative 1sg. has the desinence *-u* for both conjugations. This is to be explained by the complementarity between the maximally marked value of the grammatical form and the status of /u/ as the least marked vowel in the Russian system, this sound being unmarked for the two relevant distinctive features, flatness and diffuseness (cf. Shapiro 1976:38). 3pl. distinguishes two desinential vowels, *u* vs. *a*, just as do the forms outside 1sg. and 3pl. (*o* vs. *i*). The latter are to be explained by the coherence of an unmarked stem (IIC) and the [M flat] vowel /i/, on the one hand; and that of a marked stem (IC) with the [U flat] vowel /o/, on the other. The former (*u* vs. *a* in 3pl.) presents the same complementarity of stem and desinential vowel, except that the relevant distinctive feature is diffuseness rather than flatness. The [M dif] vowel /a/ combines with unmarked stems, the [U dif] vowel /u/ with marked stems.

The desinences of the finite forms (i.e., all forms but the infinitive, participles, and gerund) in Russian all either begin with or consist of a sonorant or zero. Put negatively, a finite desinence cannot begin with or consist of an obstruent. The specific sonorants involved are: the vowels *a, i, u, o;* and liquids *l, l'*.

In the nonpreterite indicative the nonterminal portion consists of a vowel, the terminal portion of a consonant, or zero (see chart below). In the preterite, the order is reversed: the nonterminal portion consists of the liquids *l* (sg.) or *l'*(pl.), the terminal portion of the vowels *a* (fem.), *o* (neut.), *i* (pl.), and zero (masc.). This means that in the unmarked indicative category of the nonpreterite the nonterminal portion (tense marker) of the desinences is diagrammatically expressed by segments which are unmarked for vocality (vowels), whereas in the corresponding marked indicative category of the preterite the nonterminal portion (tense marker) is diagrammatically expressed by segments which are marked for vocality (liquids).

	sg	pl
1	u-$\emptyset$	o/i-m
2	o/i-š	o/i-t'e
3	o/i-t	u/a-t

The markedness values of the three genders and two numbers in the preterite are likewise diagrammed by the markedness values of the sounds expressing these categories. The gender hierarchy of Russian is dominated by the opposition feminine vs. nonfeminine, the latter bifurcating further into masculine vs. neuter (Figure 33).[36] The set of desinences expressing gender consist of two real vowel desinences (*a, o*) and $\emptyset$. The maximally unmarked category masculine is represented diagrammatically by the unmarked zero (whose value varies inversely with the synthetic markedness value of the categories it implements—here the marked preterite and the unmarked masculine, hence with the synthetic value M). The singly marked feminine is realized by *a*, which is [M dif]. The doubly marked neuter is realized by *o*, which is also [M dif]. The greater degree of markedness for the feature diffuse of *a* vis-à-vis *o*, in virtue of the former's

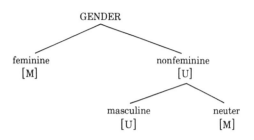

FIGURE 33.

specifications as [+ cmp] and the latter's as [— cmp], mirrors the higher rank (hierarchical dominance) of the feminine/nonfeminine distinction.

Getting back to the nonpreterite, the diagram of sound and meaning in the desinences is constituted by coherence of markedness values between expression and content. First, in comparing the terminal consonants of desinences by numbers, there is no differentiation in the third person: this accords with the maximally unmarked value of that category. The marked category (vis-à-vis the third person) of 2nd person is, however, differentiated. The š of the 2sg. is opposed as [U abr] to the [M abr] value of *t* 'in the 2pl. Within the two numbers, in the singular the š of the marked second person is opposed as [M cmp] to the [U cmp] value of *t* in the unmarked third person. In the plural, the *t* 'of the 2nd person is opposed as [M shp] to the [U shp] *t* of the 3rd person, and the *m* of the 1st person is opposed to both *t* and *t* ' as [M nas] to [U nas]. The only apparently unmotivated relationships in this pattern are that of 1sg. to 2sg. and 3sg.; and 1pl. to 1sg. However, we should note that the maximally marked status of 1sg. is mirrored in its having the only desinence devoid of a consonantal terminal. Accordingly, the pertinent locus of comparison shifts to the vocalic portions (Figure 34).

Here, however, the diagram changes from a replicative to a complementary one, since marked categories are expressed—insofar as the nonterminal (vocalic) portions of the desinences are concerned—by unmarked values of the relevant features and corresponding unmarked categories by marked values for the features involved. This dichotomy between the replicative diagram for terminal (consonantal) desinences, on the one hand, and the complementary diagram for nonterminal (vocalic) desinences, on the other, is to be understood as an instance of markedness reversal. Since nonterminal desinences are marked vis-à-vis terminal, the straightforward diagrammatization of the unmarked context is reversed in the dominant marked context, and the signs apply with opposite markedness values.

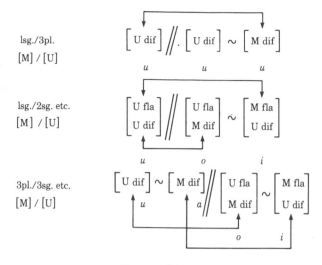

Whereas replication is the norm for sound/meaning cohesions in desinences whose realization is morphophonemically independent of the properties of the stems with which they fuse, complementation is the norm in desinences (like that of the imperative above) whose realization is contingent on stem structure. This is the case with the infinitive, which (we have seen) has four regular desinence alternants: *č, st'i, st', and t'*. Their distribution is as follows (cf. n. 32):

1. if stem is consonantal and ends in *k* or *g*, then *č*
2. if stem is unstressed in preterite, then *st'i*
3. If consonant stem ends in obstruent other than velar, then *st'*
4. If stem is vocalic, or consonantal ending in sonorant, then *t'*

This distribution makes semeiotic sense if we assume, to begin, that the desinence alternants themselves have a relational structure. The two polar members of the continuum of stem types are clearly: (1) obstruent stems in *k* or *g;* and (2) sonorant stems (including vowel stems). The former utilize a desinence which consists of one segment, and that segment is marked for compactness and stridency. The velars *k* and *g* are also marked for compactness; they are, however, unmarked for stridency. This means that one feature value (compactness) is replicated as between the stem-final and the infinitive desinence, one feature value (stridency) complemented (Figure 35).

In the other polar case, that of sonorant and vowel stems, the desinence utilized is also monosegmental, *t'*. Here as in the two other (transitional) stem/desinence relationships mentioned above, the final

FIGURE 35.

sounds of consonant stems are uniformly noncompact. But they are either marked for nasality (*n* and *m*) or marked for consonantality (vowels and glides). Since, as with velar stems and *č*, there is an identical markedness value for a common feature, that of stridency,[37] between sonorants and the [M str] *t'*, it is the sole feature of nasality and its unmarked realization in the desinence alternant *t'* that informs the complementary relation between stem and desinence (Figure 36).

The transitional stem/desinence cohesions, which involve obstruent stems, manifest the alternants *st'í* and *st'*, differentiated by stress and the concomitant final vowel. Here stridency is not the relevant feature because the obstruent can be either strident or nonstrident (e.g. *krad* 'steal'/ *krá-st'* alongside *griz* 'gnaw'/ *grí-st'*, *v'od* 'lead'/ *v'o-st'í* alongside *v'oz* 'carry'/ *v'o-st'í*, etc.). The identically valued common feature is nasality (in addition to the unmarked value for compactness that separates velar stems from all the rest): both the stem-final consonants and the desinence alternants are composed entirely of [U nas] segments. The difference in the case of *st'í* infinitives is the complementary value for stress. Since stems which take *st'í* are invariably stressless, the complementation here is between the prosodically marked stem and the prosodically unmarked desinence. Conversely, when the stem is stressed, hence unmarked prosodically, the desinence alternant is unstressed, hence marked prosodically, i.e., *st'-∅*.

The only other fact requiring explanation is the presence of the (historically metanalytic) segment *s* before the *t'* in the two transitional alternants of the infinitive desinence. Remembering that the two polar terms in this pattern are *č* and *t'*, we should start by reiterating the function of the compactness feature as the pivotal one. Consonant stems not having a final compact consonant have *t'* in their infinitive form. Of these, the obstruent stems (plus *kl'an* 'curse'/ *kl'á-st'*) exhibit *s*, which is [U cns] and/or [U nas], just like the contiguous *t* and (more importantly) all

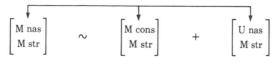

FIGURE 36.

obstruents. The *s* does not appear when the stem ends in a [M nas] or [M cns] segment. This distribution, then, is the expression of the following hierarchy of stems[38] (Figure 37).

This brings us to the stem shapes of the nonpreterite and preterite.[39] Aside from completely automatic phonological variations in the shape of verb stems (e.g. reduction of vowels in unstressed position, contextual assimilation of consonants, etc.), the predesinential portion of a stem assumes two alternating shapes depending on the grammatical category of the form. As has become abundantly clear, the alternation involves the presence vs. absence of one segment (consonant or vowel). Thus in comparing the preterite and nonpreterite forms of a verb like *igrát'* 'play,' one observes the presence of a stem-final *j* in the nonpreterite that is absent in the preterite and the infinitive (Jakobson's 'rule of truncation').

Infinitive   igrá'-t'
Nonpreterite

	SG	PL
1	igráj-u	igráj-om
2	igráj-oš	igráj-ot'e
3	igráj-ot	igráj-ut

Preterite

MASC	FEM	NEUT	PL
igrá-l-∅	igrá-l-a	igrá-l-o	igrá-l'-i

Consequently, there are two stem shapes, differing only in respect of the final, *igráj-* vs. *igrá-*. A comparison of the stem shapes in the two unmarked categories of infinitive and nonpreterite shows the maximally unmarked infinitive with a shape lacking the consonant that is present in the partially marked nonpreterite. This signifies that in consonantal stems, defined as those which display a predesinential consonant in the non-preterite absent in the infinitive, the shorter or consonant-less alternant is

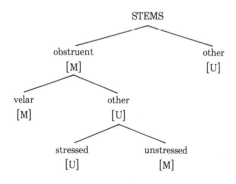

FIGURE 37

evaluated as unmarked (but cf. n. 22). This applies partly (but see below) to verbs like *beréč'* 'guard' (cf. *péč'* 'bake' above) that retain the stem-final consonant in the preterite as well as the nonpreterite.

Infinitive   b'er'é-č
Nonpreterite

	SG	PL
1	b'er'og-ú	b'er'ož-óm
2	b'er'ož-óš	b'er'ož-ót'e
3	b'er'ož-ót	b'er'og-út

Preterite

MASC	FEM	NEUT	PL
b'er'óg-∅	b'er'og-l-á	b'er'og-l-ó	b'er'og-l'-í

Complementarily, in verbs whose infinitive and preterite display a stem-final vowel that is lacking in the nonpreterite, the shorter or vowel-less alternant is evaluated as marked. Hence in a verb like *letét'* 'fly,' the stem shape of the infinitive and preterite *l'et'é-* is unmarked, while that of the nonpreterite *l'ot'-/l'oč-* is marked.

Infinitive   l'ot'é-t'
Nonpreterite

	SG	PL
1	l'oč-ú	l'ot'-ím
2	l'ot'-íš	l'ot'-ít'e
3	l'ot'-ít	l'ot'-át

Preterite

MASC	FEM	NEUT	PL
l'ot'é-l-∅	l'ot'é-l-a	l'ot'é-l-o	l'ot'é-l'-i

Within the class of consonant stems, however, there is a differentiation (with semeiotic consequences) of verbs whose stem shape in the preterite has a final consonant from those that lack this consonant. Thus alongside the pattern of *beréč'* above, cf. that of *klást'* 'place.'

Infinitive   klá-st'
Nonpreterite

	SG	PL
1	klad-ú	klad'-óm
2	klad'-óš	klad'-ót'e
3	klad'-ót	klad-út

Preterite

MASC	FEM	NEUT	PL
klá-l-∅	klá-l-a	klá-l-o	klá-l'-i

The segmental pattern represented in the preterite by *b'er'óg-*

∅/*b'er'og-l-á*/*b'er"og-l-ó*/*b'er'og-l'-í* is found when the final consonant of a consonantal stem is any of *s, z, k, g, b, r*.[40] The pattern represented in the preterite by *klá-l-∅*/*klá-l-a*/*klá-l-o*/*klá-l'-i* occurs when the final consonant of a consonantal stem is any of *v, j, t, d, n, m*. These two sets of consonants exhaust the class of possible consonantal stems in Russian. Apparently, the reason that the first set is retained in the preterite is that all of them are [U str].[41] This means, moreover, that the subclass of consonantal stems in which these unmarked consonants are retained in the preterite is evaluated accordingly as the unmarked subclass vis-à-vis the marked subclass of stems whose final consonants are [M str] and therefore drop before the desinences of the preterite. In the face of the overall principle of complementation that governs the combination of stems and desinences, the fusion of consonant + consonant that one observes in the preterite of verbs like *berèč'* can only be seen as motivated when the stem shape of the preterite is understood to be unmarked via its unmarked (for stridency) final consonant.

In the marked context of the preterite, then, the same formal material (not counting automatic alternations) as in the nonpreterite is evaluated differently from that in the latter. For if the stem shape of the infinitive is juxtaposed to its nonpreterite counterpart, the consonant-less alternant is unmarked and the consonantal one marked (see below).

b'er'é-č	b'er'og-ú etc.
[U]	[M]

But in the preterite the value of the shape *b'er'og-* is U, owing to the unmarked value of its final consonant. By contrast, verbs of the *klást'* type have formally different stem shapes in the preterite and nonpreterite (see below).

klá-l-∅ etc.	klad-ú
[U]	[M]

This completes our survey of alternation in the stem shapes of the categories of the indicative. The complementarity principle (4) explains in each set of cases the appearance of a particular stem shape in a particular conjugational form and does it via the semeiotic terms of markedness as a coherence of oppositely valued entities.

The asymmetric principle of combination of linguistic units also informs the behavior of stress in the Russian conjugational patterns. This transpires if the following assumptions are made. First of all, as in the whole of Russian grammar, stress differentiation (mobility) in the paradigm is marked, nondifferentiation (fixed stress) unmarked. Consequently, to the extent that differentiation exists and is perpetuated, it serves a semeiotic function. With regard to conjugation specifically and in conformity with the markedness complementation established earlier, unmarked stem types generally exhibit the marked stress type, marked stem types generally exhibit the unmarked stress type (v. below for exceptions). Hypermarked stem types, furthermore, occasion reversal in the basic relation, and the stress types apply with reversed values. In the nonpreterite, where the only kind of mobility is that of a 'retraction' of stress from desinence to stem-final syllable, unmarked stems like *nos'í* or *v'ert'e* are desinentially stressed in 1sg. but stem-stressed in the remaining forms. Historically, the tendency is most decidedly in the direction of establishing mobile stress in unmarked stems (Voroncova 1959), although there remain many with fixed desinential stress even among the commonest verbs (e.g. *s'íd'é* 'sit,' *govor'í* 'talk,' etc.). There are clearly semantic constraints on the establishment of mobile stress, such as the features abstract vs. concrete or figural vs. literal that determine fixed vs. mobile stress in contrasting stems like *vozbud'í* 'arouse'/*vozbuž-ú, vozbud'-íš*, etc. vs. *razbud'í* 'wake'/*razbuž-ú, razbúd'-iš*, etc.; *opr'ed'el'í* 'determine, define'/ *opr'ed'el'-ú, opr'ed'el'-íš*, etc. vs. *razd'el'í* 'divide'/*razd'el'-ú, razd'él'-iš*, etc.; *kos'í* 'bend, make crooked, look askance'/*koš-ú, kos'-íš*, etc. vs. *kos'i* 'mow'/*koš-ú, kós'-iš*, etc. (correlated with *kosá* 'scythe').

In marked stems, on the other hand, the general pattern is to have fixed—hence unmarked—stress (*p'ok*/*p'ok-ú, p'oč-óš*, etc.), and there are very few exceptions (e.g. *t'anu* 'pull'/*t'an-ú, t'án'-oš*, etc.; *tonu* 'drown'/ *ton-ú, tón'-oš*, etc.; *mog* 'be able'/*mog-ú, móž-oš*, etc.).[42] In hypermarked stems, the reversal may be superseded by other marked contexts such as syllabicity and anaptyxis. Thus in monosyllabic *-a* stems which are anaptyctic in the nonpreterite like *bra* 'take'/*b'or-ú, dra* 'flay'/*d'or-ú, zva* 'call'/*zov-ú*, as well as in nonanaptyctic ones like *rva* 'tear'/*rv-ú, vra* 'lie'/*vr-ú*, and *tka* 'weave'/*tk-ú*, expected mobile stress does not ensue due to the supervening marked context of syllabicity.[43]

Hypermarked stems have in common with unmarked stems that they both display mobility in the nonpreterite, obligatorily in polysyllabic hypermarked stems and as a general tendency in unmarked stems. The mobility differentiates 1sg. from the rest of the nonpreterite paradigm, and this is due to the fact that 1sg. is the maximally marked form and hence exhibits the complementary unmarked stress (defined as stress on any syllable other than stem-final, excluding the theme vowel). The other forms, being unmarked vis-à-vis 1sg., accordingly exhibit the complementary marked stress.

The picture in the preterite follows similar lines. In unmarked and hypermarked stems the stress is generally fixed on the theme vowel, except that monosyllabic *-a* stems mostly have desinentially stressed feminine forms, e.g. *rva-l-á, žra-l-á, žda-l-á, lga-l-á, vra-l-á, zva-l-á*, etc. Thus the overwhelming majority conforms to the patterns *xoxotá-l-∅, xoxotá-l-a,* *xoxotá-l-o, xoxotá-l'-i;* as in *govor'í-l-∅, govor'í-l-a, govor'í-l-o, govor'í-l'-i.*[44]

Consonant stems in the preterite split up into two groups depending on whether the consonant is obstruent or sonorant. Obstruent stems (which include those in *r—tr/t'ór/t'er'é* 'rub,' *mr/m'ór/m'er'é* 'die,' *pr/p'ór/p'er'é* 'push') are marked vis-à-vis sonorant stems, and these semeiotic values show up in the stress pattern of the two types: the former does not admit of differentiation in either the nonpreterite or the preterite, the latter permits differentiation in both.[45] The preterite of obstruent stems can thus have either 'desinential' stress (actually, stress falls on the last stressable syllable, which is mostly the desinence) or stem stress: *v'oz* 'carry'/*v'óz-∅, v'oz-l-á, v'oz-l-ó, v'oz-l'-í; griz* 'gnaw'/*gríz-∅, gríz-l-a, gríz-l-o, gríz-l'-i.* Stem stress is limited to a handful of stems: *str'ig* 'shear, pare,' *s'ek* 'whip,' *l'éz* 'climb,' *griz* 'gnaw,' *jed* 'eat,' *klad* 'place,' *krad* 'steal,' *pr'ad* 'weave,' *jéd/jéxaj* 'ride,' *pad* 'fall,' *s'ád/s'éd* 'sit,' *šib* 'hit.' The difference between the two patterns is rooted in the relation between stem vocalism and/or stem-final consonant and stress (cf. Shapiro 1969:19-26); the principle informing the relation is complementarity. The presence of a vowel with the value [M fla] is coherent with the placement of stress on that syllable, owing to the unmarked status of stressed syllables in Russian. This accounts for all of the stem-stressed items listed above that do not have *a* as their stem vowel. As for the latter, given that *a* is nondistinctively [+ fla] and hence [U fla], the determination of stem vs. desinence stress hinges on the presence vs. absence, respectively, of an obstruent evaluated as [M str]. Thus, on the one hand, we have stem stress in *klad, krad, pr'ad;* but desinence stress in *pas* 'graze' and *tr'as* 'shake'—the only two stems with *a* as the preterite stem vowel and a final [U str] obstruent.[46] This means that in the preterite the unmarked stressed syllable of consonant stems containing the vowel *a* coincides with the stem vowel in case the stem ends in an obstruent marked for stridency; and with the last stressable vowel in case it ends with an obstruent unmarked for stridency.

Precisely the same relations characterize the infinitives of these stems. In each case where the stress in the preterite falls on the stem vowel throughout the four forms, the corresponding infinitive also has stem stress (and the desinence alternant *-st'* rather than *-st'í*): *lé-st', grí-st', jé-st', klá-st', krá-st', pr'á-st', pá-st', s'é-st'.*[47]

It is now time to summarize the theoretical and methodological implications of the analysis of Russian conjugation presented here. What needs underscoring first is the role of asymmetry in the manifestation of linguistic signs, specifically in its conceptual bond with complementarity and markedness. The unequal evaluation of the terms of oppositions in language has been an important notion of linguistic theorizing since at least the heyday of the Prague School's chief Russian representatives, Trubetzkoy, Jakobson, and Karcevskij. The clearest early expression of its role is given in Jakobson's 'Zur Struktur des russischen Verbums' ([1932] 1971:15), where the asymmetry of correlative grammatical forms in morphology is characterized as two antinomies: (1) between the signalization of A and nonsignalization of A; (2) between the nonsignalization of A and the signalization of non-A. In the first case two signs making reference to the same objective reality differ in semeiotic value in that the signatum of one of the signs specifies a certain 'mark' A of this reality while the meaning of the other makes no such specification. In the second case, the antinomy is between general and special meaning of the unmarked term, where the meaning of the latter can fluctuate between leaving the content of the 'mark' A unspecified, neither positing nor negating it; and specifying the meaning of the unmarked term as an absence.

In focusing on the paradigmatic asymmetry of linguistic signs expressed by the polar semeiotic values of marked and unmarked superimposed on oppositions in phonology, grammar, and lexis, the early structuralists appear to have glossed over a cardinal syntagmatic consequence of markedness: complementarity. If the conceptual system underlying and informing grammar, and language broadly conceived, consists of oppositely valued signs and sign complexes, then whatever syntagmatic coherence linguistic phenomena have in their actual manifestation must likewise be informed by principles of organization diagrammatic of this underlying asymmetry. The only aspect of the asymmetric nature of linguistic opposition that allows access to structural coherence is the complementarity of the terms of the asymmetry, the markedness values. The systematic relatability of the complementary entities and of their semeiotic values is assured by the binary nature of all opposition, which balances the asymmetry of the axiological superstructure by furnishing the system of relations with the symmetry needed for the identification and perpetuation of linguistic units by learners and users.

In explaining the cohesions between form and meaning in Russian conjugation above, moreover, complementation of markedness values was seen to be the dominant mode of semeiosis—so much so that replication was confined to the structure of desinences and the expression of further undifferentiated members of the hierarchy of categories. Given the common understanding of undifferentiated contexts, statuses, and categories as marked in value (Brøndal's principle of compensation), it is clear that replication is itself the marked (more narrowly defined) principle of semeiosis vis-à-vis its unmarked (less narrowly defined) counterpart, complementation.

Complementation actually has two aspects or modes of manifestation, which are semeiotically distinct and need to be understood as such. The more usual effect of complementation, well known in linguistic analysis, is the distribution of phonetic properties in complementary but mutually exclusive contexts. This widespread fact of language structure serves as a diagnostic in the determination of the nondistinctiveness of a particular feature, so that, to repeat an earlier example, the complementary distribution of short and long vowel realizations in English before obstruents indicates the nonphonemic status of quantity. The general effect of variation rules is augmented by their correlation of complementary phonetic properties with specific contexts. More significantly, we have seen that the assignment of particular properties to particular contexts is governed by a universal semeiotic principle—markedness assimilation—which assigns the unmarked value of an opposition to the unmarked context and the marked value of an opposition to the marked context. Complementary distribution can thus be understood as the semeiotic instantiation of markedness assimilation.

It is not difficult to perceive that this first, familiar sense of complementation is a manifestation of symmetry, since 'variation rules . . . transform relations of similarity—equivalence in markedness—into relations of contiguity in phonetic realization' (Andersen 1979:381). What has not been perceived, however, is that this form of complementation is peculiarly characteristic of the expression system of language (phonology, phonetics). By contrast, as the analysis of Russian conjugation has repeatedly made manifest, the morphophonemic system of a language largely eschews the symmetrical, replicative patterns of semeiosis which are so favored by phonology. Indeed, morphophonemics systematically exploits a second, less studied form of complementation which is antisymmetrical in its effects, as an inversion, and can accordingly be called *chiastic*.[48] The predominant use of chiastic complementation comports perfectly with the semeiotic nature of morphophonemics, which is the part of grammar that is constituted by the 'relations between the contextual variants of the same linguistic sign(s)' and contrasted to morphology, constituted by the 'relations between [basic] linguistic signs' (Andersen 1969a:807). The fact that morphophonemics privileges chiasmus is, in other words, in complete alignment with its function: the manifestation of morphological alternation.

Conversely, the prevalence of symmetrical modes of semeiosis in the specification of the basic signs of morphology—such as the structure of Russian verbal desinences illustrated above (cf. Shapiro 1972b:356-61)—accords with the semeiotic status of morphological units. Thus when the constitution of hierarchically independent (invariant) entities in grammar is at issue, correspondences reflecting relations on the content level (grammatical meaning) in the relations of the expression level (sounds) function as iconic signs. More precisely, they are a variety of icon, or hypoicon in Peirce's trichotomous classification, which Peirce called metaphors and defined as 'those which represent the representative character of a representamen [= sign] by representing a *parallelism* in something else' (2.277; emphasis mine). This idiosyncratic understanding of metaphor reflected in Peirce's typically difficult diction seems to imply that the more familiar kind of hypoicon—diagram (image being the third)—is a more general species of sign which subsumes parallelistic semeiosis (replication of relational values) and chiastic semeiosis (alternation of relational values) as variants. If this is so, then the metaphoric relations of parallelism entail the characterization of the relations contracted by chiasmus as metonymic, owing to the status of antisymmetry as a species of metonymy via its negational quotient (cf. chapter 5, section 2).

The invocation of a framework based on markedness, to explain the coherence of linguistic entities syntagmatically, also implies the ineluctable and necessary consideration of these entities as signs, as parts of a semeiotic. Whereas heretofore things like verb stems and desinences, including their positional shapes and alternants, have been looked upon simply as artifacts of description which facilitate an economical, mutually consistent statement of distributional facts, the semeiotic analysis presented here reposes on the fundamental assumption that all of these linguistic units have values—markedness values—which vary coherently and uniformly in alignment with contexts and the values (hierarchy) of contexts. The fusion of stems and desinences owes its coherence, its semeiotic raison d'être, to the form of the meaning on both sides of the expression/content 'solidarity,' to what Hjelmslev (1969:54-6) so astutely called 'content-form' and distinguished from 'expression-form.'

The coherence of linguistic units amongst each other is by no means a static one, for we have incontrovertible empirical evidence that languages change over time. But the fact of change must be understood correctly as a dynamic based on teleology, where the telos is greater goodness of fit (iconicity, coherence) between underlying structure and its overt manifestation in speech (cf. Anttila 1974:19-25). The picture of Russian conjugation and of its system drawn above differs strikingly little from that of Old Russian (Bulaxovskij 1958:250-3; cf. Kiparsky 1967:180), i.e., from the state of the language with respect to verb inflection dating as far back as 900-1000 years ago! Given such a long span for testing, encompassing vast upheavals in the morphophonemics of Russian occasioned by the sound change known as the 'jer shift' (cf. Isačenko 1970), we have every reason to suppose that present-day conjugation has a teleological coherence which has given shape to it diachronically and enables it to subsist in its present form synchronically.

3. Counter-etymological Vowels in Russian

Russian is quite punctilious about maintaining the etymologically pristine or 'correct' shape of stems and desinences, so that the morpho-phonemics of contemporary standard Russian is for the most part a faithful representation of the language's attested history. There are, however, cases where the segmental shapes have been altered, particularly in regard to unstressed vowels and connected with the introduction of akan'e and ikan'e. Thus O(ld) R(ussian) *poromъ* 'ferry' came to be spelled *parom* (Bulaxovskij 1958:106). As long as the vowel never appeared under stress, this sort of 're-etymologization' remained a largely orthographic phenomenon (at least in the literary language), e.g. *kalač* 'kolatch' (OR *kolačь*'), *barsuk* 'badger' (OR *borsukъ*), *rabota* 'work' (OR *robota*), etc. (Bulaxovskij 1958:105-6). It cannot be gainsaid, however, that some quotient of morphophonemic relevance could have attached to the forms in question as a result of even a purely orthographic change. Moreover, as soon as a counter-etymological vowel appeared in a stressed syllable as part of a morphophonemic alternation, its status changed palpably and systematically. Thus, whereas it was immaterial from the morphophonemic point of view that OR *rjasnica* 'eyelash' came to be spelled *resnica* (conceding, of course, the *not* immaterial concomitant loss of semantic correlation with *rjasa* 'cassock'; v. Fasmer 1971:473-4), since the syllable in question was never stressed, the change of OR *djasna* 'gum' to *desna* gave rise to a morphophonemically relevant counter-etymological vowel in the stem-stressed plural forms *dësny*, *dësnam*, etc. (Bulaxovskij 1958:107). In one known case of this type, a doublet has arisen consisting of the normative paradigm *kajmá* 'border,' pl. *kajmý*, *kaëm*, *kajmám*, etc.; and the non-standard (proscribed) alternation *kajmá*, pl. *kójmy*, *kojm*, *kójmam*, etc. (Avanesov and Ožegov 1959:207). This singular example among substantives is paralleled by the morphophonemically identical change (especially widespread in Russian dialects) to a counter-etymological vowel in the present indicative forms (excluding 1sg.) of a group of verbs with the theme vowel -*i* (Bromlej and Bulatova 1972:253n; cf. Orlova 1970 and Obnorskij 1953:94-9). Putatively by analogy (thus Obnorskij 1953:98; cf. Bulaxovskij 1958:106) with verbs like *nosít'* 'carry,' 1sg. *nošú* [nʌšú], 2sg. *nósiš'* [nós'iš], wherein a so-called stress retraction from desinence to stem conditions the alternation of /a/ and /o/, the two verbs *(po)sadít'* 'plant, seat' and *platít'* 'pay' in particular were accepted in the literary language through the beginning of the present century (at least as alternates) with the conjugation [sažú], [sód'iš], etc.; and [plačú], [plót'iš], etc. To the extent that the pronunciation with counter-etymological *o* in these verbs is still extant today, it is especially characteristic of the grammar of older generations of Muscovite speakers of CSR (Graudina 1977:103). But forms such as [plót'it] and past passive participle [ʌplóč'ьn:ɨj] are also to be heard from non-Muscovite speakers of the standard language. Less common are [pʌsód'iš], etc. These forms were considered standard by those grammarians (Grot and Šaxmatov; v. Bulaxovskij 1958:106) who were among the first to think in terms of a standard language in Russia. The counter-etymological forms of *platít'* are explicitly proscribed as non-standard by normative sources today (e.g. Avanesov and Ožegov 1959:396). The form *sódiš'* is not mentioned by Avanesov and Ožegov; however, Ušakov (1935:22) cites it as a Muscovite alternate of *sádiš'* (cf. Ušakov 1964:15). It should be noted, moreover, that non-standard forms like *provozgósiš'* and *priglósiš'* have reportedly begun to make inroads into CSR (Voroncova 1959:145).

Another set of data relating to counter-etymological vowels has been adduced by Janko-Trinickaja (1971). Her examples, while pertaining to current speech, are strictly limited to proper names (nicknames and sobriquets) and more generally to the affective sector of the Russian lexicon. While it is typical of names to preserve their presumed etymological vowels when serving as deriving bases for nicknames (diminutive and hypocoristic), e.g. *Nadéžda → Nádja, Vasílij → Vásja, Polína → Pólja, Bor'ís → Bórja, Svetlána → Svéta, Veniamín → Vénja,* etc., there are cases where the stressed vowel in the derivative is counter-etymological: *Tamára → Tóma, Matrëna → Mótja, Matíl'da → Mótja, Matvéj → Mótja, Afanásij (Afanásija) → Afónja, Fónja, Larísa → Lóra (~ Lára).* Most of the examples involve the substitution of /o/ for /a/. There are, however, a few examples of /i/ being substituted for /e/: *Venedíkt → Vínja (~ Vénja), Semën → Síma (~ Sénja, Sëma), Revékka → Ríva (~ Réva).*

One of the most favored processes in current affective formations is truncation as applied to surnames and sobriquets. Here again the norm is preservation of the original vowel: *Kamergérov → Kam, Bočkarëv → Bóča, Drebínskij → Dréba, Sivkóv → Síva,* etc. Counter-etymological substitution is possible too: *Krašenínnikov → Kroš, Speránde → Spírka;* cf. the toponym *Peterbúrg → Píter* (all examples from Janko-Trinickaja 1971:292). In one interesting attestation, a pet pelican's hypocoristic displays the same sort of alternation: *pelikán → Pílja, Píl'ka.*

The phenomenon of counter-etymological vowels is not restricted to proper names; nor is concomitant truncation. Alongside the expected derivatives *tramváj* 'streetcar' → *tram, dopolnítel'nyj (paëk)* 'extra ration' → *dop, preferáns* 'preference' [card game] → *pref, psixíčeskij (bol'noj)* 'mental patient' → *psix, televízor 'TV set'* → *télik, xorošó* 'good' [a mark] → *xórik, diréktor* 'director' → *dírik* (note the accompanying suffixation in the latter three examples), Janko-Trinickaja (1971:292) cites instances like *otolaringólog* 'otolaryngologist' → *lor, spekuljánt* 'speculator' → *spíkul',* and *špargálka* 'crib' → *špóra.* Cf. *bárxat* 'velvet' → *bárxatka ~ barxótka* 'velvet ribbon,' which Ušakov (1935:91) does not differentiate in meaning while assigning stylistic value (specifically, *prostorečie* 'low style') to the variant with the counter-etymological vowel, whereas Ožegov and

Sapiro (1959:50) gloss the first as *kusóček bárxata* 'a piece of velvet' and the
second as *bárxatnaja lentočka* 'velvet ribbon.'

What is remarkable and in need of explanation is the fact that among
affectives the substitution of vowels is invariably /o/ for /a/ and /i/ for /e/
(Janko-Trinickaja 1971 cites only one [apparent nonce] ex. to the contrary,
Kitáj → Kéta). This is not so with regard to the verb alternation discussed
earlier. There exist dialects in which /a/ is substituted for /o/, although the
phenomenon appears to be much more restricted geographically than the
reverse: *lovít'* 'catch' → [láv'iš], *solít'* 'salt' → [sál'iš] (Orlova 1970:119).

If we wish to understand counter-etymological vowels in the two
categories of examples adduced above, we need first to distinguish the two
types from each other. In the Russian verb the 'retraction' of stress from
desinential to predesinential position has a semeiotic function (see above
section 2). In conformity with the overall principle of markedness
complementation governing the structure of Russian conjugation, unmarked stem types generally exhibit the marked stress type (i.e., mobility),
whereas marked stem types generally exhibit the unmarked stress type (i.e.,
fixity). In the nonpreterite, where the only kind of mobility is the
'retraction' in question, it is the unmarked stem types like *nos'i-* or *v'ert'e-*
'twirl' that productively exhibit this alternation (the *p'isa-* 'write' type being
hypermarked and unproductive). The 1sg. as the most marked form of the
paradigm displays desinential stress, furthermore, because in Russian
stressed syllables are unmarked, unstressed syllables marked (Trubetzkoy
1975:182); in other words, the fact of the grammatical form's being marked
is complemented by the incidence of stress—the unmarked value for
stress—on the desinence. Conversely, then, all the other forms of the pres.
indic. paradigm (excluding 1sg.) are unmarked; hence the desinences of
these forms are complemented by the marked value for stress, viz.
stresslessness. It is these semeiotic relations that motivate the pronounced
tendency of *-ít'* verbs to develop this sort of stress pattern diachronically
(Voroncova 1959).

The role of complementarity in the morphophonemic patterning of
Russian conjugation is crucial to solving the problem of counter-
etymological vowels in verbs. While in standard Russian the complementary relationships do not extend beyond the desinence/stress nexus,
it seems that dialects which have forms like *sódiš'* have gone one step
further in realizing the semeiotic potential of the complementary relation
between segmental and suprasegmental values by widening its compass to
embrace stems. Specifically, the stem final or predesinential vowel, on
which the retracted stress falls in forms other than 1sg., may change
counter-etymologically, thus manifesting an alternation defined by complementary values.

The relation between /o/ and /a/ in terms of markedness values is such that /o/, being [— compact], is marked for compactness, whereas /a/, being [+ compact], is unmarked for this feature. The complementarity between stress value and vowel value thus emerges in these examples: /o/ as the marked sound coheres semeiotically with the incidence of stress on the syllable containing it.

The explanation of counter-etymological /o/ and /i/ in affectives hinges ultimately on similar considerations. Just as in the relation of /a/ to /o/, the relation of /i/ to /e/ is that of a marked to an unmarked vowel for the same diacritic category, compactness, since the former, being [+ diffuse], is relatively less compact ([+ compact] being the unmarked value) than the latter, which is [— diffuse]. Thus while both /i/ and /e/ are marked for compactness vis-à-vis the [+ compact] vowel /a/, the former is nonetheless marked vis-à-vis the latter for the feature.

Janko-Trinickaja (1971:293) is at a loss to explain the phenomenon of counter-etymological vowels phonologically. The missing ingredient, and one she takes no systematic note of, is the stylistic value of the items she adduces. Nicknames and sobriquets are part of the affective lexicon of Russian, as are appellatives like *otolaringólog* → *lor* that manifest the same vowel alternation. Indeed, it is highly significant that not one of the examples falls outside the affective category. This seems to suggest strongly that the alternation is coherent with the value of affectives as a lexical class.

Another invariable aspect of these formations overlooked by Janko-Trinickaja is that they all involve a morphophonemic 'truncation,' i.e., elements present in the deriving base are absent in the derivative. But truncation as a semeiotic process involves an unmarking (see chapter 2 and chapter 3, section 1). A term of a derivational correlation taken to be primary (the deriving base) vis-à-vis a specific secondary counterpart (its derivative) is marked, and the latter is unmarked. This assignment of markedness values accords well with the common notion that the absence (*signe zéro*) of something is normally unmarked, whereas the presence of that same something is normally marked.

If truncation (and, for that matter, all reduction) is to be understood normally as an unmarking, then it follows that all augmentation (affixation) is normally a marking. In an opposition dominated by a marked context, however, the reverse may obtain, in conformity with this semeiotic universal by which the normally unmarked value is construed as marked and the normally marked value as unmarked. Markedness reversal can be seen to operate in the context of affectives, since reduction applies with reversed sign values in diminutives, like the proper name *Míša* 'Mike' which is marked vis-à-vis its neutral counterpart *Mixaíl* 'Michael.' An analysis of reduction in terms of markedness not only reveals the semeiotic coherence of the derivational relations involved but accounts as well for the widespread incidence of truncation as a preferred means of forming hypocoristics and diminutives. Moreover, this observation is fully compatible with the knowledge that (to repeat) ellipsis, abbreviation, and univerbation are particularly favored processes in the formation of marked (i.e., non-neutral) vocabulary and the marked (social/professional) use of language.

A second semeiotic universal is pertinent to the problem at hand, namely markedness assimilation. In the case of both markedness assimilation and reversal, context is to be understood in the broadest possible sense encompassing a whole range of features, from phonetic environments (simultaneous and sequential) to the most abstract social environments.

Coming back to the analysis of items like *Tamára* → *Tóma* and *Revékka* → *Ríva,* we are now in a position to suggest that the counter-etymological vowels have a definite semeiotic function, in that they replicate the markedness value (as an instance of markedness assimilation) of the stylistic status of the words in which they appear as affective alternants. It is the marked characters of the words as a stylistic class that is indicated by and coherent with the marked value of the vowels /o/ and /i/. Since this is admittedly a sporadic phenomenon, truncation in and of itself must be adjudged to be sufficient in realizing the marked character of affective vocabulary in Russian.

Although there is an almost perfect overlap in the results of the counter-etymological substitution in the two categories of examples, the motivations are different. In the verb the appearance of /o/ is associated with stress on this vowel as its complement. In the affectives the vowels /o/ and /i/ are replicative in one respect and complementary in another. Their marked status for compactness replicates the marked status of affectives as a class and complements the unmarked value of stress, i.e., their stressedness. The fact that the second category exhibits replication of values primarily and complementation secondarily, while the first evinces only complementation, is in alignment with the two different types of grammatical alternation each implements. The formation of affectives by means of truncation (with or without accompanying affixation) is subsumed by *derivational* morphology/morphophonemics, whereas the formation of conjugational paradigms falls under the rubric of *inflectional* morphology/morphophonemics. Counter-etymological vowels, therefore, can be perceived via their disparate semeiotic motivation as (Peircean) indexes of the fundamental division of grammar into derivation and inflection. In this respect their sign function is compatible with that of vowel/zero alternations in Russian (cf. above, section 1). But whereas vowel/zero alternations have a stable and productive role to play in Russian morphophonemics, counter-etymological vowels, as episodic occurrences, exploit a semeiotic potential that is basically covert, presumably on the common principle of linguistic diagrammatization, something like 'the more, the merrier' (cf. Anttila 1980:277).

V
Semantics

1. Meaning and Semantic Change

Symbols—despite the indirectness of their signification—are the species of (legi)sign capable of constituting linguistic discourse. 'The most characteristic aspect of a symbol is its aspect as related to its interpretant; because a symbol is distinguished as a sign which becomes such by virtue of determining its interpretant' (NE 4:260). Here we note the full power of Peirce's definition as it applies to the notion of language as a symbolic system. And if we accept Jakobson's statement that 'everything language can and does communicate stands first and foremost in a necessary, intimate connection with meaning and always carries semantic information' (1972:76), we are forced to the conclusion that all linguistic phenomena must ultimately be comprehended as instantiations of symbolicity. The semeiotic perspective articulated by Peirce encompasses symbols as the epitomical signs, and 'language is an example of a purely semiotic system' (Jakobson 1971:703). In order to make progress in the exploration of meaning, it thus appears we must probe the ontology of the symbol.

The successful investigation of semeiosis, including symbols, cannot proceed, however, without taking due account of Peirce's three categories. It is Thirdness that figures most prominently in the structure of a semeiotic system such as language. Whereas Firstness is fundamentally a quality of feeling or a mere possibility and Secondness 'the experience of effort, prescinded from the idea of a purpose' (H 25), Thirdness alone informs the notion of mediation or representation; that is to say, precisely the triadic relation that obtains between sign, object, and interpretant (cf. H 31). Thirdness is generality governing lawlike change and transformation, which distinguishes it from Firstness, the possibility of a single unitary and immutable quality. Thirdness is accorded functional prominence in the

Peircean concept of the interpretant. Since it is the interpretant that is indispensable to the integrity of the sign relation, semeiosis—and, consequently, meaning—are ineluctably contingent on Thirdness via the role of the interpretant: 'every genuine triadic relation involves meaning, as meaning is obviously a triadic relation' (1.345).

The categorial framework of Firsts, Seconds, and Thirds provides (in addition to other advantages) a way of understanding the different, seemingly incompatible aspects of meaning to which linguistis have been attuned traditionally. To begin with the perceived 'ungraspability' (Lyons 1977) of meaning which has led some to relegate the concept to the status of a 'pre-theoretical term' (Lyons 1977:1), we can now correctly judge this property to be inherent and highly necessary as the systematically built-in quotient or margin of inchoateness which allows meaning to subsist and to change. Firstness of meaning is tantamount to infinite regress, which is actually the inherent potential of an infinity of translatable signata indispensable to the fulfillment of new communicative needs as they arise in the course of cultural growth. The relation between sign and object cannot, of course, remain ultimately inchoate, and the mediational or interpretative system which comprises semantic structure comports an element of Secondness, of what Peirce terms 'brute reaction' between actual meanings as they are differentiated from each other, in the imposition of pragmatically definite choice that language makes on the potentially infinite continuum of reference. Simple reaction as represented by selection (the segmentation of the semantic continuum) does not complete the picture, however. This role is reserved for Thirdness, manifested in the rule or law, the patterning and coherence, which facilitate understanding between speakers through the system of interpretants that places practical communicative limits on infinite regress, thereby creating the condition of structure in meaning. Peirce himself puts it tellingly: 'Reality is compulsive. But the compulsiveness is absolutely *hic et nunc*. It is for an instant and it is gone . . . . The reality only exists as an element of the regularity. And the regularity is the symbol. Reality, therefore, can only be regarded as the limit of the endless series of symbols' (NE 4:261).

Symbols by their very nature, while producing an endless series of interpretants that are themselves symbols, tend towards definiteness, towards interpretants that are continually more determinate than their antecedents. Growth—a tendency to become determined via interpretation —inheres in the structure of the symbol as its fundamental definiens. That is why Peirce goes so far as to assert that 'a symbol is an embryonic reality endowed with power of growth into the very truth, the very entelechy of reality' (NE 4:262). (So much for truth-conditional semantics!)

The structure and development of tropes is particularly suited to an illustration of the teleological nature of symbols. The dynamic or life cycle of tropes (perhaps more aptly to be called their 'life spiral') typically involves (as we shall see in the next section) the lexicalization of an initially living metonymy or metaphor (by what Stern 1931:390 calls adequation). This aspect is especially common to the diachronic accretion of terminology in a specialized (e.g. scientific) sector of the vocabulary. As Quine has it, 'the neatly worked inner stretches of science are an open space in the tropical jungle, created by clearing tropes away' (1978:162). To take an example from the idiom of contemporary sports, specifically basketball in America, within the last decade an expression—*back door*—has entered common parlance to describe a maneuver whereby one of the offensive team's players (without the ball) manages to penetrate unnoticed behind the opposing team's defenses close enough to the basket to attempt an unobstructed short shot (usually a so-called 'layup'). When this play first came into existence, its linguistic designation was patently metaphorical (cf. *getting in through the back door*). Both the play and the expression, indeed, arose spontaneously, by chance, as instantiations of the 'brute force' of Secondness. But as the play spread and grew in frequency, it ceased to be the spontaneous result of chance configurations in game situations. It became what is known as a 'set play,' that is a maneuver planned and perfected in practice sessions, designed to take its place among the stock of plays in a team's repertoire or 'play book.' At this crucial point, the metaphor had largely lost its figural status, having become a term. Now, *back door* became a deriving base for terminological exfoliations such as *to go back door, to back door, to pull a back door* (*play*), etc. Indeed, here we can legitimately speak of a lexicalization of the original trope. In a Peircean perspective, this is the predicted teleological result of the very ontology of a symbol. In its status as the epitomically indeterminate sign, the symbol is defined by its preeminent power of growth and development, of determining itself increasingly, of making its meaning more concrete (= clear, not non-abstract) by engendering successive interpretants with which it maintains a semantic affinity along a gradient simultaneously synchronic and diachronic.

What is particularly significant about the playing out of this preordained development in terminology is the semeiotic connection between the gradual attenuation of indeterminacy and the concept embedded in the word *term* itself. The end result of the growth of symbols is precisely the etymologically veridical *term*(*inus*)!

Linking this process to Peirce's pragmatistic conception of habit as the ultimate logical interpretant, we can see with clarity that the intellectual, rational core of habit presupposes a concomitant loss of the spontaneous, the emotive quotient of sign function. In the Peircean idiom, we have here a progression away from the emotional interpretant toward the final interpretant, viz. a mental habit subtending a habit of action. An immediate morphological parallel that suggests itself is lexicalization in affective (expressive) formations. In a language as replete with diminutives and hypocoristics as Russian, it is common to observe the transition of an original expressive derivation into the category of terms broadly conceived (i.e., neutral substantives with no affective meaning). A word such as *nosok* 'sock, spout, toe (of footwear or hose)' shows an effacement (not completely) of the historically primary meaning 'little nose' via an intermediate stage involving figuration, whereby the protuberance charac- teristic of a nose is transferred onto objects occupying the same position vis-à-vis an anchoring mass. Hardly an isolated example in Russian, it has, moreover, analogous counterparts in many other languages.

But the power of a symbol does not stop with the demise of a trope or the eclipse of affective meaning resulting from fading and lexicalization. The entombed history of the linguistic sign can always be disinterred—by poets, or by those who recur to the poetic function for aesthetic effect in an otherwise discursive context (such as that of advertising slogans). Third- ness, with its definitional *esse in futuro,* always teleologically transcends the limitations of Secondness, of the here and now.

The telos of the symbol, its teleological thrust, is not confined to this kind of sign; it is only most prominent therein. For signs are entelechies (NE 4:299), and entelechy is just 'the third element . . . which brings things together . . . the element which is prominent in such ideas as Plan, Cause, and Law' (ibid., 195-6).

We thus come to the notion that linguistic semeiosis necessarily presupposes the involvement of the most important member of the semeiotic triad, the interpretant, whose role is defined by the only fallible mode of inference—abduction. This definition accords perfectly with the essential nature of the symbol and with symbolicity. Collocated within the matrix of Peirce's categories and his pragmaticism, semeiotic fallibilism renders change in meaning understandable as an inalienable part of the sign situation and, consequently, as an aspect of semantic continuity assuring interpretability across discontinuous generations. What is even more important, change itself becomes an ontological component of linguistic meaning and the nature of meaning. A semeiotic perspective thus leads without fail to the position that synchronic grammar (including lexis) cannot be validated without recourse to diachrony: every structure incorporates a dynamic.

Or as Jakobson put it (1971:562), 'when the time factor enters into such a system of symbolic values as language, it becomes a symbol itself.'

2. Tropes and the Structure of Meaning

From antiquity to the present day the study of tropes, or figures of speech, has always been at or near the center of scholarly interest in language. The preponderant mass of research on tropes (both traditional and more recent[1]) has had as its primary goal the explication and typologization of the semantic relations contracted by figures of speech, rather than the analysis of what can be called the *ontological structure* of tropes. As conceptualized with reference to Schema A below representing the simultaneous aspects inherent in all tropes, the emphasis heretofore has been on setting forth the precise details of the 'preexisting conditions' entered into by the two signata, figural and literal, i.e., a kind of relational algebra; and on the combinatorial logic or 'operations' to which the relations are subjected when the signata are juxtaposed. Furthermore, although many studies purport to deal with the ontological structure of tropes (their essential *definientia*), none appears in my opinion to have had noteworthy success.

Nor has there been much effort by modern investigators, with the prominent exception of Stern (1931; rpt. 1965), to collocate tropes in a general theory of semantic change. This is, nonetheless, precisely where tropes ought to be placed in order to be understood in their diachronic subaspect as verbal entities with a structurally marked dynamic. What has been insufficiently apperceived, indeed, is the fact that all figures of speech are a particular kind of abductive innovation. As such they necessarily project a historical dimension, which involves change in meaning; and even a kind of 'life cycle.'

To elaborate on the ontological structure of tropes, one might begin by noting that for Aristotle the genus/species relationship in its four exhaustive substitutions of terms—genus for species, species for genus, genus for genus, and species for species—defines the domain of metaphor. Indeed, metaphor is the all-encompassing trope for Aristotle, as for all succeeding analysts of figural language. The opulence of studies focusing on metaphor and the marked paucity of those focusing on metonymy issue directly from this (tacit) understanding (I return to this matter below to suggest a natural and precise cause).

In a pioneering article (1965; rpt. 1971:345-59) on the semeiotic essence of language, Jakobson includes in passing the following perspicuous characterization (355) of metaphor and metonymy:

> A partial similarity of two signata may be represented by a . . . total identity of signantia, as in the case of lexical tropes. *Star* means either a celestial body or a person—both of preeminent brightness. A hierarchy of two meanings—one primary, central, proper, context-free; and the other secondary, marginal, figurative, transferred, contextual—is a characteristic of such asymmetrical couples. The metaphor (or metonymy) is an assignment of a signans to a secondary signatum associated by similarity (or contiguity) with the primary signatum.

In this passage the notions of similarity and contiguity are somewhat subordinate to the notion of hierarchy, which tends to belie their prominence in Jakobson's conception of the two tropes promulgated elsewhere. An earlier and better-known exposition is to be found in his *Fundamentals of Language,* in connection with the linguistic analysis of aphasia. There the notion of hierarchy is only implicit at best, and the entire thrust of the argument hinges on defining metaphor as a relation of similarity and metonymy as a relation of contiguity between signata. Clearly, both the ranking of signata vis-à-vis each other and their specific relational connection are equally pertinent to an understanding of the structure of tropes. But the relative importance of these two aspects of the 'figural situation' (as I shall call it) has not heretofore been fully assessed.

The figural situation is comprised by three fundamental components or conjugate aspects which are copresent and rank ordered in every trope. There is first the preexisting condition or quality in which the terms of tropes, the signata, must inhere; which is to say the requirement of *relatability*—the perceptual and cognitive potential underlying the actual relationship of two signata—that must be satisfied by the terms in order for tropes to have an *esse in futuro.* The state of being relatable is defined logically by three partially unranked specificity conditions on trope signata: (1) membership in a certain *species,* with a concomitant relatability by similarity; (2) membership in a certain *context,* with a concomitant relatability by contiguity (logical as well as spatial); (3) adumbration, vis-à-vis each other, of a potential *rank order* tantamount to value (in the strict axiological sense) or dominance. Second, there is the actualization of that substance represented *in posse* by the preexisting condition of trope formation; which is to say the *juxtaposition* or *relation* of signata. This juxtaposition is, more accurately, an *opposition* of terms, since the configuration of meanings in tropes is necessarily dyadic. In parallel to the first aspect, the second is defined logically as a partially unranked triad of operations comprehended by the signata: (1) *selection,* implying simultaneous reference to the paradigms of which the signata are representative; (2) *combination* of the signata into simultaneous syntagms; (3) imposition of *ranking* on the signata so selected and combined, or their hierarchization. Notice should be taken that the second operation is, strictly speaking, not prescindable from the third. Their relationship is, however, not biunique: ranking implies combination, but combination does not imply ranking.

In reviewing the parallel tripartite subdivisions of the first two conjugate aspects of the figural situation, then, we should say that species denotes class membership; the signata of tropes are either of the same or of different species. Context denotes the ground in which the signata are embedded; the ground can be either shared or discontinuous. And rank is the evaluative component which is superimposed on relatable, ultimately correlate, signata. These three terms are coordinate with three distinct types of relation which they implement: similarity, contiguity, and value (dominance). In turn, the three types of relation are coordinate, respectively, with three types of juxtapositional operations: selection, combination, and ranking. Again, ranking or hierarchization represents an evaluative superstructure imparting form to selection, or paradigmatization, and combination, or syntagmatization. Note that an implicit claim is here being made to the effect that similarity and contiguity relations are copresent in and underlie *all* tropes, not just metaphor and metonymy. The traditional association of metaphor with similarity and metonymy with contiguity is not thereby rendered incorrect. It must, nevertheless, be revised to render explicit the fact that these two kinds of relation are present in both major tropes but are so in opposed rank order; in metaphor, similarity predominates over contiguity; in metonymy, the order is inverted.

The preexisting condition, which acts as a springboard for the onset of the figural situation, simultaneously imposes a constraint on the combinability of the signata: they must differ in respect of at least one of the signata. This is the constraint, for instance, which prevents *knife* from being a trope for *fork,* or vice versa (*ad* Todorov: 1974:128), since both words do not differ in species, context, or rank. Note, characteristically, that in aphasic (i.e., pathological) speech *knife* and *fork* can be commuted for each other (Jakobson 1971:250).

Finally and most significantly, the figural situation manifests a third aspect—the resultant state or the *representation* articulated by the signata. This is the ontological *definiens* of the trope. It hinges on the concept of rank or hierarchy; here, more precisely, on the rank order of the signata in the set presented by the figural syntagm. Specifically: *Metonymy* is defined as that trope in which a hierarchy of signata is either established or instantiated. Complementarily: *Metaphor* is defined as that trope in which the (simultaneously) established hierarchy of signata is either reversed or neutralized. Metonymy places two previously unconnected signata into a dominance relation vis-à-vis each other; or it gives overt semantic expression to the specific hierarchical relationship which the signata contract independent of the trope. Metonymy goes no further than the establishment or the instantiation of a hierarchy; metaphor, on the other hand, reverses or neutralizes a hierarchy, even if the hierarchy is one established during the metaphoric process only to be reversed.

The entire purport of the foregoing fairly abstract argument can perhaps be made more palpable by resort to the following tabular framework (Schema A).

COPRESENT RANK ORDERED ASPECTS OF THE FIGURAL SITUATION

1. **preexisting condition or quality**
   a. species (similarity)
   b. context (contiguity)
   c. rank (value)
2. **juxtaposition or relation**
   a. selection (paradigmatization)
   b. combination (syntagmatization)
   c. ranking (hierarchization)
3. **resultant state or representation**
   a. metonymy: establishment/instantiation of hierarchy
   b. metaphor: reversal/neutralization of hierarchy
   c. relation between metonymy and metaphor

SCHEMA A

It is important to clarify at this juncture just what is meant by the phrase 'establish a hierarchy.' We may start by noting that Jakobson (1971:232) considers contiguity to be an 'external' relation and similarity an 'internal' relation. This nomenclature can be understood in the terms we adopted by observing that semantic hierarchies (simultaneous syntagms) necessarily project two dimensions, referential and significational, corresponding to the processes, respectively, of denotation and connotation (Frege's *Bedeutung* and *Sinn*). Within the dimension of reference the syntagm is characterized by the several denotata (referents) which correspond to the several signata. Here, then, is an articulation of the patterned set of correspondences between physical or material objects or events, on the one hand; and their mental or conceptual correlates as embodied linguistically in words and sentences, on the other. A focus on the referential dimension is tantamount to an emphasis on the external aspect of meaning. Simultaneously, each semantic syntagm has an internal organization—a focus on the relations contracted by the signata *amongst each other*—which corresponds to and is interdependent with the denotata that constitute the universe of referents we call reality.

In diagrammatic form these relations can be represented as follows (where S = signatum and D = denotatum) (Schema B).

The distinction between external and internal can be aligned, following Jakobson, with the distinction between metonymy and metaphor. In metonymy the referential dimension predominates over the significational, whereas in metaphor this dominance relation is inverted. An external or referential focus is thus tantamount to the priority of message over code, while an internal or significational focus is equivalent to the reverse priority of code over message.

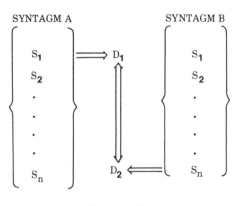

SYNTAGM A   SYNTAGM B

SCHEMA B

To take a pair of concrete examples (borrowed and adapted from Le Guern 1973:14), if it is suggested to someone that he 'reread his Shakespeare,' this does not entail an internal modification in the sense (*Sinn*) of the word 'Shakespeare.' The metonymy constituted by the implementation of an author's name to designate a work by that author hinges on a shift of reference; the internal, or semic, organization has remained unaltered even though the referent has been displaced from author to book. Similarly, when Zola writes about the 'loud voices [that] wrangled in the corridors' ('de grosses voix se querellaient dans les couloirs'), the hierarchy of semantic features or range of connotations is unchanged. The only thing that changes is the referent with which the semantic syntagm is associated. To put it another way, the message demands a partly figural interpretation while leaving the code unaltered.

It is precisely this referential shift that is captured by the phrase 'establish a hierarchy.' The two denotata that are correlated with the two feature hierarchies are not paratactic vis-à-vis each other because one is more general than the other: 'voice' stands for itself in the Zola example as well as for 'person' but *not vice versa*. The fact that 'voice' retains its meaning while simultaneously referring to something other than itself is precisely one of the *differentiae specificae* of metonymy as a trope over and against metaphor. It is the contextual locus or, more fully, the necessary presence of the contiguity relations facilitated by the context that allows the figural meaning of a metonymy to be perceived and understood as such. In saying 'figural meaning' I am designating in more general terms the establishment of an asymmetric relation between denotata *as embodied in* their correlative signata.

The dominance of external reference characteristic of metonymy is absent from metaphor. The relation between the metaphoric term and the object to which it normally makes reference is rendered discontinuous or indirect. In Pascal's 'Man is a thinking reed,' the primacy of a similarity relation means not that two referents are arranged in rank order but rather that the meaning 'reed' is incorporated *for the moment* or *ad hoc* as a nonce signatum of the simultaneous syntagm comprising 'man.' Furthermore— and this is the crucial point—there is a concomitant reversal of the rank order of the two signata 'man' and 'reed' without which the figurality of the sentence would not ensue. Another way of characterizing this reversal is to say (Le Guern 1973:15) that 'the mechanism involved in metaphor is to be analyzed . . . as a suppression, or more precisely, a bracketing ("mise entre parenthèses")' of one member of the set of meanings which constitute the word's semantic structure.

All metonymies, which are based on an inclusion relation, either establish or instantiate hierarchies of signata. The simplest non-literary example of this mode of signification is a taxonomy (cf. Bunge 1969:19), since any classification is founded on (or is transformable into) the principle of binary opposition, and the relation of binary opposition is metonymic. Specifically, the negative entails (includes) the positive term of an opposition but not vice versa. Negation is consequently a metonymy. Indeed, the negative term of an opposition necessarily and overtly makes reference to the positive term, whereas the positive term only implies or makes covert reference to its negative opposite. An opposition being a minimal (binary) paradigm, one term is *in absentia* where the other is *in praesentia* and vice versa. However, the positive is explicitly included in the negative since the latter is a specified absence of the former. The positive, on the other hand, includes its (negative) counterpart only implicitly, in virtue of the very nature of (logical and privative) opposition. This necessary, overt inclusion of the positive in the expression of the negative is what renders the negative a metonymy of the positive and demonstrates the inclusional nature of metonymy.

It is important to understand the rhetorical implications of binary opposition precisely because tropes presuppose the copresence of *two* signata, roughly labeled the literal and the figural. The opposition between these two signata is functionally construed as privative: figural meaning is juxtaposed to its opposite, non-figural meaning. Moreover, figural meaning is in a *relation of dominance* over the non-figural. If this were not so, the trope would cease to be understood as such (as happens not infrequently; see below).

In metonymy the relation of dominance (i.e., hierarchy) is something that is established with the onset of the figural situation and goes no further. This is especially clear in *pars pro toto*. The word *sail*, used to denote the totality *ship* of which it is but one (albeit an important) part, involves the differentiation of that totality. Differentiation—another mode of characterizing the process inherent in what was earlier termed taxonomy—is precisely a singling out or individuation of constituents. However, in metonymy it is not differentiation pure and simple. A necessary concomitant is the relative ranking or hierarchization of the constituents, here the two signata. In the case of *sail* for *ship,* no wonder the part chosen to represent the whole is the most prominent one; prominence is, after all, a relation of rank. One might even assert that the choice of the item singled out in metonymy is perceptually and/or cognitively well-motivated (natural). That is to say the hierarchy established by metonymy rests on yet another hierarchy. In the *sail* for *ship* case the relation between a sail and the remaining parts of the vessel is also one of rank order.

Similarly, abbreviations (a form of metonymy)—visual as well as verbal—reflect the hierarchies which inform their structure. The hiero-glyph, or the pictorial part of an emblem, consists of a visual representation. While different from a verbal representation it is nonetheless fundamentally metonymic because it represents one or more parts of an object or of an utterance taken as an object. The aspect of condensation was perceived by the quatrocento philosopher Marsilio Ficino, who praised hieroglyphs for their power of contracting many thoughts into one single form. It happens more often, however, the pictorial translation of language being at issue, that the hieroglyphic designs of emblems consist of several symbols rather than one alone. An apt example might be the amorous motto *dulce et amarum* 'sweet and bitter' illustrated by the pseudo-Theocritan idyll of Cupid stung by bees while tasting honey. The metaphoric, dominant aspect of the emblem, which submerges the aspect of narrow iconicity, is simultaneously its generalizing impetus and power. It demands that contexts be sought outside the realm of direct entailment by the pictured material itself. A massive diachronic parallel to this is instanced by Chinese writing, which began as pictographic but soon became ideographic. Over time the shape of the characters underwent an internal development entailed by functional demands which resulted in a continuous attenuation of the relation between the meaning of the character and the object which it originally depicted or imitated.

Indeed, investigation of the representational aspect of forms in the visual arts tends to corroborate the finding that the *tertium comparationis* of a symbol and its object is not external form but function; more specifically, that formal feature which fulfills the minimum requirement for the performance of the function. Accordingly, a hobby horse provides a child with a functional substitute for a real horse as long as it can be 'ridden' (Gombrich 1963), even as the metonymic aspect of the figural situation includes the metaphoric component owing to similarity. This example shows appositely the primal character of metonymy as well as the greater immediacy of its link to perception as compared to metaphor.

On the more strictly linguistic side of the ledger, an abbreviation, e.g. *USA,* reflects at least two hierarchies which condition its structure. First, only the categorematic words *United States America* are selected from among those which make up the full unabbreviated version, the syncategorematic words *the, of* being deleted. Second, not just any letters of the unabbreviated counterpart are implemented in the abbreviation but the functionally prominent initials. A further—grammatical—hierarchy underlies the variant *US*: the adnominal genitive *of America* is subordinate to the adjectival phrase *United States*; but contrast *America* (for *The United States of America*) where the lexical hierarchy reverses that of the grammatical one. In contemporary Soviet Russian, which abounds in abbreviations and acronyms, their structure typically reflects two further hierarchies within the unabbreviated version, viz. the syntagmatic precedence of (1) morphemes; (2) letters in morphemes. Thus a word like *ispolkom* 'executive committee' which abbreviates the adjectival phrase *ispolnitel'nyj komitet* presupposes a selection of the leftmost segment of each constituent word up to and including the first three letters of the first lexical morpheme (*ispol-* + *kom-*).

In these strictly linguistic, non-literary examples the metonymic relations are defined by the instantiation of a preexistent or implied hierarchy rather than by the *ab ovo* creative establishment of a hierarchy. Indeed, the difference between instantiation and establishment serves as a typological demarcation, respectively, between linguistic and poetic metonymy. If Jakobson (1971:295) is correct in labeling the relations obtaining between members of a word family as metonymic (via their 'semantic contiguity'), then the juxtaposition of items like *editor-edition-editorial-editorship* represents the instantiation of a hierarchy defined by the lexical differentiation which the grammatical signata (here: suffixes) effect in the meaning of the deriving base.

The dichotomy between linguistic and poetic is, of course, not peculiar to metonymy and is inherent in metaphor as well. Here the difference hinges, respectively, on the distinction between the neutralization and the reversal of the signata in a hierarchy. To continue with Jakobson's example, the ascription of metaphoric status (via 'semantic similarity') to the relations obtaining between words with the same suffix such as *editor-auditor-solicitor* is to be understood as the *equivalence* resulting from the neutralization of the base/suffix hierarchy which accompanies the juxtaposition of words with identical suffixes but different bases. This equivalence is the very same relation underlying *synonymy,* since two or more words are construed to possess essentially the same meaning when the difference between their respective syntagms of semantic features (signata) are suspended or neutralized. In poetic language, however, it is the reversal of a semantic hierarchy rather than its neutralization that defines metaphor. Reverting to Jakobson's statement (cited above), it is just when the ranking of the two signata of *star,* viz. 'heavenly body' and 'luminary,' is inverted that the figural situation can be said to have ensued. The meaning considered primary in a literal context (hence superordinate to other meanings in other contexts) loses its primacy in a figural context, which is to say that it becomes subordinated to the figural meaning.

When metonymy and metaphor are thus viewed in terms of hierarchies of signata, it becomes evident that these two cardinal figures cannot be hermetically sealed off from each other. More importantly, indeed, it becomes clear that their continued separation tends to distort their immanent interdependence and to obstruct a unitary understanding of the dynamic that binds them. While taking account of the high incidence of semantic fading among tropes in non-poetic discourse, we must also acknowledge the fact that a metonymy, even at its original creation in literary texts, is already on the way to becoming a metaphor. This is, as I shall explain more fully below, a function of the inherent dynamic of tropes. Homer's 'thirty sails' is a metonymy, to be sure, since the trope establishes a hierarchy between signata. At the same time, however, the very establishment of a hierarchy sows the seeds of metaphor, since the figural meaning must predominate over the literal in order for the figural situation to obtain. Every metonymy thus contains the potential for sliding into metaphor. Moreover, of course, both tropes can coexist in the same linguistic vehicle, facilitating all the more the slide of an original metonymy into metaphor. The word *head* used to denote the person in charge is metonymic in that one part of the human body is taken to stand for the entire body (person); it is simultaneously metaphoric in that an analogy (semantic similarity) is drawn between the dominance of the head physically and physiologically over the rest of the human body, on the one hand, and the dominance of a leader over the group, on the other. These two coexistent figural components of *head* are themselves, naturally, not unranked: the metaphoric component markedly dominates the metonymic. This rank order, notably, is consistent with the principle that metonymy tends strongly to be superseded by metaphor. This means that metonymy is the more basic, less complex of the two tropes (cf. Lévi-Strauss 1962:101, cit. Donato 1975:6).

All metonymies which 'pass into the public domain' become metaphors. This accounts for the overwhelming emphasis on metaphor (noted inter alia by Jakobson 1971:258) in the history of rhetoric and the impoverished state of studies in the theory of metonymy.[2] Metonymies are resistant to metaphorization only when localized in texts; similarly, metaphors are genuinely resistant to lexicalization (fading) only when firmly anchored to the literary text. Once metaphors have also passed into the public domain, they can be said to have commenced on a trajectory which will lead ultimately to their effacement: 'a language is nothing but a necropolis of dead metaphors' (Sparshott 1974:84).

The context-sensitive nature of metonymy as a *modus significandi* comports well with its high incidence in works of art, including literature, which fall under the rubric of realism (Jakobson 1971:255 ff.). Metonymy subsists on overt terms of reference for its very figurality, while metaphor (as e.g., the pun) can get by on the eduction of an implied context.

Certain types of metonymy depend on context in resisting metaphorization. In personification, for example, the new signatum does not enter into the syntagm of signata because the focus is invariably on the establishment of a hierarchy that did not exist before rather than on the reversal of a preexistent or newly generated hierarchy. Harald Weinrich (1970:31) has pointed out that in the Middle Ages personifications approach in function certain mythological personages who play an extremely active role within the boundaries of the courtly universe. These symbolic personifications arise upon the attachment of degenerate mythological structures that have lost their narrative element to the allegorism of medieval thought.

For both metonymy and metaphor, their figural power is thus either crucially dependent on and/or significantly enhanced by a textual locus. In most non-poetic discourse communication may be impaired directly as the quotient of figural expressions rises; that is to say, as the number of coded (fully lexicalized) units decreases. Beyond the obvious difficulties attendant on speaking in verse (for the encoder), people communicate in 'prose' precisely because the prefabricated coded units, including idioms (among which are no small number of dead figures), need no spontaneous glossing since their meanings are relatively fixed and well-known. Literary discourse, on the other hand, provides the author with a great latitude of creativity in fulfilling the poetic function but entails a possibly burdensome interpretative load for the reader (decoder). Aristotle is clearly very close to the mark when he avers that the poet is to be measured in part by his skill at metaphor, meaning not simply the high incidence of tropes but their freshness. This notion is convergent, for instance, with the Russian Formalist tenet of deautomatization or defamiliarization. The spontaneous creative aspect of novel (not necessarily 'unusual') locutions is conveyed by Monroe Beardsley's 'metaphorical twist' or by Paul Ricoeur's notion of 'event.' Ricoeur correctly stresses the role of context in regulating and limiting the figural power of tropes (1974:99-100):

> This contextual action [shift in meaning] creates a word meaning which is an
> event, since it exists only in this context; but it can be identified as the same

when it is repeated; in that way the innovation of an 'emergent meaning' (Beardsley) may be recognized as a linguistic creation; if it is adopted by an influential part of the speech community it may even become a standard meaning and be added to the polysemy of the literal entities, contributing in that way to the *history* of the language as *langue,* code, or *system.* But, at that ultimate stage, metaphor is a dead metaphor. Only genuine metaphors are at the same time 'events' *and* 'meaning.'

As mentioned earlier, tropes which are or become part of the language at large (the public domain) have a decided tendency to lose their figural status (cf. Anttila 1972:145). Examples abound in all languages. To take a familiar Romance one, the literal meaning of Latin *pastor* 'shepherd' was augmented by the Christian figural meaning 'head of the congregation.' Over time, however, the figural meaning faded even though, notably, the original metaphor of shepherd and sheep survived. As pointed out by Anttila (1972:145-6), the fading of tropes (i.e., a kind of lexicalization) is particularly frequent in the formation of euphemisms. Since euphemisms tend to run in diachronic chains whose individual links are subject to progressive loss of marked status, it is not uncommon to find a synchronic distribution of such items which makes reference to parameters of style or speakers' age (so with words, for instance, denoting the locus for discharging bodily functions).

Lexicalization actually involves two distinct stages of what might be termed the *dehierarchization* of trope structure. Where the opposition between figural and literal has faded without being totally effaced, the item (word or phrase) has entered the category of *idiom.* Thus at some early point in its historical trajectory, *pastor* faded but continued to maintain a connection with 'shepherd.' Ultimately, of course, this bond was severed for all practical purposes; only a specialized acquaintance with the word's etymology permits the connection to be revivified. While the connection still lived a common life, the new meaning was an idiom: there was an idiomatic (here: religious) transference of meaning. The lexicalization was complete only when the transferredness ceased to be a part of the perceived meaning. The intermediate stage between the life and death of tropes constituted by idioms is most aptly exemplified by *proverbs,* for it is in these longest of idioms that the semantic parts fail to add up to the meaning of the whole despite the presence of a delineated constituent structure. The absence or demise of a perceived constituent structure in idioms is, indeed, the proximate cause of their petrification, i.e., of the passage of idioms into the category of genuine lexicalizations.

Idioms and other species of lexicalization are, however, not immutably petrified. The poetic function, whether in verse proper or in other varieties of discourse parasitic on poetry, often involves the revivification of dead or faded tropes. This process results in paronomasia or punning, of a kind especially favored by the slogans of modern advertising.

The specious equivalence relation established by the pun reverses the hierarchy between signans and signatum. This reversal and transposition mocks the referential function of language by substituting a virtual (covert) meaning for the contextually anticipated one. The resultant metaphor identifies two objects, each of which retains its own form. A literary variation of the pun is the use of a word in play, alternately in its normative dimension, on the one hand, and its connotative (figural) dimension, on the other.

The general framework of our structural analysis suggests that paronomasia (including punning) constitutes a *rehierarchization* of signata into a new figural syntagm, and thereby a remetonymization and/or remetaphorization of lexicalized material. This return to tropehood (as it were) means that the process has come full circle. Indeed, we have every reason to construe the voyage from metonymy to paronomasia via metaphor, idiom, and lexicalization as the 'life cycle' of tropes. While not every trope need complete the entire cycle, many obviously do. It should be emphasized that the full dynamic of trope development is inherent in all figures regardless of the arrested growth manifested by this or that particular example. To summarize in schematic form see Schema C.

INHERENT DYNAMIC (LIFE CYCLE) OF TROPES

1. metonymy————→metaphor (metaphorization)
2. metaphor ————→ idiom————————→lexicalization
                                        (dehierarchization)
3. idiom/lexicalization————————→paronomasia
   (revivification, i.e., rehierarchization =
   remetonymization/remetaphorization)

SCHEMA C

In an analysis of the structure of tropes the figure known as oxymoron is a particularly useful diagnostic, for as Beardsley points out (1962:298), 'in oxymoron we have the archetype, the most apparent and intense form, of verbal opposition.' Now, as was noted earlier, an opposition is a minimal paradigm, one term being *in praesentia* and the other *in absentia* and vice versa. In oxymoron, however, both terms are *in praesentia,* since qualitative opposites are understood to be or are reinterpreted as privative opposites. In an example like 'the living dead,' if we represent the two terms as A (living) + B (dead), we then note that A = non-B and B = non-A, which is to say that both terms are negations of each other. This logical condition on the structure of the oxymoron as a figure means that oxymoron is fundamentally metonymic (via the mutual negation). At the same time, the oxymoron has a metaphoric component which pre-dominates—in accord with our expectations. Oxymoron is metaphoric, more precisely, in that the paradigm/syntagm hierarchy is reversed: mutual exclusion (the condition of paradigmaticity) is subordinated to mutual inclusion (the condition of syntagmaticity). Put another way, disjunction is superseded by conjunction. But this resultant state or *definiens* of the trope is only the *form of the meaning* of an oxymoron. So long as the substance of the linguistic items in oxymoron is genuinely polar the meaning of their juxtaposition will remain epitomically abstract, which explains, inci-dentally, just why one is so hard pressed to distill a meaning from pure oxymoron. The superlative degree of vividness and intensity noted by Beardsley derives, then, from oxymoron's canonic status as *pure form.*

Since it is the very terms of the conception of figurality themselves (as well as their rank order)—i.e., paradigm and syntagm—that are subject to manipulation in oxymoron, one is tempted to characterize oxymoron as a *metafigure,* corresponding to Beardsley's archetype.

In underscoring the dynamism implicit in the structure of tropes and articulating their life cycle, we have actually approached a trichotomy of ontological categories corresponding to the triad of Peirce's phenomeno-logical categories viz. Firstness (quality), Secondness (reaction), and Thirdness (mediation).

Echoing the discussion of chapter 1, the categories are defined by Peirce (8.328) as follows:

> Firstness is the mode of being of that which is such as it is, positively and without reference to anything else.

> Secondness is the mode of being of that which is such as it is, with respect to a second but regardless of any third.

> Thirdness is the mode of being of that which is such as it is, in bringing a second and third into relation to each other.

It is the category of Thirdness that is of special pertinence to the study of tropes since all linguistic units, including figures of speech, are thirds. Indeed, tropes are epitomical instances of Thirdness, since Peirce himself conceives of it as involving the idea of 'composition' (1.297) or combina-tion, defined as 'something which is what it is owing to the parts which it brings into mutual relationship' (1.363). Peirce also recognizes the inherent complexity which is embodied by all thirds and hence by thirdness itself, which is a 'conception of complexity' (1.526). This requires, of course, that thirds have a part-whole structure. Peirce's description of the conceptual correlates of this hierarchy are quite precise and strikingly relevant to tropes (which are genuine thirds):

In genuine Thirdness, the first, the second, and the third are all three of the nature of thirds, or thought, while in respect to one another they are first, second, and third. The first is thought in its capacity as mere possibility; that is, mere *mind* capable of thinking, or a mere vague idea. The *second* is thought playing the role of Secondness, or event. That is, it is of the general nature of *experience* or *information.* The third is thought in its role as governing Secondness. It brings the information into the mind, or determines the idea and gives it body. It is informing thought, or *cognition.* But take away the psychological or accidental human element, and in this genuine Thirdness we see the operation of a sign. (1.538)

This passage is helpful in understanding that Peirce's semeiotic is a theory of cognition. Not only is the sign in the category of Thirdness but so is the *interpretant,* defined by Peirce as 'that determination of which the immediate cause, or determinant, is the Sign, of which the mediate cause is the Object' (6.347). Moreover:

A sign therefore is an object which is in relation to its object on the one hand and to an interpretant on the other in such a way as to bring the interpretant into a relation to the object, corresponding to its own relation to the object. (8.334)

As I have argued in chapter 2, Peirce's interpretant in relation to linguistic signs is to be understood as the *evaluative* component of sign structure, i.e., the expression of hierarchy among coordinate sets of signantia and signata in syntagms (both simultaneous and linear). Hierarchy is, as we saw, the syntagmatic counterpart of the paradigmatic asymmetry known as markedness.

Peirce's notion of Thirdness, his tripartite division of it, and its manifestation in the semeiotic are in perfect accord with the ontological analysis of trope structure summarized in Schema A and the diachronic progression of the inherent dynamic of tropes articulated in Schema C. The *qualitative* aspect of the figural situation corresponds to 'thought in its capacity as mere possibility'; it is the relatability of some two signata as conceived by mind. Their actual *relation* in tropes is the potential of quality realized by specific juxtapositions of signata. Finally, the *representation* achieved thereby, which gives shape to the informational bond forged by the correlate signata, is a cognitive structure defined by reference to an interpretant, viz. hierarchy or the embodiment of Thirdness.

3. Style as an Aspect of Meaning

Style as a term is so much a part of common parlance and has such a wide range of application (language, literature, art, music, dance, clothing, coiffure, behavior generally), yet paradoxically it has never been studied as a global phenomenon, across disciplinary lines. There is no dearth of studies of style in individual fields, particularly literature, art, and music. Nor have scholars refrained from attempting general definitions of style (e.g. Enkvist 1969, Cassirer 1975, Thoma 1976), although such essays have inevitably failed to go beyond ever more inclusive cataloguings of previous attempts. This lack of success has even led one investigator to deny any legitimacy to style as a conceptually discrete object of study (Gray 1969, 1973).

This last position is, of course, a *reductio ad absurdum*. The complexity of style simply requires a far richer conceptual framework and a greater concern for its ontological specificity than have either been available or heretofore been accorded the problem. Peirce's semeiotic provides just such a framework and all the tools of analysis as well. In particular, it is Peirce's notion of interpretant that will be seen to suggest an articulated solution.

Style in language has been characterized as 'a marked—emotive or poetic—annex to the neutral, purely cognitive information' (Jakobson 1972:77). In literature, painting, architecture, dress, etc., style is usually associated with a choice of features expressive of the affective intention of the subject (utterer, writer, maker, etc.). Style involves the notion of appropriateness, a goodness of fit between the context (whole) and the features chosen (parts); and/or between proper function and actual use. Where a choice is possible, the particular feature or set of features selected from a pre-established stock (paradigm, code) are in virtual opposition to those which are absent. Something is given prominence, something suppressed by being excluded. Indeed, as one goes from the maximally coded signs in human culture—the distinctive features, or diacritic categories, of phonology—to those aspects of behavior which transcend language, there is a corresponding increase in freedom of choice. While features or units do not cease to be coded as one ascends the hierarchy of parts and wholes, there is a graded gamut of codedness, including important distinctions of degree of freedom or variability at certain crucial nodes.

When Jakobson speaks of a 'marked annex' to the purely cognitive information, we can interpret this to mean the investment of a certain linguistic form with a certain value. The notion of markedness defines the asymmetry attending the terms of a paradigmatic opposition: one term is marked, the other unmarked. These terms are signs. Terms of oppositions combine into sign complexes called syntagms. To a varying degree (depending on the kind of complexus), the terms in syntagms are ranked, which is to say that the paradigmatic asymmetry know as markedness is mirrored in the syntagmatic asymmetry known as hierarchy or ranking. Hierarchy corresponds to value, and since value can be defined as preferential behavior, there emerges an obvious connection between style and markedness/hierarchy. The interpretant of a true sign mirrors the latter's *fundamentum relationis* and is itself a true sign. The triadic relation defining the non-degenerate sign hinges on the interpretant in that it is the interpretant (and only the interpretant!) that gives the semeiotic triad its 'assurance of Form' (Sanders 1970:10) which subsumes assurances of Experience and Instinct. In short, the form of relation is hierarchy.

This definition of hierarchy, which involves the notion of interpretant and thereby places the subject in a semeiotic frame, appears to facilitate the search for a global conception of style in a remarkably productive fashion. The sought-after definiens must apply uniformly to undifferentiated feelings or mere intimations of style (as signified in the phrase 'to have style') and to its full-blown manifestations as recurrent patterns in synchrony and in diachrony.

In global terms there is no principled difference between the instantiations of style as an aspect of semeiosis in objects of variable aesthetic significance. Hence, the analysis of styles of popular clothing is no less revealing theoretically than that of art objects. When a person 'has style' by virtue of the clothing he or she is wearing (or wears habitually), the aggregate of clothes and accessories is marked vis-à-vis possible other ensembles which manifest no prominence of features *primarily by imputation,* i.e., in which the semeiotic dimension of hierarchy (value) is relatively absent. The unmarked aggregate thus can either be a specified absence (the more usual function of unmarked generally) or it can be neutral, i.e., semeiotically vague or noncommittal. The latter value of the unmarked term encompasses not only the stylistically neutral but what is called customary or normal as well. A functional match between items of clothing and the context in which such items are customary is tantamount to the absence of a hierarchization which is anything other than purely 'factual.' The choice of denim as a cloth for use in work clothes does not rise to the status of a semeiotic datum as long as there is no interpretant and, therefore, no semeiosis. But a student who wears jeans to a college classroom for the first time in an institution's history elevates denim to the status of a sign. The act is perceived as an *innovation,* i.e., as something with incipient intellectual purport. This is the beginning of a style, semeiotically completely parallel to all such stylistic beginnings whether they occur in the history of art (cf. Schapiro 1953:304-6) or, more proximately, in the rarefied world of haute couture. At this stage wearing jeans is marked; its semeiotic value is in its perceivability/interpretability as preferential (albeit singular) behavior. This fledgling sign is what Peirce calls 'rheme' and defines as a 'sign which is represented in its signified interpretant as *if it were* a character or mark' (H 34). If it continues to be manifested, this innovation may become a *change,* having a social rather than purely individual dimension. Peirce categorizes a relation of this sort as a gradience in 'the Mode of Being of the Dynamical Object' (8.344) or in the 'Nature of their [i.e., the signs'] dynamic objects' (8.366): a 'concretive' dynamic object is becoming a 'collective' one (8.365-367). Simultaneously, and in conformity with the nature of style as a semeiotic phenomenon, the signatum corresponding to the signans becomes more intelligible in that the interpretant becomes what Peirce calls a dicent and defines as 'a sign represented in its signified interpretant *as if it were* in a Real Relation [i.e., a relation of factual contiguity] to its Object' (H 34). Since ideas (interpretants) have, according to Peirce, a tendency to grow by begetting related ideas, what started as an innovation can become a change—a social datum in the full sense—when 'the Nature of the Influence of the Sign' (8.373) reaches its full fruition as an 'argument,' defined by Peirce as 'a sign which is represented in its signified interpretant *as if it were* a Sign of the Interpretants' (H 34).

What is particularly important in this application of Peircean semeiotic for the global theory of style is the structured dynamic inherent in even as trivial an example as the spread of jeans as an item of clothing among college students. We know that jeans have lost their marked status; indeed, they have become customary (the 'norm'), a habit. But while they were still perceived as a phenomenon of style proper, the signatum or object was identified *with the wearer*. In Peircean terms, the sign was predominantly a dicent (more specifically, a Dicent Indexical Legisign). But the teleology of all semeiotic situations predetermines a movement towards Thirdness, towards full 'Lawlike-ness.' This telos is, however, at odds with the ontology of style. Style loses its particularity and becomes custom when the signantia of style lose their epitomically dicential common signatum—Man as Object. Buffon's famous dictum, 'le style est [de] l'homme même' (cit. Cooper 1907:179), is semeiotically perfect. Peirce himself expressed just this view when he wrote: 'The word or sign which man uses *is* the man himself' (5.314). This implied object of the dicent explains (inter alia) the preoccupation in art-historical circles with connoisseurship and attribution as an unceasing search for the missing signatum.

Style as code is, accordingly, not style in its proper semeiotic sense. However, style extended to include fully coded units and matrices is, like all such semantic transfers, an inevitable result of the teleology of signs and meanings. As Anttila has noted (1977:38), 'affective words are largely signs for signs.' Moreover, there appears to be a change in ranking ('shift in semantic mode') as between affective and cognitive: 'The object of the affective sign seems to be the cognitive signs' (loc. cit.). This kind of semeiotic relationship appears to be almost completely analogous to the structure of tropes. The ontological definiens of metonymy and metaphor (along the lines of Peirce's pragmatic maxim) resides, as we have seen, in their significate effects. In both species of cardinal trope these effects have to do with hierarchy, with the ranking of figural and literal signata in a semantic syntagm. The ontological structure of tropes, moreover, determines—as we saw was true of style—a characteristic dynamic or 'life cycle.' Metonymy, the primary trope, tends to be submerged in metaphor, and metaphor in turn has a decided tendency toward lexicalization (fading, petrification, idiomatization). The fully coded metaphor is no figure at all. Its demise is defined by a dehierarchization.

The semeiotic parallel between troping and style suggests a common *modus significandi,* determined by what appears to be a common definiens. In terms of Peirce's interpretant, style can be seen to establish a hierarchy of interpretants (a hierarchy of hierarchizations) in which the emotional interpretant is dominant vis-à-vis the energetic and the logical interpretants; it is thus a metonymization. As style loses its quotient of freshness (the 'gratific' portion of Peirce's logical interpretant, 8.372) and gains in codedness, the hierarchy of interpretants is inverted or metaphorized. Drawing the parallel to its natural conclusion, this means that *style is to be defined as a trope of meaning*: the annexed, or stylistic, signatum is ranked higher than the cognitive, neutral, or nonstylistic signatum.

Just as the teleology inherent in the relation of phenomena to ends leads ineluctably (as Peirce has it) to the triumph of Law or Thirdness, so the lexicalization of tropes and the normalization of style furnish us with the ground, via patterning and regularity, for the recovery of meanings embedded in texts and artifacts from past generations (cf. Schapiro 1953). Change as an aspect of continuity in human culture thus arises as a concomitant of the teleology of function in all semeiosis.

Peirce brings this matter down—in his typically idiosyncratic way—to a question of 'ethics.' For him, 'the only moral evil is not to have an ultimate aim' (5.133).

NOTES

III. Phonology

1. Cf. Polivanov. I am thinking specifically of instances of lenition $(p > \emptyset > h)$ and gemination (*pp, tt, kk,* etc.) which are characteristic typologically (cf. e.g., Early Germanic, Latin) of languages with the distinctive feature tense vs. lax. See Andersen 1969b, 1969c.

2. In citing morphophonemic evidence, I do not wish to create the impression that morphophonemic rules have the same semeiotic function as phonological ones; they do not (see Ch. 4; cf. Andersen 1969a:826-7, Shapiro 1972b:354-6). Phonological markedness values are nonetheless made reference to and exploited by rules in the morphophonemic component.

3. Mutatis mutandis, the argumentation developed for the preterit is applicable equally to the gerund, conditional (provisional), and representative (alternative).

4. The other verbal categories (mentioned in the preceding footnote) are also marked relative to the nonpreterit (= indicative).

5. The substantive universals (i.e. features within brackets) coincide with those of Jakobson and Halle 1971. Slashes through originally assigned markedness values (e.g. M̸) mean a reversal. To recapitulate the pertinent formal universals briefly: in the consonantal subhierarchy, if a superordinate node is constituted by a feature with a plus specification, then the markedness value of the subordinate node will be the opposite of that assigned to the superordinate feature. Note that the special status assumed for the features nasal vs. non-nasal and tense vs. lax in Shapiro 1974b is shown here to be unmotivated. These features appear as subordinate to both the consonantality and the vocalicity features—not only and directly to the consonantality feature as erroneously assumed in my Bologna Congress report.

6. Prosodic problems have not hitherto been treated systematically in markedness-theoretic terms, the exception being my exploratory essay on Russian stress (Shapiro 1969).

7. Or as Andersen (1973:790) puts it: 'The study of phonetic correspondences divorced from phonemic relations is tantamount to the study of effects isolated from their causes.'

8. How is it, for example, that the distinction between sharp and plain consonants, so 'naturally' and effortlessly discerned by all native speakers of Russian (including children), creates such monumental problems of perception and reproduction for the German or the Czech? (cf. Jakobson 1962:300-1). Why is it we speak of octopuses as having 'arms' in English, whereas they are said to have 'legs' in Japanese and Russian?

9. The testimony on this point of Avanesov 1968:144-5 and Reformatskij 1955:13 is at variance with that of Panov 1967. This suggests free variation, at least as a possibility.

10. The appearance of items like *anšlágščik* 'headline writer' [ʌnšláкš'ik] (cf. *peredërgščik* 'exaggerater' [p'ьr'id,órkš'ik]) and possible pronunciations like *flejtščik* 'flutist' [fl'éjč'š'ik] show the continuing loss of productivity of the syncope rule in morphophonemic environments (here: suffixation) and instances the veracity of the notion that morphophonemic rules—in contradistinction to phonological rules—are inherently unproductive. Their persistence through time depends on the preservation of a semeiotic relation to the phonology (cf. Shapiro 1972b).

11. The pronunciation [énšp'il'], cited by Miloslavskij 1963: 140 for *èndšpil'* 'end-game,' corroborates the supposition that *n*, despite its sonority, may function contextually as an obstruent.

12. Exceptional are *sólnce* [sóncə] 'sun,' *zdrávstvovat'* [zdrástvəvət'] 'be healthy,' and *čúvstvovat'* [čustvəvət'] 'feel' (and all the appropriate derivatives). These are all rare lexicalizations, reflecting phonological relations of a historically earlier state of Russian (cf. modern *vdóvstvovat'* 'be widowed,' *neístovstvovat'* 'rage,' etc. where the *v* is not syncopated). Note that *bezmólvstvovat'* [b'izmólstvəvət'] 'be silent' is regular: *v* is marked for the categories of gravity and stridency, while *s* is unmarked for them.

13. Diachronically, this is reflected in the fact that the previously more common syncopated forms like *gollandka* 'Dutchwoman' [gʌlánkə] and *mašinistka* [məšin'ískə] 'typist' are giving way to the newer unsyncopated forms [gʌlántkə] and [məšin'ístkə]. In conjunction with the change from pronunciations like *namórdnik* [nʌmórn'ik] 'muzzle' and *póldnik* [póln'ik] 'lunch,' cited by Reformatskij (1955:14), to the all but universal [nʌmórdn'ik] and [póldn'ik], this supports the analysis that dental stops in Russian are distinctively abrupt.

14. There is some slight disagreement among Soviet phoneticians as to whether geminates before stressed syllables are obligatorily subject to simplification. Reformatskij 1955:13 says yes, Avanesov 1968:138-48 no. For that matter, Avanesov allows geminates before pause, which neither Reformatskij nor Panov 1967 admit as normal.

15. This is the sort of free variation which gives rise to incorrect pronunciations like [gʌs't'ín:əjə] for *gostínaja* 'living room.'

16. A great deal has been written about the unstressed vowel system of Russian. For a good bibliography, particularly of the older materials, see Panov 1967. Other sources worth noting are Bondarko, Verbickaja & Zinder 1966, Panov 1968 and 1979, Jones 1959, Finedore & Scatton 1978, Verbickaja 1970 and 1976, Bondarko 1977, Matuševic 1976, Thelin 1971, Ward 1975, Romportl 1973, and the articles in the two collections edited by Vysotskij et al. (1966, 1971). Košutíc 1919 remains to this day the best description of the so-called Old Muscovite norm, which must still be taken into account in discussing contemporary normative speech. Avanesov 1972 (and its earlier editions) is the basis for the description of the contemporary standard in the present section which limits itself to unstressed vowels that are indeed reduced qualitatively and are, moreover, unsyncopated (for treatments of vowel syncope, see Barinova 1971 and Kodzasov 1973). Vowels that

remain qualitatively unreduced despite being in unstressed syllables are practically limited to loan words, whose special status (hypermarking—see below) could easily be invoked to account for the failure of reduction to take place in such words.

No glosses are provided for most Russian items because their meaning is irrelevant to the discussion.

17. There is evidence of dialectal inroads into standard pronunciation of the sort where the diffuse vowels do change in quality; see Paufošima 1980, discussed in detail below (I am indebted to Dean Worth for calling my attention to this paper). It should be understood that in characterizing /i u/ as undergoing no qualitative change in unstressed position, the changes in their pronunciation occasioned by consonantal environments—specifically, by the presence before and/or after of hard vs. soft consonants—has no bearing on the problem addressed in this paper. The relatively more acute pronunciations of these vowels in the environment of a soft consonant are in complete accord with the general phenomenon of such tonality changes in Russian (not to speak of the other relevant Slavic languages) and is to be explained as an instance of markedness assimilation (see n. 24). In this connection, it is assumed that the relatively more acute (nongrave) and less acute (grave) variants of /i/—specifically, [i] and [ɨ]—are in complementary distribution, hence not to be reckoned with as phonologically independent. Note that under any interpretation of their phonological status, the latter does not bear on the problem at hand. From this point on, therefore, unless indicated otherwise the symbol /i/ is used to subsume the phonetic variants of /a e o/ after soft consonants.

18. The phrase 'diacritic categories' (first used by Andersen 1978) is equivalent to Jakobson's 'distinctive features' and to Andersen's (1979) other term 'diacritic paradigms.'

19. Jakobson 1972:76. The conception of markedness, particularly the idea of graded markedness (see below), applied here is different from that of Jakobson, who characterizes it in terms of 'logical contradictories' as if to exclude logically contrary oppositions. Actually, the two conceptions are readily compatible once it is understood that 'nonpresence' is always interpreted as specified absence in the relational structure of language, whether in the content side or the expression side. Needless to say, neither mine nor Jakobson's conception of markedness is compatible with that of generative grammarians.

20. It might be objected that what is called a cohesion here reduces to a 'tautology' so long as there are no independent ('paradigmatic') grounds for saying what the value of a given context or unit is. The fact of the matter is language and its users do not wait for linguists to decide whether something in structure is 'independently motivated' or not. What appears circular or 'tautological' is part and parcel of the structure, whence its coherence. A good example of this state of affairs is represented by Figure 10 (below), where the unmarked value of initial unstressed syllables appears to be 'derived' from the unmarked value of the vowel realized in that context. Context and unit cohere (match values): no more need be said. The whole idea of independent motivation is beside the point here, as it is generally in language structure, contrary to the scientistic methodological bias of modern linguistics, which erroneously views language as if it were a scientific theory subject to all of the usual tests of such a theory, including falsifiability. The position represented here (cf. Introduction and Ch. 2) is that language is a hermeneutic

object, whose structure is defined by patterns of cohesions between forms and contents. What is theoretically and explanatorily interesting is discovering precisely what sorts of cohesions there are, while relying on a uniform exegetical framework, i.e., one which considers all components of language (phonology, grammar, lexis) to be isomorphous with each other and to be analyzed using a unitary set of explanantes.

21. Panov 1979:160 attributes the introduction of the caret into Russian phonetic notation to S. Boyanus (cf. Panov 1967:45).

22. Supplemented, for the formant frequencies of unstressed [e], by Verbickaja 1976:95. In absolute initial position the duration of [ʌ] is ca. 100 micro-seconds. The first formant represents the vertical movement of the tongue which changes the openness/closeness of the aperture; the second formant corresponds to the horizontal, i.e., fronting/backing, movement.

23. The other reduced vowels after hard consonants are varieties of the phoneme /i/, viz [ɨ] and [ɨᵉ]. Since the phonetic realizations in unstressed position of /i/ are reduced only in duration, they are irrelevant for the present study. To be sure, [i] and [ɨᵉ] are possible as phonetic outcomes of unstressed /a e o/ after hard consonant, and in that event they are certainly relevant; cf. n. 17.

24. This characterization is valid for the (redundant) grave/acute variation of /i/ after hard, resp. soft consonants, as well (cf. n. 17).

25. There is a discrepancy in the form of the pronoun in this example (dative vs. genitive) as cited by Panov; the correct form is the dative, the phrase being an elliptical version of *čtob t'eb'e pusto bylo!* Another possible example is *ved'* when followed by pause (as a hesitation phenomenon). Examples in the body of the text are cited in *phonological transcription,* which bears a superficial resemblance to so-called morphophonemic transcription but is different both from it and from traditional phonemic transcription. Transliteration, where resorted to, will be noted.

26. GRAM. abbreviates 'grammaticalized,' LEX. 'lexicalized'; FIRST PRE-TONIC means the syllable immediately preceding the stress.

27. There is a great deal of variation in this class of examples; see Thelin 1971 and Kuz'mina 1966, 1968.

28. There is much variation possible here, particularly of the sort that, from the standpoint of Avanesov (1972:76-80), would be called 'nonstandard' speech. Panov (1967:65, 1979:162), for instance, admits pronunciations with schwa which Avanesov explicitly proscribes.

29. Panov 1967:63. The lack of examples is not crucial because the pronunciation of nonce words (or propria) would conform to that of the extant ones.

30. The examples are cited first in transliteration, followed by a transcription intended to reflect that of Paufošima. Whether any of the speakers from whom the examples were recorded deviate consistently from the norm is not noted.

31. The latter work (tacitly) incorporates the former, which is the written version ('Zur Struktur des Phonems') of two lectures delivered in Copenhagen in 1939.

32. Note that after /c/ the sound /o/ was reduced irregularly when the initial vowel of a suffix, e.g. *špricevát'* 'inject' [špr'iceɪvát'] (cf. *špricóvka* 'injection'), *licevój* 'facial' [l'iceɪvói] (cf. *licóvka* 'facade'). And this is still the situation in

Contemporary Standard Russian. In two verbs, however, the regular (phono-logical) reflex of / o/ after / c/ prevailed despite the morphophonemic environment: *tancevát* 'dance' [tɔncɑvát'] and *garcevát* 'caracole' [gɔrcɑvát']. The contemporary pronunciation of these items is identical except that [ɑ] has been replaced by [ʌ]. Cf. also the OM pronunciation of *pocelúj* 'kiss' [pɔcɑlúj] —corresponding to CSR [pɔciᵉlúj]; and the appearance of irregular [iᵉ] in the oblique cases of the numerals 20 and 30: *dvadcatí* [dvɔc:iᵉt'i], *tridcatí* [tr'ic:iᵉt'i].

33. The equivalent situation obtains in Contemporary Standard Russian (reported by Verbickaja 1970) where both forms are frequently pronounced [m'iᵉlá] alongside the somewhat more usual (and normative) [m'ilá].

34. /e/ does not occur (in native vocabulary) after plain consonants other than the [M str] sounds /š ž c/, so that practically one is dealing here with /a o/.

IV. Morphophonemics and Morphology

1. The special notational and abbreviational conventions utilized in this section include the following: italicized foreign items are in transliteration; grammatical morphemes (stems, suffixes, desinences) are also italicized; the doublecross (#) represents a vowel alternating with zero; INA = inapplicable; grave stress (`) means a vowel that is never stressed; a slash between Russian forms divides the nominative or accusative singular (to the left of the slash) from the genitive singular (to the right of the slash, as a representative of the oblique case endings); adj = adjective, pej = pejorative, dim = diminutive, aug = augmentative, nom = nominative, gen = genitive, ins = instrumental.

2. A phonological rule accounts for the implementation of the basic *ta* as *ita* after *s* (Japanese is an 'open syllable language'). The substitution of *š* for *s* is an automatic phonological consequence of the latter's position before *i*. There is no change morphophonemically in stems ending in *s* and *n* (*sasu/sasita, sinu/sinda*) because these two segments are both [U str].

3. Cf. Čurganova 1971, Isačenko, 1972, Klagstad 1954, Stankiewicz 1968, Worth 1967a, 1968c, Zaliznjak 1967.

4. The accent is on 'pertinent.' Thus gender is not relevant to the workings of the system, specifically to the synthetic markedness values.

5. The criterion for the assignment of synthetic markedness values is misstated in Shapiro 1969, 1971, and is rectified here.

6. The occurrence of markedness reversal here can be understood as an assimilation. Since the absence of a vocalic alternation in stems is unmarked and its presence marked, the value of stems in the presence of such an alternation is the reverse of the one that holds in the absence of the alternation.

7. Cf. *Ljubóv'/Ljubóvi* 'Love' [forename]; also *vosem'jú* ∼ *vos'm'jú* 'eight' [ins]. The stress of the latter doublet indicates that it should not be considered with *ljubóv'*, etc.

8. In current morphophonemic practice as applied to Russian (e.g. Worth 1968a), the ins sg desinence is set up as (# jù) by comparison with (oj(u)) of the 2nd declension. I dispense with the zero (#) and treat the desinence simply as *ju*. The explanatory advantage of this treatment will soon become clear.

9. This does not occur in feminine and neuter stems because their pre-zero shape is marked; see below.

10. Of all nonderived masc stems only *bagór/bagrá* engenders a doublet *bagórik* ∼ *bagorók*. In spoken Russian, naturally, *bagórčik* is also extant.

11. Cf. *ízvest'* ∼ *izvëstka* 'lime'; *zvezdá* ∼ *zvëzdočka* 'star' indicates another way of dealing with the exceptional clusters, viz. by reduplication of suffixes—here (# k). Cf. the two diminutives of *skátert'*'tablecloth': *skatërka* (*t* has been deleted, eliminating the cluster altogether) and *skaterëtka* [dialectal] (anaptyxis).

12. Further exceptions: *flejtščik* 'flutist,' *litávrščik* 'tympanist,' *kórmščik* 'helmsman.' I can propose no way of accounting for these aberrancies.

13. The varying position of stress is irrelevant.

14. Cf. on the one hand, *magístérskij* 'magistral,' *ministérskij* 'ministerial,' *burgomísterskij* 'mayoral': on the other *rótmistrskij* 'platoon leader' [adj]. The correlate substantives all have no vowel/zero alternation.

15. *t* alternates with *s* before *t*; hence *čest'*.

16. Cf. *skóbel'/skóbelja* 'scraper' ∼ *skoblít'*, wherein the directionality (if any) is not as clear to me as to Worth 1968c:121. The latter errs in relating *rákel'/rákelja* 'printshop knife' to *raklíst*, also glossed erroneously as 'printing shop foreman.' The correct gloss is 'textile printer,' and the correct correlate is *rákjla* 'steel ruler used in textile printing,' which has no vowel/zero alternation at all.

17. The environment condition of this rule needs some elucidation. The consonants between which a vowel is epenthesized must be either both marked for stridency or both marked for abruptness, so that a sequence of segments marked for a different feature will not be susceptible of anaptyxis. In what I am about to say I concentrate largely on sequences of [M str] segments.

18. Panov 1967, incidentally, does not draw the same conclusion from the evidence he cites.

19. For a complete set of bibliographical references to Slavic language studies carried out on the Jakobsonian model, see Shapiro 1974c:48-9; cf. now also Čurganova 1973 and Thelin 1975.

20. Following Jakobson 1948, I am limiting myself to an examination of the simple verbs (with unprefixed monoradical stems) and to the purely verbal categories (the finite forms and the infinitive). Verb stems and inflected form are cited in a transcription superficially equivalent to morphophonemic but which is actually phonological (in contrast to phonemic transcription). Other items are transliterated. The definitions of the elements of conjugation below are also based on Jakobson 1948.

21. The assignment of markedness values is not explicitly motivated by Trubetzkoy but coincides with the well-argued one of Jakobson 1932 and 1957.

22. Verb stems in *-nu* (about which more below) form a special class. Also, consonantal stems may have vocalic shapes (alternants) before the desinence of the infinitive (*v'e-st'í* 'lead,' etc.) which represent a 'truncation'; three cases in *-r* (*p'er'é-t'* 'push,' *t'er'é-t'* 'rub,' *m'er'é-t'* 'die') and one in *-b* (*šib'í-t'* 'hit' which does not occur unprefixed) represent an augmentation.

23. For lack of better names, I have designated the categories in Figure 3 enclosed in solid lines as 'outer' and those enclosed in dotted as 'inner.'

24. This apportionment of desinences by stem structure has several exceptions.

Among *-a* verbs, monosyllabic *mčá* 'drive,' *gna* 'herd,' *spa* 'sleep,' and *ssá* 'piss' belong to IIC; *b'ežá* is mixed, IIC in the outer forms and IC in the inner; *ržá* 'neigh,' *sm'ejá . . . s'a* 'laugh' are IC. The *-e* stems *r'ov'é* 'howl' and *xot'é* 'want' are IC.

25. For a complete set of correspondences (extending to nonverbal alternations), consult Jakobson [1948] 1971:126. Hard labials appear as alternants of soft labials in the infinitive and the nonpresent forms of the indicative; but also in 1sg. (e.g. *spl'ú* ~ 2sg. *sp'í-š*, etc.). The motivation for the 'epenthetic *l'*' appears to reside in the situation that it marks a stem which would otherwise be unmarked for all of the first four features in the Russian consonant hierarchy (labials are unique in this respect). The *l'* is, notably, marked for vocalicity and for sharpness.

26. Exceptions are discussed below.

27. This form is colloquial; cf. Panov 1968:142.

28. IIC stems have an inherently 'soft' final consonant due to the fact that the *-i* and *-e* cannot be preceded by hard consonants anywhere in verbal inflection; and that the consonants represented by *Č-a* are functionally equivalent to their soft congeners via their marked status for compactness (palatals) or acuteness (yod).

29. The phonological markedness values are assigned here and throughout this paper in accordance with the principles of Shapiro 1972, 1976. They apply, notably, to redundant as well as to distinctive features. The exceptional *sosá* 'suck' is discussed below.

30. This stem has both anaptyctic and nonanaptyctic forms in the nonpreterite (with and without 'outer' marking of *-r*): *sr-ú, sr'-óš, sr-út/s'er'-ú, s'er'-oš, s'er'-ut/s'er-ú, s'er'-oš, s'er-ut.*

31. These are defined as having identical consonants on either side of the root vowel.

32. Generally, the distribution of desinence alternants is governed by the structure (including prosody) of the stem: *t'* combines with sonorant (including vocalic) stems; *st'* with stressed and *st'í* with unstressed obstruent stems; and *č* with velar stems. Exceptions: *id/šod* 'walk' (infinitive *id-t'í*) and *job* 'fuck' (*jë-t'* or *je-t'í*), *kl'an* 'curse' (*kl'á-st'*).

33. Exceptions in stem-final yod and of the type *pórt'-∅* 'ruin' are discussed below. Note also *kráp'-∅* 'sprinkle' and *síp'-∅*, both of which lack the epenthetic *l'* characteristic of all other imperatives from stems with a labial final consonant.

34. It makes no difference whether the vowel system is that of Old Muscovite or Contemporary Standard Russian, since only the relevant feature would change (from diffuseness in CSR to compactness in OM) but not the values. Cf. ch. 3, sec. B2.

35. The possibility of imperatives like *pl'úšč-∅* 'squoosh' (cf. Zaliznjak 1977:740) argues, incidentally, for the recognition of *š'* as a separate phoneme and supports the conclusions of Ch. 3, sec. C above.

36. My analysis conflicts with that of Jakobson 1957 and 1960. He argues (1971:185-6) that the gender hierarchy and the corresponding markedness values differ in the 'caseless' forms (i.e., short forms of positive adjectives and the preterite forms of the verb), so that the neuter becomes 'the least specified, unmarked gender opposed to a more specified, marked feminine or to a less specified, unmarked masculine.' However, all of the examples Jakobson cites in support of these apparent 'shifts in the distribution of marked and unmarked categories in the

caseless forms, as compared to the case-forms' can be explained as instances of markedness reversal, which suggests that there is only one hierarchy (not two) for all forms in which gender is specified.

37. It is not clear to what extent if any features (like stridency) which are distinctive only for consonants have any relevancy to vowels, and vice versa.

38. The picture in Russian dialects and in the historical development of the language as a whole is quite variegated; see Flier 1978b.

39. In this connection it should be noted that the tense marker *l* drops out in ths masculine after those consonants which are retained in the preterite, e.g. *n'ós-∅* /*n'os-l-á*, *gr'ób-∅*/*gr'ob-l-á*, etc. This is to be explained by the principle of markedness complementarity. The suffix *l* is consonantal and hence a marked desinence, and ∅ is likewise marked because it implements the unmarked masculine. At the same time, as far as the general principle of Russian verb stem structure is concerned, consonantal stem shapes are also marked. The sequence of three marked entities is not tolerated, hence the omission of *l* after stem-final consonants before ∅.

40. To this list can be added the *x* and *p* which precede *-nu* stems that drop this suffix in the preterite, e.g. *sóxnu* 'dry,' *slépnu* 'go blind,' etc. For the peculiarities of *-r* stems, see n. 22.

41. This assignment differs in part from that in Shapiro 1976 and is based on the realization that stridency is superordinate to abruptness in the feature hierarchy of Russian for both grave and acute obstruents.

42. The situation in (necessarily prefixed) verbs with the stem *-jm*/*n'ím* is special. The nonsyllabic stem alternant, as the marked one, coheres with unmarked desinential stress, e.g. *p'er'e-jm-ú*, *p'er'e-jm'-óš*, etc. 'intercept'; and the unmarked syllabic alternant with marked mobile stress, e.g. *ot-n'im-ú*, *ot-n'ím'-oš*, etc. 'remove.' The exceptional cases of *pr'-im-ú*, *pr'-ím'-oš*, etc. 'accept' and *vo-z'm-ú*, *vo-z'm'-óš*, etc. would appear to be explained by just the bizzare metanalysis indicated by this segmentation.

43. Cf., however, *stla* 'spread'/*st'el'-ú*, *st'el'-oš*, etc.; and *sra* (n. 30). Also the *ková* 'forge'/*kuj-ú*, *kuj-óš*, etc. type (of which there are 7) vs. the regular pattern for polysyllabic roots, e.g. *nočova* 'spend the night'/*nočúj-u*, *nočúj-oš*, etc., the only exception being *dn'ova* 'spend the day'/*dn'új-u*, *dn'új-oš* (usually explained as the result of having a deriving base with an anaptyctic vowel).

44. The only exception in unmarked stems is the perfective meaning of *rod'í* 'give birth'/*rod'í-l-∅*, *rod'í-l'-a*; *rod'í-l'-i*; likewise in the corresponding reflexive forms.

45. This appears to be an instance of Brøndal's principle of markedness compensation (1943:105 ff.).

46. Cf. also differing position of stress in the two subparadigms of the indicative of *l'ág*/*l'og* 'lie': nonpret. *l'ág-u*, *l'áž-oš*, etc.; pret *l'óg-∅*, *l'og-l-á*, *l'og-l-ó*, *l'og-l'-i*.

47. Infinitives in *č* always stress the predesinential vowel. The irregular stems *jéd*/*jéxaj* and *-šib*/*-šib'í* stress the initial and the final syllable, respectively.

48. Drawing the comparison to its full conclusion, this phenomenon can in turn be construed as a kind of *markedness dissimilation*.

V Semantics

1. For a useful bibliography, consult Shibles 1971; also Ricoeur 1975. Particularly worthy of mention are Dubois et al. 1970, Henry 1971, Le Guern 1973, and Ricoeur 1975. It should be noted that the latter (English translation: *The Rule of Metaphor,* Toronto: University of Toronto Press, 1977) is a splended achievement. In my view, however, its methodological thrust is blunted (if not vitiated) by two dubious tenets: (1) the supposed nonexistence of simultaneous syntagms; or, to put it more accurately, the restriction of the notion of syntagm to a purely successive, linear dimension; and (2) the apportionment of the word to semiotics and the sentence to semantics. The two are obviously interconnected. The second is adopted by Ricoeur from Benveniste. Nonetheless, there can be no cleavage between semiotics and semantics in anything that has to do with natural language. Ricoeur apparently fails to understand that the structure of the expression plane is *isomorphous* with the structure of the content plane. Anything short of this understanding is tantamount to a rejection of the systematic nature of linguistic phenomena—regardless, nota bene, of whether or not one accepts Saussure's arbitrariness doctrine. In this regard, Andersen 1974b is most instructive. Finally, word and sentence are hardly orthogonal; they are both members of a *hierarchy of contexts,* i.e., are hypotactic vis-à-vis each other to be sure.

2. Jakobson explains this conjuncture differently: 'Similarity in meaning connects the symbols of a metalanguage with the symbols of the language referred to. Similarity connects a metaphorical term with the term for which it is substituted. Consequently, when constructing a metalanguage to interpret tropes, the researcher possesses more homogeneous means to handle metaphor, whereas metonymy, based on a different principle, easily defies interpretation. Therefore nothing comparable to the rich literature on metaphor can be cited for the theory of metonymy' (1971:258).

REFERENCES

Andersen, Henning. 1966. *Tenues and Mediae in the Slavic Languages: A Historical Investigation.* Unpublished Ph.D. thesis, Harvard University. Cambridge, Massachusetts.

_____. 1968. 'IE *s after *i, u, r, k* in Baltic and Slavic,' *Acta Linguistica Hafniensia* 11.171-90.

_____. 1969a. 'A Study in Diachronic Morphophonemics: The Ukrainian Prefixes,' *Language* 45.807-30.

_____. 1969b. 'Indo-European Voicing Sandhi in Ukrainian,' *Scando-Slavica* 15.157-69.

_____. 1969c. 'Lenition in Common Slavic,' *Language* 45. 553-74.

_____. 1969d. 'The Phonological Status of the Russian "Labial Fricatives,"' *Journal of Linguistics* 5.121-7.

_____. 1972. 'Dipthongization,' *Language* 48.11-50.

_____. 1973. 'Abductive and Deductive Change,' *Language* 49.765-93.

_____. 1974a. 'Markedness in Vowel Systems,' *Proceedings of the Eleventh International Congress of Linguists,* II, ed. L. Heilmann, 891-6. Bologna: il Mulino.

_____. 1974b. 'Towards a Typology of Change: Bifurcating Changes and Binary Relations,' in Andersen and Jones, II, 17-60.

_____. 1975. 'Variance and Invariance in Phonological Typology,' *Phonologica 1972,* ed. W. Dressler and F. Mareš, 67-75. Munich: Fink.

_____. 1978. 'Vocalic and Consonantal Languages,' *Studia linguistica A. V. Issatschenko oblata,* ed. H. Birnbaum et al., 1-12. Lisse: Peter de Ridder.

_____. 1979. 'Phonology as Semiotic,' *A Semiotic Landscape,* ed. S. Chatman et al., 377-81. The Hague: Mouton.

_____. 1980. 'Morphological Change: Towards a Typology,' *Recent Developments in Historical Morphology,* ed. J. Fisiak, 1-50. The Hague: Mouton.

_____. MS. 'Language Structure and Semiotic Processes.'

Anderson, John M., and Charles Jones (eds.). 1974. *Historical Linguistics.* 2 vols. (*North-Holland Linguistic Series* 12a-12b.) Amsterdam: North Holland.

Anttila, Raimo. 1972. *An Introduction to Historical and Comparative Linguistics.* New York: Macmillan.

_____. 1974. 'Formalization as Degeneration in Historical Linguistics,' in Anderson and Jones, I, 1-32.

_____. 1977. 'Toward a Semiotic Analysis of Expressive Vocabulary,' *Semiosis* 5.27-40.

_____. 1977a. Review of Elisabeth Walther, *Allgemeine Zeichenlehre, Lingua* 42.226-31.

_____. 1980. 'Language and the Semiotics of Perception,' *The Signifying Animal: The Grammar of Language and Experience*, ed. I. Rauch and G.F. Carr, 263-83. Bloomington: Indiana University Press.

Avanesov, R. I. 1948. 'O dolgix šipjaščix v russkom jazyke.' *Doklady i soobščenija filologičeskogo fakul'teta* [MGU] 6.23-30.

———. 1956. *Fonetika sovremennogo russkogo literaturnogo jazyka*. Moscow: MGU.

———. 1968. *Russkoe literaturnoe proiznošenie*, 4th ed. Moscow: Prosveščenie.

———. 1972. *Russkoe literaturnoe proiznošenie*, 5th ed. Moscow: Prosveščenie.

Avanesov, R. I., and S. I. Ožegov. 1959. *Russkoe literaturnoe proiznošenie i udarenie: slovar'-spravočnik*. Moscow: GIINS.

Barinova, G. A. 1966. 'O proiznošenii [ž':] i [š':],' *Razvitie fonetiki sovremennogo russkogo jazyka*, 25-54. Moscow: Nauka.

———. 1971. 'Redukcija glasnyx v razgovornoj reči,' in Vysotskij et al. 1971, 97-116.

Baudouin de Courtenay, J. A. [1912] 1963. 'Ob otnošenii russkogo pis'ma k russkomu jazyku.' *Izbrannye trudy po obščemu jazykoznaniju*, II, 209-35. Moscow: AN SSSR.

Beardsley, Monroe. 1962. 'The Metaphorical Twist,' *Philosophy and Phenomenological Research* 22.293-307.

Birnbaum, Henrik. 1970. *Problems of Typological and Genetic Linguistics Viewed in a Generative Framework*. The Hague: Mouton.

Bloch, B. 1950. 'Studies in Colloquial Japanese IV: Phonemics,' *Language* 26.86-125.

Bloomfield, Leonard. 1933. *Language*. New York: Holt, Rinehart and Winston.

Bondarko, L. V. 1977. *Zvukovoj stroj sovremennogo russkogo jazyka*. Moscow: Prosveščenie.

Bondarko, L. V., L. A. Verbickaja, and L. P. Zinder. 1966. 'Akustičeskie xarakteristiki bezudarnosti,' *Strukturnaja tipologia jazykov,* ed. V. V. Ivanov, 50-64. Moscow: Nauka.

Borunova, S. N. 1966. 'Sočetanija [š'č'] i [š':] na granicax morfem,' *Razvitie fonetiki sovremennogo russkogo jazyka*, 55-71. Moscow: Nauka.

Brock, Jarrett. 1975. 'Peirce's Conception of Semiotic,' *Semiotica* 14.125-41.

Bromlej, S. V., and L. N. Bulatova. 1972. *Očerki morfologii russkix govorov*. Moscow: Nauka.

Brøndal, Viggo. 1943. *Essais de linguistique générale*. Copenhagen: Munksgaard.

Bühler, Karl. 1934. *Sprachtheorie*. Jena: Fischer.

Bulaxovskij, L. A. 1958. *Istoričeskij kommentarij k russkomu literaturnomu jazyku*. 5th ed. Kiev: Radjans'ka škola.

Bulygina, T. V. 1971. 'O russkix dolgix šipjaščix,' *Fonetika. Fonologija. Grammatika*, 84-91. Moscow: Nauka.

Bunge, Mario. 1969. 'The Metaphysics, Epistemology and Methodology of Levels,' *Hierarchical Structures,* ed. L. L. White et al., 17-28. New York: American Elsevier.

Cairns, Charles E. 1969. 'Markedness, Neutralization, and Universal Redundancy Rules,' *Language* 45.863-85.

Cassirer, Peter. 1975. 'On the Place of Stylistics,' *Style and Text: Studies Presented to Nils Erik Enkvist,* ed. Hakan Ringbom et al., 27-48. Stockholm: Skriptor.

Chao, Y-R. [1934] 1963. 'The Non-Uniqueness of Phonemic Solutions of Phonetic Systems,' *Readings in Linguistics,* 3rd ed., 38-54. New York: ACLS.

Chomsky, N., and M. Halle. 1968. *The Sound Pattern of English*. New York: Harper and Row.

Cooper, Lane. 1907. *Theories of Style*. New York: MacMillan.

Čurganova, V. G. 1971. 'Vokalizacija imennoj osnovy v russkom jazyke,' *Izvestija AN SSSR, Serija literatury i jazyka* 30.531-41.

_____. 1973. *Očerk russkoj morfonologii*. Moscow: Nauka.

Dal', V. I. 1934. *Tolkovyj slovar' živogo velikorusskogo jazyka*, 4th ed., 4 vols. Tokyo: Tachibana Shoten.

Donato, Eugenio. 1975. 'Lévi-Strauss and the Protocols of Distance,' *Diacritics* 5/3.2-12.

Dubois, Jacques et al. 1970. *Rhétorique générale*. Paris: Larousse.

Enkvist, Nils. 1969. 'On Defining Style,' *Modern Essays on Writing and Style*, ed. Paul C. Wermuth, 21-34. New York: Holt, Rinehart and Winston.

Esposito, Joseph L. 1980. *Evolutionary Metaphysics: The Development of Peirce's Theory of Categories*. Athens: Ohio University Press.

Fasmer, Maks. 1964-73. *Ètimologiceskij slovar' russkogo jazyka*, trans. O. N. Trubačev, 4 vols. Moscow: Progress.

Feibleman, James K. 1970. *An Introduction to the Philosophy of Charles S. Peirce*. Cambridge, Mass.: The M.I.T. Press.

Finedore, Paula G., and Ernest A. Scatton. 1978. 'Towards a Typology of Vowel Reduction: The Phonology of Unstressed Vowels in Russian,' *Lingua* 45.301-17.

Fisch, Max H. 1978. 'Peirce's General Theory of Signs,' *Sight, Sound and Sense*, ed. T. A. Sebeok, 31-70. Bloomington: Indiana University Press.

Fitzgerald, John J. *Peirce's Theory of Signs as Foundation for Pragmatism*. The Hague: Mouton.

Flier, Michael S. 1978a. 'Is *kljast'* Iconoclastic?' *Studia linguistica A. V. Issatschenko oblata*, ed. H. Birnbaum et al., 111-27. Lisse: Peter de Ridder.

_____. 1978b. 'On the Velar Infinitive in East Slavic,' *American Contributions to the Eighth International Congress of Slavists*, I, ed. Henrik Birnbaum, 269-306. Columbus: Slavica.

_____. 1980. 'The Sharped Geminate Palatals in Russian,' *Russian Linguistics* 4.303-28.

_____. 1982. 'The Russian Sharped Geminate Palatals in Functional Perspective,' *Russian Linguistics* 6.277-91.

Ganiev, Ž. V. 1966. 'O proiznošenii sočetanij <stk>, <zdk>, <ntk>, <ndk>,' *Razvitie fonetiki sovremennogo russkogo jazyka*, ed. S. S. Vysotskij et al., 85-95. Moscow: Nauka.

Gombrich, Ernst H. 1963. *Meditations on a Hobby Horse*. London: Phaidon.

Graudina, L. K. 1977. 'Razgovornyc i prostorečnyc formy v grammatike,' *Literaturnaja norma i prostorečie*, 77-111. Moscow: Nauka.

Gray, Bennison. 1969. *Style: The Problem and Its Solution*. The Hague: Mouton.

_____. 1973. 'Stylistics: The End of a Tradition,' *Journal of Aesthetics and Art Criticism* 31.501-512.

Greenberg, Joseph H. 1966. *Language Universals*. The Hague: Mouton.

Haiman, John. 1980. 'The Iconicity of Grammar: Isomorphism and Motivation,' *Language* 56.515-40.

Halle, Morris. 1959. *The Sound Pattern of Russian*. The Hague: Mouton.

_____. 1965. 'On the Bases of Phonology,' *The Structure of Language*, ed. J. A. Fodor and J. J. Katz, 324-33. Englewood Cliffs, N.J.: Prentice-Hall.

_____. 1977. 'Roman Jakobson's Contribution to the Modern Study of Speech Sounds,' *Roman Jakobson: Echoes of His Scholarship*, ed. Daniel Armstrong and C. H. van Schooneveld, 123-43. Lisse: Peter de Ridder.

Henry, Albert. 1971. *Métonymie et métaphore*. Paris: Klincksieck.

Hjelmslev, Louis. 1969. *Prolegomena to a Theory of Language*, trans. Francis J. Whitfield. Madison: The University of Wisconsin Press.

_____. [1938] 1970. 'Essai d'une théorie des morphèmes,' *Essai linguistique*, 2nd ed., 152-64. Copenhagen: Nordisk Sprog-og Kulturforlag.

Isačenko, A. V. 1969. 'The Development of the Clusters *sk', *zg,' etc. in Russian,' *Scando-Slavica* 15.99-110.

―――. 1970. 'East Slavic Morphophonemics and the Treatment of the Jers in Russian: A Revision of Havlík's Law,' *International Journal of Slavic Linguistics and Poetics* 13.73-124.

―――. 1971. 'Morfonologičeskaja interpretacija dolgix mjagkix šipjaščix [š,:], [ž,:] v russkom jazyke,' *International Journal of Slavic Linguistics and Poetics* 14.32-52.

―――. 1972. 'Rol' usečenija v russkom slovoobrazovanii,' *International Journal of Slavic Linguistics and Poetics* 15.95-125.

Jakobson, Roman. 1932. 'Zur Struktur des russisches Verbums,' *Charisteria Guilelmo Mathesio oblata,* 74-84. Prague: Pražský Linguistický Kroužek. Reprinted in Jakobson 1971, 3-15.

―――. 1939/1962. 'Zur Struktur des Phonems.' Two lectures published for the first time in Jakobson 1962, 280-310.

―――. 1948. 'Russian Conjugation,' *Word* 4.155-67. Reprinted in Jakobson 1971, 119-29.

―――. 1957. *Shifters, Verbal Categories, and the Russian Verb.* Cambridge, Mass.: Department of Slavic Languages and Literatures, Harvard University. Reprinted in Jakobson 1971, 130-47.

―――. 1960. 'The Gender Pattern of Russian,' *Studii si Certetări Lingvistice* 11.541-3. Reprinted in Jakobson 1971, 184-86.

―――. 1960. 'Linguistics and Poetics,' *Style in Language,* ed. T. A. Sebeok, 350-77. Cambridge, Mass.: The M.I.T. Press.

―――. 1962. *Selected Writings, I: Phonological Studies.* The Hague: Mouton.

―――. 1965a. 'Information and Redundancy in the Common Slavic Prosodic Pattern,' *Symbolae linguisticae in honorem Georgii Kuryłowicz,* 146-51. Wrocław: Polska Akademia Nauk.

―――. 1965b. 'O budowie ukraińskiego rozkaźnika,' *Studia z filologii Polskiej i Słowiańskiej* 5.213-18. Russian version in Jakobson 1971, 190-7.

―――. 1965c. 'Quest for the Essence of Language,' *Diogenes* 51.21-37. Reprinted in Jakobson 1971, 345-59.

―――. [1941]. 1968. *Child Language, Aphasia and Phonological Universals.* The Hague: Mouton. Original German version reprinted in Jakobson 1962, 328-401.

―――. 1971. *Selected Writings, II: Word and Language.* The Hague: Mouton.

―――. 1972. 'Verbal Communication,' *Scientific American* 227/3.72-80.

―――. 1974. 'Mark and Feature,' *World Papers in Phonetics,* 37-9. Tokyo: Phonetic Society of Japan.

―――. 1977. 'A Few Remarks on Peirce, Pathfinder in the Science of Language,' *MLN* 92.1026-32. Reprinted in Jakobson 1980, 31-38.

―――. 1978. *Six Lectures on Sound and Meaning.* Cambridge, Mass.: MIT Press.

―――. 1980. *The Framework of Language.* Ann Arbor: Horace H. Rackham School of Graduate Studies, University of Michigan.

Jakobson, R., and M. Halle. 1971. *Fundamentals of Language,* 2nd ed. The Hague: Mouton.

Jakobson, R., and K. Pomorska. 1980. *Dialogues.* Paris: Flammarion.

Jakobson, R., and Linda R. Waugh. 1979. *The Sound Shape of Language.* Bloomington: Indiana University Press.

Janko-Trinickaja, N. A. 1971. 'Tamára—Tóma,' *Razvitie fonetiki sovremennogo russkogo jazyka: fonologičeskie podsistemy,* 291-3. Moscow: Nauka.

Jimbo, K. 1927. *Kokugo onseigaku.* Tokyo: Meiji Tosho Kaisha.

Jones, Lawrence G. 1959. 'The Contextual Variants of the Russian Vowels,' in M. Halle, *The Sound Pattern of Russian*, 155-97. The Hague: Mouton.

Kiparsky, Valentin. 1967. *Russische historische Grammatik, II: Die Entwicklung des Formensystems*. Heidelberg: Carl Winter.

Klagstad, H. L. 1954. *Vowel ~ Zero Alternations in Contemporary Standard Russian*. Unpublished Ph.D. Thesis, Harvard University, Cambridge, Mass.

Kodzasov, S. V. 1973. 'Fonetičeskij èllipsis v russkoj razgovornoj reči,' *Teoretičeskie i èksperimental'nye issledovanija v oblasti strukturnoj i prikladnoj lingvistiki*, ed. V. A. Zvegincev, 109-133. Moscow: MGU.

Košutić, Radovan. 1919. *Gramatika Ruskog Jezika, I: Glasovi; A: Opšti Deo (Književni Izgovor)*, 2nd ed. Petrograd: Imp. Akademija Nauk.

Krysin, L. P. (ed.). 1974. *Russkij jazyk po dannym massovogo obsledovanija*. Moscow: Nauka.

Kuz'mina, S. M. 1966. 'O fonetike zaudarnyx fleksij,' in Vysotskij et al. 1966, 5-24.

―――. 1968. '"Fonetizacija" zaudarnogo vokalizma vo fleksijax,' in Panov 1968a, 42-56.

Ladefoged, P. 1971. *Preliminaries to Linguistic Phonetics*. Chicago: University of Chicago Press.

Le Guern, Michel. 1973. *Sémantique de la métaphore et de la métonymie*. Paris: Larousse.

Lévi-Strauss, Claude. 1962. *La Pensée sauvage*. Paris: Plon.

Lieb, Irwin C. (ed.). 1953. *Charles S. Peirce's Letters to Lady Welby*. New Haven: Whitlock's.

Lyons, John. 1977. 'Basic Problems of Semantics.' *Plenary Report to the XII International Congress of Linguists. Abstracts*, 1-3. Vienna: Interconvention.

McCawley, J. 1968. *The Phonological Component of a Grammar of Japanese*. The Hague: Mouton.

Martin, S. 1952. *Morphophonemics of Standard Colloquial Japanese* (Language Dissertation, 47). Baltimore: Waverly Press.

Martinet, A. 1939. 'Un ou deux phonèmes?' *Acta Linguistica* 1.94-103.

―――. 1955. *Economie des changements phonétiques*. Berne: Francke.

Matusevič, M. I. 1976. *Sovremennyj russkij jazyk: fonetika*. Moscow. Prosveščenie.

Miloslavskij, I. G. 1963. 'Sočetanija perednejazyčnyx šumnyx soglasnyx fonem v sovremennom russkom jazyke,' *Naučnye doklady vysšej školy* 31/3.133-40.

Obnorskij, S. P. 1953. Očerki po morfologii russkogo glagola. Moscow: AN SSSR.

Orlova, V. G. 1970. 'Mesto udarenija i kačestvo udarennogo glasnogo v ličnyx formax nekotoryx glagolov II sprjaženija,' *Obrazovanie severnorusskogo narečija i srednerusskix govorov*, 118-24. Moscow: Nauka.

Ožegov, S. I., and A. B. Šapiro. 1959. *Orfografičeskij slovar' russkogo jazyka*, 4th ed. Moscow: GIINS.

Panov, M. V. 1967. *Russkaja fonetika*. Moscow: Prosveščenie.

―――. (ed.). 1968a. *Russkij jazyk i sovetskoe obščestvo: sociologo-lingvističeskoe issledovanie.' Fonetika sovremennogo russkogo literaturnogo jazyka. Narodnye govory*. Moscow: Nauka.

―――. (ed.). 1968b. *Russkij jazyk i sovetskoe obščestvo: sociologo-lingvističeskoe issledovanie. Morfologija i sintaksis sovremennogo russkogo literaturnogo jazyka*. Moscow: Nauka.

―――. 1979. *Sovremennyj russkij jazyk: fonetika*. Moscow: Vysšaja škola.

Paufošima, R. F. 1980. 'Aktivnye processy v sovremennom russkom literaturnom jazyke (Assimiljativnye izmenenija bezudarnyx glasnyx),' *Izvestija AN SSSR: Serija literatury i jazyka* 39/1.61-68.

Polivanov, E. D. 1959. 'Kategorii soglasnyx v japonskom jazyke (Glava iz istoričeskoj fonetiki),' *Japonskij linvisticeskij sbornik,* ed. A. A. Paškovskij, 17-34. Moscow: Izdatel'stvo vostočnoj literatury.

Quine, W. V. 1978. 'A Postscript on Metaphor,' *Critical Injury* 5.161-2.

Reformatskij, A. A. 1955. 'Soglasnye, protivopostavlennye po sposobu i mestu obrazovanija, i ix var'irovanie v sovremennom russkom literaturnom jazyke,' *Doklady i soobščenija Instituta jazykoznanija AN SSSR* 8:3-23

―――. 1967. '(Ж),' *To Honor Roman Jakobson,* 1650-6. The Hague: Mouton.

―――. 1970. *Iz istorii otečestvennoj fonologii.* Moscow: Nauka.

Reilly, Francis E. 1970. *Charles Peirce's Theory of Scientific Method.* New York: Fordham University Press.

Ricoeur, Paul. 1974. 'Metaphor and the Main Problem of Hermeneutics,' *New Literary History* 6.95-110.

―――. 1975. *La Métaphore vive.* Paris: Seuil.

Romportl, Milan. 1973. 'On the Vowel System of Russian,' in his *Studies in Phonetics,* 37-58. Prague: Academia.

Sanders, Gary. 1970. 'Peirce's Sixty-six Signs?' *Transactions of the Charles S. Peirce Society* 6.3-16.

Saussure, F. de. 1960. *Cours de linguistique générale,* 5th ed. Paris: Payot.

Savan, David. 1976. *An Introduction to C. S. Peirce's Semiotics.* Toronto: Victoria University.

Ščerba, L. V. 1957. 'Teorija russkogo pis'ma,' in his *Izbrannye raboty po russkomu jazyku,* 144-79. Moscow: GIMP RSFSR.

Schane, S. A. 1968. 'On the Non-Uniqueness of Phonological Representation,' *Language* 44.709-16.

Schapiro, Meyer. 1953. 'Style,' *Anthropology Today,* ed. A. L. Kroeber, 287-312. Chicago: University of Chicago Press.

Shapiro, Michael. 1967. 'Concatenators and Russian Derivational Morphology,' *General Linguistics* 7.50-66.

―――. 1968. *Russian Phonetic Variants and Phonostylistics.* Berkeley: University of California Press.

―――. 1969. *Aspects of Russian Morphology: A Semiotic Investigation.* Cambridge, Mass.: Slavica.

―――. 1970. Review of Daniel Jones and Dennis Ward, *The Phonetics of Russian, The Slavic and East European Journal* 14.514-16.

―――. 1971. 'The Genitive Plural Desinences of the Russian Substantive,' *The Slavic and East European Journal* 15.190-8.

―――. 1972a. 'Consonant Syncope in Russian,' *The Slavic Word,* ed. D. S. Worth, 402-23. The Hague: Mouton.

―――. 1972b. 'Explorations into Markedness,' *Language* 48.343-64.

―――. 1974a. 'Markedness and Distinctive Feature Hierarchies,' *Proceedings of the Eleventh International Congress of Linguists,* II, ed. L. Heilman, 775-81. Bologna: il Mulino.

―――. 1974b. 'Morphophonemics as Semiotic,' *Acta Linguistica Hafniensia* 15.29-49.

―――. 1976. *Asymmetry: An Inquiry into the Linguistic Structure of Poetry.* Amsterdam: North-Holland.

―――. 1981. 'Peirce's Interpretant from the Perspective of Linguistic Theory,' *Proceedings of the C. S. Peirce Bicentennial International Congress,* ed. K. L. Ketner et al., 313-18. Lubbock: Texas Tech Press.

Shibatani, M. 1973. 'The Role of Surface Constraints in Generative Phonology,' *Language* 49.87-106.

Shibles, Warren. 1971. *Metaphor: An Annotated History.* Whitewater, Wisc.: Language Press.

Shirota, S. 1971. 'Nihongo oninron ni yosete,' *Gengo Kenkyū* 59.15-42.

Short, T. L. 1981. 'Semeiosis and Intentionality,' *Transactions of the Charles S. Peirce Society* 17.197-223.

———. 1982. 'Life Among the Legisigns,' *Transactions of the Charles S. Peirce Society* 18. 285-310.

———. MS. 'Peirce's Division of Interpretants.'

Sparshott, F. E. 1974. '"As," or The Limits of Metaphor,' *New Literary History* 6.75-94.

Stankiewicz, E. 1962. 'The Interdependence of Paradigmatic and Derivational Patterns,' *Word* 18.1-22.

———. 1968. *Declension and Gradation of Russian Substantives.* The Hague: Mouton.

———. 1976. 'Prague School Morphophonemics,' *Sound, Sign and Meaning: Quinquagenary of the Prague Linguistic Circle,* ed. Ladislav Matejka, 101-18. Ann Arbor: Department of Slavic Languages and Literatures, The University of Michigan.

Stern, Gustaf. [1931] 1965. *Meaning and Change of Meaning.* Bloomington: Indiana University Press.

Superanskaja, A. V. 1966. *Udarenie v sobstvennyx imenax v sovremennom russkom jazyke.* Moscow: Nauka.

Terexova, T. G. 1966. 'Proiznošenie sočetanij trex soglasnyx v sovremennom russkom literaturnom jazyke,' in S. S. Vysotskij et al., 72-84. Moscow: Nauka.

Thelin, Nils B. 1971. *On Stress Assignment and Vowel Reduction in Contemporary Standard Russian.* Uppsala: Skriv Service AB.

———. 1974. 'On the Phonological Status of the Russian Geminate Palatals,' *Russian Linguistics* 1.163-76.

———. 1975. *Towards a Theory of Verb Stem Formation and Conjugation in Modern Russian.* (Studica Slavica Upsaliensia, 17). Stockholm: Almquist & Wiksell International.

———. 1981. 'On the Phonemic Status of the Geminate Palatals in Russian—One More Time,' *Russian Linguistics* 5.301-13.

Thoma, Werner. 1976. 'Ansätze zu einer sprachfunktional-semiotisch orientierten Stilistik,' *Zeitschrift für Literaturwissenschaft und Linguistik* 22.117-141.

Todorov, Tzvetan. 1974. 'On Linguistic Symbolism,' *New Literary History* 6.111-34.

Toporov, V. N. 1971. 'O distributivnyx strukturax konca slova v sovremennom russkom jazyke,' *Fonetika. Fonologija. Grammatika,* 152-62. Moscow: Nauka.

Trubetzkoy, N. S. 1934. *Das morphonologische System der russischen Sprache.* (*TCLP,* 5²). Prague: Harrassowitz.

———. 1936. 'Die Aufhebung der phonologischen Gegensätze,' *Travaux du Cercle linguistique de Prague* 6.29-45.

———. 1958. *Grundzüge der Phonologie,* 3rd ed. Göttingen: Vandenhoeck & Ruprecht.

———. 1969. *Principles of Phonology,* trans. C. Baltaxe. Berkeley: University of California Press. Translation of Trubetzkoy 1958.

———. 1975. *Letters and Notes,* ed. R. Jakobson. The Hague: Mouton.

Ušakov, D. N. 1935-40. *Tolkovyj slovar' russkogo jazyka,* 4 vols. Moscow: Sovetskaja ènciklopedija.

———. 1964. 'Izvlečenie iz stenogrammy vystuplenija na zasedanii sektora slavjanskix jazykov instituta jazyka i pis'mennosti AN SSSR 16 fevralja 1940 g.,' *Voprosy kul'tury reči* 5.17-9.

Vennemann, T. 1972. 'Phonetic Detail in Assimilation: Problems in Germanic Phonology,' *Language* 48.863-92.

Verbickaja, L. A. 1970. 'Nekotorye voprosy russkoj orfoèpii,' *Russkij jazyk za rubežom* 2(14).65-72.

————. 1976. *Russkaja orfoèpija.* Leningrad: LGU.

Veyrenc, J. 1966. 'Un ou deux phonèmes? Le cas de щ, en russe,' *La linguistique* 1. 111-23.

Vinogradov, V. V. and N. Ju. Švedova (eds.). 1964. *Očerki po istoričeskoj grammatike russkogo literaturnogo jazyka XIX veka: glagol, narečie, predlogi i sojuzy v russkom literaturnom jazyke XIX veka.* Moscow: Nauka.

Voroncova, V. L. 1959. 'O normax udarenija v glagolax na -it' v sovremennom russkom literaturnom jazyke.' *Voprosy kul'tury reči* 2.117-56.

Vysotskij, S. S. et al. (eds.). 1966. *Razvitie fonetiki sovremennogo russkogo jazyka.* Moscow: Nauka.

————. 1971. *Razvitie fonetiki sovremennogo russkogo jazyka: fonologičeskie podsistemy.* Moscow: Nauka.

Ward, Dennis. 1975. 'Unaccented Vowels in Russian,' *Russian Linguistics* 2.91-104.

Weinreich, Uriel, William Labov, and Marvin I. Herzog. 1968. 'Empirical Foundations for a Theory of Language Change,' *Directions for Historical Linguistics,* ed. W. P. Lehman and Y. Malkiel, 95-188. Austin: University of Texas Press.

Weinrich, Harald. 1970. 'Structures narratives du mythe,' *Poétique* 1.25-34.

Wenck, G. 1966. *The Phonemics of Japanese: Questions and Attempts.* Wiesbaden: Otto Harrassowitz.

Worth, D. S. 1967a. 'On Cyclical Rules in Derivational Morphophonemics,' *Phonologie der Gegenwart,* 173-84. Graz: Hermann Böhlaus.

————. 1967b. 'The Notion of "Stem" in Russian Flexion and Derivation,' *To Honor Roman Jakobson,* 2269-88. The Hague: Mouton.

————. 1968a. 'Notes on Russian Stress, 2: *ljubov', voš',* etc.,' *Studies in Slavic Linguistics and Poetics in Honor of B. O. Unbegaun,* 279-87. New York: NYU Press.

————. 1968b. '"Surface Structure" and "Deep Structure" in Slavic Morphology,' *American Contributions to the Sixth International Congress of Slavists,* I, 295-427. The Hague: Mouton.

————. 1968c. 'Vowel ∼ Zero Alternations in Russian Derivation,' *International Journal of Slavic Linguistics and Poetics* 11.110-23.

————. 1972. 'Morfonologija nulevoj affiksacii v russkom slovoobrazovanii,' *Voprosy jazykoznanija* 6.76-84.

Wright, Georg H. von. 1963. *Norm and Action: A Logical Enquiry.* New York: Humanities Press.

Zaliznjak, A. A. 1967. *Russkoe imennoe slovoizmenenie.* Moscow: Nauka.

————. 1977. *Grammatičeskij slovar' russkogo jazyka.* Moscow: Russkij jazyk.

Zinder, L. R. 1963. 'Fonetičeskaja suščnost' dolgogo palatalizovannogo [š':] v russkom jazyke,' *Naučnye doklady vysšej školy. Filologičeskie nauki* 2.137-42.

INDEX

Abelard, Peter: as one of the Schoolmen, 5
Alexandrian grammarians: on language governed by analogy, 1
American structuralists: transformational-generative grammar as reaction to, 8
Anaptyxis: in Russian 147-150; in Russian derivation, 150-154; in Russian genitive plural, 152, 158-162; in Russian nominal inflection, 152-153, 157-162, 218; in Russian verb/substantive derivational relations, 153-154; effect of syllabicity on, in Russian, 154-155; role of stress in, in Russian, 155-156; in Russian conjugation, 181; sign function of, compared with that of counter-etymological vowels in Russian, 190
Andersen, Henning: on relationship between expression plane and content plane in language, 75, 76, 77, 78, 79, 81, 82, 83, 93; on markedness, 76, 79, 80, 84-85, 86, 87, 93, 94, 100, 109, 184; on diacritic signantia in speech, 81, 82, 136, 215; on variation and neutralization rules, 82, 86, 94, 111-112, 184; on adaptive rules in phonology, 83, 84, 88; on iconicity, 89; on English plural desinences, 100; on tenseness vs. laxness as distinctive feature in Japanese obstruents, 104-105; on function of phonological rules, 111; on syllable slopes, 115; on differences between Russian and Japanese vowel systems, 138-139; mentioned, 79, 83, 84, 86, 87, 88, 89, 90, 93, 99, 118, 121, 156, 172, 184, 208, 213
Anttila, Raimo: *Introduction to Historical and Comparative Linguistics,* x; diagram of Peirce's three sign types adapted from, 63; on tropes, 205, 211; mentioned, 185, 190
Apel, Karl-Otto: revived hermeneutics, 10
Aristotle: *De Interpretatione,* 12; on metaphor as trope, 195, 204; mentioned, 28
Assurance of interpretation, 60-63
Avanesov, R. I.: on Russian geminates, 118, 214; on status of ž' in Russian, 119; on Russian unstressed vowels, 124, 214, 216; on acuteness as distinctive in Russian

liquids, 158; on Russian third person plural, 168; on counter-etymological vowels in Russian, 186-187

Bally, Charles: endorsed Saussure, 2
Barinova, G. A.: on status of ž' in Russian, 119; on unstressed vowels in Russian, 214
Baudouin de Courtenay, J. A.: founder of structural linguistics, 2; unaware of Peirce's writings, 6; on biphonemic status of ž' in Russian, 119
Beardsley, Monroe: "metaphorical twist" of, 204; on oxymoron, 206, 207
Benveniste, Emile: "La nature du signe linguistique," 2; on the arbitrariness of language, 2, 3; mentioned, 221
Birnbaum, Henrik, 162
Bloch, B., 104
Bloomfield, Leonard: endorsed Saussure, 2; as American structuralist, 8; on phoneme as "bundle of distinctive features," 80
Boas, Franz, 2
Boeckh, August: *Encyclopaedia,* 10
Bolinger, Dwight, 3
Bondarko, L. V.: on unstressed vowels in Russian, 127, 214
Borunova, S. N.: on status of ž' in Russian, 119, 120
Boyanus, S.: introduced caret into Russian phonetic notation, 216
Brock, Jarret: on Peirce's Speculative Grammar, 26, 27; on Peirce's idea of sign, 27
Bromlej, S. V.: on vocalic stem shapes before infinitive desinences in Russian, 170; on counter-etymological vowels in Russian, 186
Brøndal, Viggo: on principle of markedness compensation, 120, 220
Buffon, George L. L. de, 211
Bühler, Karl: on physiognomic signs, 77
Bulatova, L. N.: on vocalic stem shapes before infinitive desinences in Russian, 170; on counter-etymological vowels in Russian, 186
Bulaxovskij, L. A.: on Russian conjugation,